TASTE & TECHNIQUE

RECIPES TO ELEVATE YOUR HOME COOKING

NAOMI POMEROY

WITH JAMIE FELDMAR

PHOTOGRAPHY BY

CHRIS COURT

TEN SPEED PRESS

BERKELEY

Contents

Introduction

When I was seven years old, my mother taught me how to make a soufflé. An expert in making something from nothing, my mom was a military brat who spent her early adolescence in rural France and grew up loving food and rock and roll. Fast-forward to the late 1970s and early 1980s and she was a single mom raising me in Corvallis, Oregon. Getting by on clever resourcefulness, we lived in a house meticulously decorated with thrift-store finds and tended the little garden behind it.

Our food-stamp stipend always included rations of flour, eggs, milk, cheese, and butter. Luckily, they also happen to be the ingredients for a soufflé. We'd add all sorts of extras: in the winter, it might just be cheese; in the summer, we'd mix in puréed vegetables from the garden. Nowadays when I tell people that my mom and I ate soufflés three times a week, they're always impressed. What I learned from my mother in all of this is that you can't really ruin a soufflé. Even if it doesn't rise as dramatically as a glossy magazine would have you believe it should, chances are it still tastes great. It's just a few eggs. They shouldn't intimidate you.

Both of my parents were big into food. In the same year that I made my first soufflé, my dad and stepmom ripped out their front lawn and planted an edible garden, and I learned pretty quickly that cooking was a good way to take care of people. My dad's mother, a tough southern lady if ever there was one, spent hours with my grandfather picking through hundreds of pounds of pecans, hand-shelling each one, to send out as gifts to the family. That's hospitality at its most stripped-down level. There's a joy that comes from making something for someone, and that's part of the reason why I spent more time baking elaborate birthday cakes and throwing dinner parties for my friends during my college years than I did writing history essays.

During those same years, I started working summers at a catering company in Ashland, Oregon. The owner, Jean Kowacki, a Culinary Institute of America–trained chef, kept saying, "You're so young and smart, you shouldn't get into this business. It's not a business for nice people—it's for alcoholics and assholes." But I knew I couldn't follow her advice. I was falling in love with cooking and the adrenaline rush that came from acting on your feet. It was totally addictive.

Early Days

After college, I began dating Michael Hebb, the man with whom I eventually founded several businesses and who later became the father of my child. He suggested that we start our own catering company, which we called Ripe. For our logo, we "borrowed" the woodblock print of chickpeas from the *Chez Panisse Vegetables* cookbook. We didn't have a commercial kitchen, or any professional equipment. Everything happened out of our house, the lower level of a duplex in a shady part of Portland, Oregon. We had a small electric range, a twenty year-old BMW, and not much else.

Despite all that, word about Ripe spread quickly, and I began cooking like crazy, teaching myself to do everything, from butchering to making stock, using cookbooks that I read voraciously. I must have cooked through *The Kitchen Sessions with Charlie Trotter* a hundred times, finally getting the sear on my scallops just so. I learned about balance, acidity, and seasoning from *The Elements of Taste* by Gray Kunz and Peter Kaminsky; worked my way through all of the different types of duck confit in Madeleine Kamman's *The New Making of a Cook*; and learned how to shop for produce from Alice Waters's *Chez Panisse Vegetables*. The more I cooked, the more I realized that great food starts with a handful of great building blocks. Once I knew how to make stock, then I could make demi-glace. Once I mastered the basic *pâte sucrée* recipe in Nancy Silverton's *Pastries from the La Brea Bakery,* I could turn out dozens of different tarts. I still had a lot to learn, but I was starting to see how the pieces fit together.

In 2000, after our daughter, August, was born, Michael and I decided to start hosting dinner parties at our house as a way to see our friends and meet new people. We didn't really own what we needed to throw a dinner party, however, so Michael "built" a table by setting a couple of hollow-core doors on top of sawhorses, we asked guests to bring their own chairs, and we rented plates and silverware. We also suggested that everyone chip in a few dollars to help cover costs. I cooked whatever I was in the mood for. It was a chance for me to experiment in the kitchen.

The first dinner was a hit, so we did it again. We had an e-mail list, and the first eight people to respond got a seat, the only requirement being that they had to bring someone new. That way, we were always assured a mix of different people. We started doing the dinners twice a month, but the list kept growing, and people started clamoring for seats. Our underground dinner parties dovetailed with the strong DIY ethos pervading Portland, and we started getting some attention from the press. Eventually we gave the dinners a name: Family Supper. We even received a letter from Charlie Trotter in praise of our efforts.

A few months later, we took over a commercial kitchen space in a renovated mattress factory and moved the dinners to the sprawling, raw space of beautiful old Douglas fir floors, a skylight, and exposed brick walls. We'd prep for our catering gigs during the day and throw Family Supper, which was now operating as a legitimate restaurant, at night. A lot of chefs were moving to Portland at the time, and they wanted to break out of the routine of toiling in other people's kitchens and instead work with other young, high-energy chefs who weren't following the old rules. I had no formal culinary training and little traditional restaurant experience, so the way we worked was totally different from the traditional model, a suppressive approach where one person (usually an older man) was in charge and always right. Some chefs are afraid to hire people who are better than them, but I was thrilled to learn from experienced cooks.

In 2004, we opened clarklewis. Our amazing chef, Morgan Brownlow, taught me the importance of seasonality and how to choose our purveyors carefully. He knew how to talk to the farmers at the market. He showed me how to set up a *mise en place* (literally "to put in place," or the process of organizing yourself and your ingredients) to maximize efficiency and minimize mess. Morgan also taught me how to move in the kitchen. He was like a ninja; all of his actions were so graceful. Even when hurried, he was still calm and focused. That's when I began to realize that cooking is a dance, and knowing this has had an enormous impact on the way I carry myself at work to this day.

In April 2005, we opened Gotham Tavern with Tommy Habetz, one of our favorite chefs from the catering business, running the kitchen. We billed it as a gastropub, and it is where I picked up a lot of the little tricks that set professional chefs apart from home cooks, like how to emulsify pasta with a bit of the cooking water for starch, which is something Tommy had learned from working with Mario Batali in New York. I also honed my skills at writing of-the-moment menus that captured the best of what was in season that week, and I spent a lot of time thinking about how all of the elements of a dish should work together on the plate.

Michael and I had broken up as a couple by this point, but we were still running the restaurants together. In April 2006, things started to fall apart. Michael came to me privately and said, "We're not going to make payroll." We had never really paid attention to costs at any of the restaurants, foolishly thinking that because we were busy we were making money. As it turned out, we were spending more than we were making. There was no way we'd be able to pay back our investors. We shut down Gotham Tavern immediately to avoid incurring more debt, and Michael distanced himself from the situation. I spent a few more months working with lawyers and accountants to restructure clarklewis so it could be sold to the investor to whom we owed the most money, and I filed for bankruptcy.

I took some time to lick my wounds and figure out what my next move was. I had just very publicly closed three restaurants and had lost ninety employees and a significant amount of money. I had the seeds of a new idea in mind, but I was nervous about going ahead with it. A big voice in my head said, "You're a failure," but a bigger voice said, "You have nothing left to lose." So I decided to go back to my roots, and that's how Beast was born.

The Rise of Beast

I started throwing underground dinner parties at my house again with one of the best cooks from clarklewis, Mika Paredes. These back-to-basics meals—no waitstaff, BYOB, composed plates served in the backyard—became the basis for Beast. When it opened in September 2007, I really didn't know if it would be successful. I was afraid my passion

wouldn't carry me and that the whole thing might fail. But I had a choice about how I reacted to what happened in my life, and I realized how important it was to move forward, rather than let my failures paralyze me. So, I picked up the pieces and got back to the stove.

When Beast first opened, Mika and I had virtually nothing. It was like the start of my catering days all over again. There was no stove, only two tiny electric induction burners and no hood, so we'd go to the restaurant next door to sear all of our meat. We put together two big communal tables for a purely practical reason: you can seat more people that way. We decided to have only two seatings each night, and we settled on a set menu because we had to. With only a tiny open kitchen, we could not cater to dozens of different orders. It was like planning a dinner party every evening, and we deliberately went with an aesthetic that made the space feel comfortable, like a home.

From the start, we were committed to creating an enjoyable environment, for both our customers, who were eating in what was essentially our home, and for us, because the mood you take into the kitchen really does translate to the food. We had fun cooking, and people picked up on that. Our cooking at Beast has grown more polished over the years, but we've always worked to create an enjoyable atmosphere as much as we work to make great food.

The most valuable thing I've learned since opening Beast is the importance of teaching, and how to translate my experiences in a way that helps others learn to cook. My staff may make a mistake the first time, but that's just part of the learning process. The key is to ensure that they improve the next time. As I've matured as a chef, I've learned to step back and take pleasure in helping others find confidence in their own ability to get the job done.

That's why I'm writing this book now. Over the years, I've learned a lot—much of it the hard way—from books and other cooks, but at the end of the day, I'm a self-taught chef. How I got here largely has to do with developing and sharpening my habits through a series of culinary "building blocks."

How This Book Works

Building blocks are the foundations that allow you to become truly comfortable in the kitchen. It can be a single technique, such as whipping cream, which you could do with an electric mixer but should do by hand to understand the mechanics of incorporating air into liquid. Or it might be an ingredient that you deploy over and over again, such as homemade stock, which can be used as is or reduced to a demi-glace or clarified for consommé. I hope that as you cook your way through this book and see how techniques and ingredients fit together and build off of one another, you will master an arsenal of building blocks that will boost your kitchen confidence.

That brings me to my next point: cooking should be a pleasure. All too often I hear home cooks talk about being scared, overwhelmed, or otherwise intimidated by the prospect of getting into the kitchen. I get it. No one has the time to spend hours shopping, preparing, and presenting a magazine-worthy spread on a daily basis. But you can go a long way toward having a better time and making a better meal by simply setting the right mood for yourself as soon as you begin to cook (or even think about cooking). I am a pragmatic person, but this is one of those times that my West Coast hippie upbringing shows through: if you're having a miserable day and you go into the kitchen carrying that energy, the food you make will absolutely not taste as good as if you entered the kitchen in a better mood. Cooking is more than a physical act. Indeed, it is every bit as emotional as any other art form.

Where should you begin? First, think about what to cook. I often start by choosing my protein. Let's say I want to prepare beef. Seasonality often naturally dictates the specifics: If it's July and humid, I won't want the oven on for hours, so I might choose to quickly sear a thin marinated flat iron steak (page 264). In the depths of winter, chances are I'll crave something rich and comforting, like braised short ribs (page 273).

From there, I start to consider what else to make with the beef. It's all about creating balance within a meal: the flavors, textures, and even colors of your dinner should be complementary but still distinct, and seasonally appropriate. Take those braised short ribs I'm making in December. Because of all of the bone and connective tissue in a rib, they're rich, with a deeply meaty

flavor. So I'll think of a side dish that contrasts with the taste, texture, and appearance of the meat and that features in-season produce, such as Orange-Caraway Glazed Carrots (page 178). The carrots provide a bright blast of color and a sweet-and-sour quality that helps cut some of the richness of the beef, and the caraway seasoning complements the earthiness of the meat, tying all of the elements together. For a final touch, I'll make a quick Horseradish Gremolata (page 40), which offers an herbaceous note that brings a needed freshness to the dish.

That's enough to make a beautiful meal: three simple ingredients—beef, carrots, horseradish—prepared with attention to how their textures and flavors interact. It's important to strive for balance within each individual component, whether it's a side dish or main course. Even something as seemingly minor as a garnish of crème fraîche deserves the attention of seasoning: salt, pepper, or a squeeze of fresh lemon juice. I say this not to make beginner cooks nervous but to encourage you to pay attention to every element of your meal. As I've matured as a cook, I have learned that balance and restraint are two of the best skills a chef can have. All of the recipes in this book are balanced, and as you cook your way through them, you too will hone your understanding of how a dish should taste. It won't take long before you start to train your palate, though it will take practice to perfect it.

When you're deciding what to cook, go to the farmers' market to see and taste what's available. If the ingredients you were planning to buy don't look or taste good, reconsider what you intended to make. The menu at Beast changes every week, largely depending on what produce looks and tastes best within those seven days. Subpar raw materials result in subpar finished dishes. And although this is something that took me a long time to learn, you must keep in mind the power of simplicity: a salad made with tender Little Gem lettuces needs nothing more than a creamy pistachio vinaigrette (see page 121) to impress.

Invest in a handful of ingredients that might be more expensive or harder to find than what you are used to, like *fleur de sel* or ten-year aged balsamic vinegar (for a full list of recommended ingredients, see page 370). Such purchases will pay off exponentially in the degree to which they will enhance

your food. I have little use for expensive professional tools, like *sous vide* machines or Combi ovens, but some of my recipes call for equipment (see the full list on page 373) that you may not already own. If you can find a way to purchase them, they will greatly improve your cooking—a high-powered blender and a black steel pan in particular.

Once you've decided what to cook, set yourself up physically to do it well and enjoyably. Chefs often talk of the importance of *mise en place*, the process of organizing and arranging ingredients and tools ahead of cooking. This is important in both professional and home kitchens, but what we often neglect to emphasize is the importance of mental *mise en place*, too. Do what you need to do to feel good going into a cooking session: crank up your favorite music, pour yourself a glass of wine, and focus on what you're about to create. You will have a more relaxed time as a cook when your space is organized, and you will enjoy the act of cooking in a more meaningful way. Get yourself a notebook to take notes as you cook your way through a recipe, so you can reference them next time. Organization allows you the freedom to relax and enjoy the act of cooking, which ultimately extends to the quality of the meal.

But most important, don't psych yourself out. All too often we fall into a trap of thinking that everything must be perfect, and all hope is lost if the fluting on your pie crust is uneven or your chicken is slightly overcooked. I often think of what my mother told me about a soufflé: you can't really ruin it. Even if it doesn't poof into that picture-perfect dome, chances are it will still taste great, and if you serve it with confidence and grace, few people will notice its minor imperfections.

This book is organized fairly classically, starting with sauces before moving into starters, soups, vegetables, proteins, and desserts. The techniques employed in the early chapters will help you master some of the recipes in the later chapters, and though you certainly don't need to cook this book from cover to cover, I encourage you to familiarize yourself with each of the chapters, as many techniques build off of one another. Do take the time to read each recipe all the way through before you begin, as it will prepare you for what is to come. Each of the main recipes focuses on learning a specific cooking method, such as braising, pan searing, or gentle poaching. With each of the main dishes, I have suggested a series of seasonal vegetable side dishes and sauces that pair with the meat, poultry, or fish. That said, nearly all of the side dishes work beautifully on their own, too.

Take Fennel-Brined Pork Loin (page 247) with its suggested summer accompaniments of baby artichokes and hazelnut romesco, for example. The flavors and textures of each component are complementary, but they each work independently, too. *Romesco* is a versatile sauce that is equally delicious on crispy baby artichokes as it is on a hunk of crusty bread. Trimming, blanching, and frying artichokes is another set of skills to learn even if you are not making the artichokes as part of this recipe. The ability to brine and sear a beautiful piece of meat will serve you well when making countless other meals. In other words, you don't have to make all three components of this dish at the same time: the meat can be prepared and served as is or with some simply dressed greens, and the side dish and sauce can either be skipped altogether or paired with a completely different main dish. In the end, every recipe stands alone as a valuable way to improve your skills as a cook.

Finally, I cannot overstate the importance of learning how to season—it's one of the easiest ways to improve your home cooking. Instead of directing you to season "to taste," I almost always provide measurements for salt and pepper, so you can learn how much to actually use—it may surprise you. When you have cooked a recipe enough times to become comfortable with its rhythms, feel free to stop measuring and season to your own taste. I use natural sea salt and recommend that you do the same. (Before making any of these recipes, see my notes on using salt on pages 371 and 375.)

It's my hope that this book will encourage you to get into the kitchen, take cooking seriously, and feel good about it. The only secret to becoming a great cook is to practice, practice, practice. If you like doing it, dedicate some time to perfecting it. Even if (and when) things don't go exactly as planned, you should take deep pleasure in the act of making and sharing food with the people you love. That, to me, is the true joy of cooking.

Sauces

My love for sauces is why I started cooking. Even in my earliest culinary experiments as a child, adding a sauce was the easiest way for me to quickly transform a dish. That's why I believe this is the most important chapter in the book. In traditional French kitchens, *saucier* is one of the highest positions, because making the perfect sauce requires great attention to detail, technique, timing, and expertise acquired through practice and patience.

Sauces elevate a dish more than any other single element, adding an extra layer of flavor that pulls everything together. They complete the taste experience and are often a connection point among all of the components on a plate. A quick sauce can lift even the simplest of meals into something extraordinary. The key to great sauce making is understanding balance, which is what every recipe in this chapter is designed to help you accomplish.

Perhaps because of the perception that sauces take years to master, many home cooks often skip making one. That's unfortunate, since plenty of sauces are actually quite easy to make and offer a return far greater than the amount of effort it took to assemble them. My definition of sauce is fairly broad. It doesn't have to be liquid, for example. It is any substance that can be spooned or poured, such as a chutney, relish, or confiture. And while a sauce is not necessary for the completion of a dish, it adds that important extra touch.

Parsley Sauce Verte

MAKES ABOUT 1 CUP

This sauce, a staple in my kitchen, was strongly influenced by a recipe in Alice Waters's *Chez Panisse Vegetables* cookbook and is one of the most versatile recipes in this book, standing next to only Demi-Glace (page 36) in terms of its usefulness and importance. You can use this sauce as a dressing for roasted vegetables, a soup garnish, a vinaigrette pick-me-up, or a *chimichurri*-like condiment for grilled steak. To be honest, I can't think of much I wouldn't put it on.

The secret is in the amount of macerated shallot and salt you use. Chopping herbs and putting them into oil is the first step, but using acid and salt to balance those flavors is what makes the process exciting. Depending on how you will be using the sauce, feel free to tweak its texture, adding more oil to make it thinner for a dressing or less oil for a garnish or dip. Just be sure to taste frequently as you work. For example, if you're adding more liquid, you'll need to add more salt, pepper, and perhaps a pinch of sugar. It's best to taste this sauce alongside whatever you're serving it with, so you can season accordingly. Should you want to experiment with different flavors in the base recipe, the variations at right offer some easy additions.

A final note: You need to do a lot of chopping in this recipe and in the Walnut-Parsley Pistou (page 6) that follows. I know it's tempting to just throw all of the herbs into a food processor, but do not take this shortcut. The processor bruises herbs instead of cleanly slicing them. When you hand chop, not only do you improve your knife skills but you also preserve the integrity of the herbs, so they will spoil less quickly. For more on how to chop herbs, see page 376.

Place the oil in a small mixing bowl. Immediately upon chopping the parsley, chives, and tarragon, add them to the oil to prevent browning. Fresh herbs start to discolor as soon as they're chopped; submerging them in oil helps keep their color and protects their flavor. Splash in more oil if needed to keep all of the herbs covered.

In a second small bowl, cover the shallot with the vinegar and add half of the salt; stir to dissolve the salt. Splash in more vinegar if needed to keep the shallot covered. Macerating the shallot helps mellow some of its sharp taste.

No more than 15 minutes prior to serving, mix together the herbs and the macerated shallot with its liquid (adding the vinegar too early will cause the herbs to brown before serving). Season with the remaining salt, the pepper, the sugar, and with more vinegar and oil if necessary. Serve immediately.

¾ cup extra-virgin olive oil

½ cup finely chopped flat-leaf parsley

2 tablespoons plus 1 teaspoon finely chopped chives

2 teaspoons finely chopped tarragon

1 tablespoon finely minced shallot

1 tablespoon plus 1 teaspoon good-quality white wine vinegar

¼ teaspoon salt

1/16 teaspoon freshly ground black pepper

1/16 teaspoon sugar

Variations

Anchovy Sauce Verte: Make the Parsley Sauce Verte but omit the salt. Add 2 teaspoons anchovy paste (from 4 to 5 fillets; see page 370), stirred in at the end. Taste and add up to ¼ teaspoon salt as needed. (This is great on roasted potatoes and/or alongside a juicy rib eye, see page 263.)

Hazelnut Sauce Verte (pictured, top): ¼ cup candied hazelnuts (see page 351), roughly chopped and added at the last minute so they keep their crunch (a good pairing with roast pork, see page 247, or Orange-Caraway Glazed Carrots, page 178).

Lemon Confit Sauce Verte (pictured, bottom): 3 tablespoons minced lemon confit (page 343), stirred in with a little bit of its oil (a great option for topping lamb dishes like Lamb Loin Chops, page 286).

Walnut-Parsley Pistou

MAKES ABOUT 1 CUP

Pistou is the French equivalent of pesto—meet my version. I've loved a lot of pestos in my time, and I never tire of playing around with different herb-nut-cheese combinations. This is one of my favorites because the pairing of fresh, bright parsley and nutty, savory walnuts works so well. It's important to buy your nuts from a farmers' market or reputable source that has a high product turnover. The difference in taste between stale walnuts (many of which are rancid) and fresh cannot be overstated. You'll know that the second you bite into a sweet, fresh one.

This *pistou* is delicious on grilled chicken or a fillet of white fish like halibut, or as a garnish atop the asparagus velouté on page 85. It will hold for up to 3 days in the refrigerator and also freezes well (bring it to room temperature before using). Before you begin, read my final note about chopping herbs in Parsley Sauce Verte (page 5).

Preheat the oven to 325°F. Spread the walnuts on a small baking sheet and toast for 3 to 5 minutes, until lightly fragrant but not overly toasted. Set aside until cool to the touch, about 10 minutes.

Place the oil in a small bowl about 4 inches in diameter and add the parsley immediately upon chopping to prevent browning. Fresh herbs start to discolor as soon as they're chopped; submerging them in oil helps keep their color and protects their flavor. Splash in more oil if needed to keep the parsley covered.

In a food processor, pulse the walnuts 3 or 4 times to break them into small pieces. Add the cheese and garlic and pulse another 5 to 10 times to incorporate and evenly disperse the garlic.

Combine the nut mixture and the parsley with its oil in a bowl and stir to mix. Adjust the consistency with more oil if necessary and then taste and adjust the seasoning.

½ cup walnut halves

½ cup extra-virgin olive oil

½ cup finely chopped flat-leaf parsley

¼ cup ground Parmigiano-Reggiano cheese (see page 376)

1 teaspoon garlic paste (page 344)

⅛ teaspoon salt

Variation

Basil Pistou: Blanch and shock (see page 375) 2 cups of tightly packed basil, cooking for 15 to 20 seconds, until tender. When cool, completely squeeze out the water and roughly chop the basil; you should have about ½ cup. Follow the recipe to toast ¼ cup pine nuts until lightly toasted and fragrant, 3 to 5 minutes; set aside to cool. Place the basil in a food processor and turn on the machine, slowly add ½ cup extra-virgin olive oil until evenly combined, 5 to 10 seconds. Transfer the basil-oil mixture to a bowl. In the same food processor (no need to wash), pulse the pine nuts 3 or 4 times to break them into small pieces. Add ¼ cup ground Parmigiano-Reggiano cheese and ¾ teaspoon garlic paste and pulse another 5 to 10 times to incorporate and evenly disperse the garlic. Follow the recipe to combine the nut and basil-oil mixture, adjusting the consistency with more oil and adjusting the seasoning with ¼ teaspoon salt as necessary.

Spring Pea–Mint Relish

MAKES ABOUT 1¼ CUPS

This versatile recipe, with its reliance on fresh English peas, announces that spring is in full swing. You can serve it alongside a cheese plate, toss it with pasta, or use it to top a crème fraîche tart (see page 50). Peas and mint combine well, but the mint can be overpowering if not used judiciously, as I have below. It's also important to use spearmint, not peppermint, which has an overwhelming minty quality.

In a small saucepan, carefully warm the oil over medium heat until it is warm to the touch but not hot (about 150°F). Add the peas and salt, turn down the heat to the lowest setting, and cook until the peas are beginning to turn bright green and taste just barely cooked, 3 to 4 minutes. Be careful not to overcook the peas or they'll be mushy, and make sure the heat is very low or you may accidentally fry them. Using a slotted spoon or spider (see page 374), transfer the peas to a plate or tray. Reserve the cooking oil.

In a small sauté pan, warm 2 tablespoons of the reserved oil over medium-low heat. Add the garlic and chile flakes and carefully sweat (see page 377) them until the garlic is very lightly cooked, about 1 minute. Taste the garlic. It should have a mild and sweet (as opposed to raw) flavor.

Add the cooked peas, the garlic-chile mixture with its oil, the mint, the lemon zest, and ¼ cup of the reserved pea cooking oil to a food processor and pulse 3 or 4 times, until the mixture is roughly chopped. It should have a nice, oily sheen and resemble a rough pesto; it shouldn't be a uniform purée. Stir in a few more tablespoons of the pea cooking oil if necessary to achieve the correct consistency. Taste for salt. Don't be tempted to add acid of any kind to this relish or the peas will change color from beautiful green to drab. Serve immediately.

1½ cups extra-virgin olive oil

1½ cups shelled English peas

2 teaspoons salt

1½ teaspoons minced garlic

¼ teaspoon red chile flakes

2 teaspoons chopped mint

1½ teaspoons lemon zest
(see page 375)

NOTE You can reuse the leftover pea poaching oil in another recipe that includes peas or in Long-Cooked Green Beans (page 156).

Savory Tomato Confiture

MAKES ABOUT 3½ CUPS

My father lived in India with his parents from the age of five to twelve, so my grandmother incorporated some Indian flavors into her cooking now and then. Mango chutney is one of the first condiments I ever played around with as a kid. I can remember mixing it with mustard to serve on plain chicken when I was barely six years old. That was an early aha moment for me: recognizing that I could do something to enhance a meal.

I serve this confiture with Seared Marinated Flat Iron Steak (page 264) and Long-Cooked Green Beans (page 156) in the summer, but because it uses canned tomatoes, you can make it year-round. Spread it on a sandwich or serve it as a savory accompaniment to a cheese course. It's also a great alternative for ketchup and one of my favorite ingredients to have on hand or give as a gift.

In a 4-quart nonreactive saucepan, heat the oil over medium heat. Add the onion, shallot, and garlic and sweat (see page 377) until translucent, 2 to 3 minutes. Add the cumin, coriander, chile flakes, orange zest, fennel pollen, salt, pepper, and the brown and yellow mustard seeds and cook, stirring frequently to ensure the garlic does not burn, until the mustard seeds begin to pop, about 1 more minute. Add the tomato paste and cook, stirring, until the oil starts to separate, about 30 seconds. Add the sugar and cook until completely melted and bubbling, about 1 minute. Add the vinegar, stir to combine, and allow the mixture to bubble for about 30 seconds, until it looks uniform.

Add the tomatoes, turn down the heat to low, and continue to cook, stirring frequently to avoid scorching, until the confiture has deepened in color and flavor, 25 to 30 minutes. Taste throughout the cooking and turn off the heat before the sugars burn (add 1 tablespoon water if the mixture starts to stick to the pan). Taste and adjust for vinegar or spice level if needed.

The confiture will keep in an airtight container in the refrigerator for up to 10 days. Bring to room temperature or warm gently before serving.

⅓ cup extra-virgin olive oil

½ cup finely minced yellow onion

¼ cup minced shallot

6 cloves garlic, thinly sliced

½ teaspoon toasted and ground cumin seeds (see page 378)

½ teaspoon toasted and ground coriander seeds (see page 378)

¼ teaspoon red chile flakes

¼ teaspoon orange zest (see page 375)

¼ teaspoon fennel pollen or toasted and ground fennel seeds (see page 378)

2 teaspoons salt

½ teaspoon freshly ground black pepper

2 teaspoons brown mustard seeds

2 teaspoons yellow mustard seeds

3 tablespoons tomato paste (preferably Italian)

¼ cup packed light or dark brown sugar

¼ cup sherry vinegar

3 cups canned diced tomatoes (see page 371 and Note, below), drained

NOTE I don't care for the taste of tomatoes from a metal can, so I seek out tomatoes packed in a glass jar or an aseptic carton (see page 371). You can also make this confiture with in-season fresh tomatoes. It is an ideal way to use up tomatoes with blemishes. Just remember to core, blanch and shock, then peel and chop them before beginning the recipe (see the techniques used in Chilled Tomato-Cucumber Soup with Bread and Almonds, page 90).

Peach Confiture

MAKES ABOUT 2 CUPS

Ripe summer peaches cooked down with a slew of spices results in a savory-sweet condiment that's as good spread across a turkey sandwich as it is on a cheese plate or alongside roasted meats. I like to serve this confiture with perfectly seared duck breasts (see page 229) because I love the pairing of crisp-skinned gamey meat and sweet, tangy fruit.

With a paring knife, cut a small, shallow X in the blossom end (bottom) of each peach, just through the skin. Blanch and shock the peaches (see page 375), cooking for about 1 minute, or until the skin begins to loosen; remove before the fruit softens too much. Immediately transfer the peaches to the bowl of ice water to cool. Remove the peaches from the ice water and, starting at the X, peel each peach. Using the paring knife, and starting at the stem end of a peach, cut through to the pit, then cut all of the way around the fruit. Separate the halves and discard the pit. Cut each half into 4 wedges, then cut the wedges into slices about ¼ inch thick. Repeat with the remaining 2 peaches.

Heat the oil in a small nonreactive saucepan over medium heat. Add the shallot and sweat (see page 377) until translucent, 2 to 3 minutes. Add the garlic and ginger and cook, stirring, until the garlic releases its fragrance, 1 to 2 minutes. Add the coriander, cloves, salt, pepper, the black and yellow mustard seeds, and the chile flakes and cook, stirring occasionally, until the mustard seeds begin to pop, about 2 minutes. Add the sugar and allow it to melt slightly. Add the vinegar and simmer, stirring occasionally, until the mixture thickens, 1 to 2 minutes. Lower the heat and stir frequently as needed to ensure that the sugars don't burn, adding 1 tablespoon water if necessary to prevent scorching.

When the mixture has thickened and is the consistency of a heavy syrup, add the peaches and simmer, stirring occasionally, until the peaches are very tender but not falling apart and all of the flavors have melded. The finished confiture should still have some discernible peach pieces and a chutney-like consistency; it should not be thin or watery. This will take 10 to 25 minutes, depending on how ripe the peaches are and their water content. Remove from the heat and let cool to room temperature before serving. If after cooling, the chutney still seems thin, return it to low heat for 5 to 10 minutes to further evaporate the water and thicken it.

The confiture will keep in an airtight container in the refrigerator for up to 10 days. Bring to room temperature before serving.

3 large yellow peaches

2 tablespoons extra-virgin olive oil

5 tablespoons minced shallot

1 tablespoon plus 1 teaspoon sliced garlic

2 teaspoons peeled and minced fresh ginger

1 teaspoon coriander seeds, toasted and ground (see page 378)

2 whole cloves, toasted and ground (see page 378)

1¼ teaspoons salt

½ teaspoon freshly ground black pepper

2 teaspoons black mustard seeds

1 teaspoon yellow mustard seeds

⅛ teaspoon red chile flakes

3 tablespoons plus 1 teaspoon muscovado sugar or dark brown sugar

3 tablespoons white wine vinegar

Hazelnut Romesco

MAKES ABOUT 2 CUPS

An excellent year-round sauce made from pantry staples, this rich, fragrant *romesco*, which was inspired by a recipe in Deborah Madison's *Vegetarian Cooking for Everyone*, is incredibly versatile. It perfectly complements a pan-seared pork chop and is equally good alongside simple roasted vegetables or even a piece of crusty artisanal bread.

You have a choice of dried chiles in this sauce, and you may need to adjust the amount of Espelette pepper to suit your spice tolerance (Espelette is often spicier than sweet paprika). When shopping for bell peppers, keep in mind that flatter ones are easier to peel after they are blackened. Try to choose peppers without prominent ridges on the bottom and a fairly uniform shape. If bell peppers aren't in season or you're in a time crunch, use jarred roasted *piquillo* peppers from Spain.

Mise en place is particularly important in this recipe because it calls for small amounts of many different ingredients, and once you get started cooking, they all come into play fairly quickly. Help yourself by measuring out each ingredient in little bowls ahead of time.

Preheat the oven to 350°F. Spread the almonds and hazelnuts on a small baking sheet and toast for 6 minutes. Carefully shake the baking sheet to ensure even toasting, then continue to toast for 2 to 4 minutes more, until the nuts are a light golden color throughout. Remove the nuts and leave the oven on. If the hazelnuts are not skinned, rub the still-hot nuts between a pair of kitchen towels to remove the skins.

Remove the stems and shake out and discard the seeds from the dried chiles. Place the chiles on a baking sheet and toast in the oven for 4 to 5 minutes, until they darken slightly and begin to puff up. (If they get too dark they will taste bitter, so keep an eye on them. They need only to puff up slightly to be ready. You can do this while you're toasting the nuts if you are careful about timing and remember to remove the chiles first.) Remove the chiles from the oven and turn the oven to broil.

Place the toasted chiles in a small heatproof bowl and pour in 1 cup of boiling water. Keep the chiles submerged by placing a small bowl or other weight on top of them. Cover the bowl and let it sit until the chiles are soft and pliable, 10 to 15 minutes.

If using bell peppers, place them on a baking sheet and brush them with about 1 tablespoon of the oil. Place the peppers under the broiler and roast, turning them every 2 to 3 minutes as they color, until all of the skin on the peppers is blackened and begins to separate from the flesh, about 15 minutes. Using tongs, transfer the peppers to a small bowl, cover tightly with plastic wrap, and allow to sit for at least 15 minutes, or until cool enough to handle. (The longer they steam, the easier it will be to peel off the skins.) When cool, lay the peppers on a cutting board. One at a time, pull out the stem from the top and discard, scrape the inside clean of any seeds, and then flip the

Continued

¼ cup unsalted Marcona almonds or roasted regular almonds (see Note, below)

¼ cup hazelnuts (see Note, below)

1½ ounces ancho or New Mexico chile (about 3 chiles)

2 red bell peppers, or 1 (4-ounce) jar Spanish piquillo peppers

1 cup plus about 3 tablespoons extra-virgin olive oil

2 tablespoons tomato paste (preferably Italian)

1 ounce crusty bread (such as ciabatta or artisanal white; piece 2 to 3 inches long and 1 inch thick)

1 rounded teaspoon garlic paste (page 344)

3 tablespoons tomato purée (preferably San Marzano)

½ teaspoon Espelette pepper or sweet paprika

½ teaspoon toasted and ground cumin seeds (see page 378)

¾ teaspoon toasted and ground coriander seeds (see page 378)

1 teaspoon sherry vinegar

½ teaspoon fish sauce (see page 370)

1¼ teaspoons salt

⅛ to ¼ teaspoon sugar (optional)

4 to 6 dashes Tabasco sauce (optional)

NOTE Even if your almonds or hazelnuts are labeled "roasted" on the package, it's okay to roast them again lightly to bring out even more of their flavor.

Hazelnut Romesco

CONTINUED

pepper over and peel off the skin from the outside. Reserve the peppers and any juices left in the steaming bowl. If using piquillo peppers, drain well and remove any seeds, if present.

Place a small nonreactive sauté pan over medium-high heat and add 2 tablespoons of the oil and the tomato paste. Let the paste cook on one side for about 1 minute, or until it starts to get a little dark, and then flip the paste over and slightly caramelize the other side, allowing the paste to dissipate into the oil. Remove the pan from the heat and set the oil-tomato mixture aside.

Cut the crust off the bread and cut the bread into 6 uniform cubes for frying. In your smallest saucepan (1 to 2 quarts or so), heat ¼ cup of the oil over medium-low heat. Add the bread cubes, turn down the heat to low, and cook until the bread very slowly turns a deep golden hue on both sides, 15 to 20 minutes total. You want the bread cubes to be evenly crispy throughout with no softness or give. Don't rush! If your oil isn't truly slow and low, the sugars on the outside of the bread will caramelize and the bread will look done but the interior will still be soft. You'll reserve the oil from this step and blend it back into the finished sauce, so it's important that it doesn't hit its smoke point and develop an unpleasant taste. (If it does, discard it and add a little more oil to your romesco during blending.) Using tongs, transfer the bread cubes to a paper towel to drain and cool. Set the oil aside.

Place the rehydrated chiles and their soaking water in a food processor and process until you have a very smooth and fully combined ketchup-like purée, about 1 minute. Add more water as needed to achieve the proper consistency, but be careful not to add too much or you will dilute the final result. Push the paste through a fine-mesh strainer to remove any skin or bitter residue; you should have between ¼ and ½ cup purée. Wash the processor bowl.

Add the fried bread, garlic paste, and nuts to the food processor and pulse until the bread is reduced to rough crumbs, 15 to 20 seconds. Remove the mixture from the processor, divide it into two batches, and set aside.

Add ¼ cup of the strained chile purée (save any leftover purée to add to a soup or sauce), the roasted bell peppers or piquillo peppers, the fried tomato paste, the tomato purée, Espelette pepper, cumin, coriander, vinegar, fish sauce, salt, and half of the bread-nut mixture to the processor (no need to wash the bowl first) and purée for about 1 minute, or until completely smooth and fully combined. With the machine still running, stream in the remaining ¾ cup oil, plus any of the reserved oil from frying the bread (likely a few tablespoons). Transfer the purée to a small bowl and fold in the remaining bread-nut mixture. Taste for seasoning and adjust with the sugar and Tabasco if desired.

The sauce will keep in an airtight container in the refrigerator for up to 1 week. Bring to room temperature before using.

Cracked Green Olive and Armagnac Prune Relish

MAKES 2 CUPS

This earthy relish was inspired by the recipe for chicken Marbella from *The Silver Palate Cookbook* by Julee Rosso and Sheila Lukins that involved a rustic mix of prunes and olives. I usually serve it alongside Lacquered Duck Confit (page 235) to help balance some of the duck's natural richness. It's also a great accompaniment to Fennel-Brined Pork Loin (page 247).

I like to use Castelvetrano olives for this relish because they are salt brined rather than vinegar brined, so the natural flavor of the olives shines through. They have a unique mild and fresh taste, but if you can't find them, Picholines are a good substitute.

1½ cups Castelvetrano olives

1 cup Armagnac-poached prunes (page 369), quartered

6 tablespoons extra-virgin olive oil

2 tablespoons finely minced shallot

1 teaspoon finely minced garlic

Generous pinch of red chile flakes

½ teaspoon fennel pollen

1 tablespoon aged sherry vinegar (see page 370)

To crack and pit the olives, using a small mallet or the flat side of a knife blade, press down firmly on each olive until it breaks, without crushing the pit. When you take the olive apart, don't crush it into tiny little bits. Instead, remove the pit and tear the olive in half, leaving it in large, rustic pieces. Place the olives in a bowl and add the prunes.

In a small sauté pan, warm 3 tablespoons of the oil over medium-low heat. Add the shallot, garlic, and chile flakes, lower the heat to ensure nothing takes on color, and then add the fennel pollen and stir occasionally. As soon as the shallot and garlic are translucent, after 2 to 3 minutes, remove from the heat and add to the prunes and olives. Add the vinegar and the remaining 3 tablespoons oil and stir to mix.

The relish will keep in an airtight container in the refrigerator for up to 1 week. Bring to room temperature before using.

Lemon Confit and Fried Caper Relish

MAKES 1½ CUPS

Here is just one of myriad ways to utilize the lemon confit on page 343. Packed with flavor, this relish has the acidity of a vinaigrette, but boasts an amazing amount of textural interest from the fried capers. It is served on Sole Piccata (page 221) and would also be great on seared tuna (see page 76) in place of the citrus and fennel salad; on Pan-Seared Salmon (page 218); or even with Lamb Loin Chops (page 286).

If the capers are in brine, drain well and press gently between paper or cloth towels until totally dry. If the capers are salt packed, soak in warm water for about 10 minutes, then remove with a slotted spoon, allowing the salt crystals to fall to the bottom. Put the capers in a bowl of fresh water and let soak for 5 minutes more. Drain well and press gently between paper or cloth towels until totally dry. (I prefer salt-packed capers, which tend to be more mature, have a better flavor, and open up like flowers when fried.)

Pour the canola oil into a 2-quart saucepan and heat to 350°F over high heat. Drop in the capers and cook for about 2 minutes, or until they open up into little flowers and begin to look crunchy. Using a slotted spoon, transfer to a paper towel. Let cool completely.

Put the lemon confit and confit oil, lemon juice, and vinegar in a small bowl and set aside.

In a small saucepan, warm the olive oil over medium heat. Add the shallot and cook, stirring occasionally, until translucent, 2 to 3 minutes. Add the garlic and cook until it, too, is translucent, about 1 minute. Stir in the chile flakes and Marsala and turn off the heat.

Add the shallot mixture to the bowl with the lemon confit and stir to mix. Add the parsley and fried capers and stir briefly to combine. Serve immediately.

¼ cup brined or salt-packed capers

1½ cups canola oil

3 tablespoons minced lemon confit (page 343), with 1 tablespoon of its oil

1 tablespoon plus 1 teaspoon lemon juice

½ teaspoon aged sherry vinegar (see page 370)

1 tablespoon extra-virgin olive oil

3 tablespoons finely diced shallot

2 cloves garlic, thinly sliced

⅛ teaspoon red chile flakes

1 teaspoon sweet Marsala

¼ cup roughly torn flat-leaf parsley leaves

NOTE This relish, minus the fried capers, can be assembled up to a day in advance. Just before serving, fry the capers and stir them into the relish.

Flavored Crème Fraîche

One of the first essential rules of cooking is that fat is flavor. A high-quality crème fraîche or sour cream (see page 370) is appealing because it's naturally fatty but also slightly tart. Take that combination and balance it with a little salt and you've just unlocked one of the keys to great cooking.

Crème fraîche carries other flavors easily and enhances everything it touches. An infused crème fraîche is easy to make because most of the ingredients are probably already in your kitchen.

The amount of seasoning for each flavored crème fraîche should depend on what you'll be serving it with and how much you'll be thinning it out, so you'll need to taste frequently as you work. For more on salting, see page 375. If the version you're making calls for lemon zest and juice, grate the zest before halving and squeezing the lemon. This will save you the annoyance of trying to grate the zest of an already squeezed lemon. All of these variations can be stored in an airtight container in the refrigerator for up to 3 days.

From top: Smoked Paprika and Espelette, Herbed, and Lemon Confit

Herbed Crème Fraîche

MAKES ABOUT 1 CUP

This light, herb-infused crème fraîche is the one I use most often, usually as a soup garnish, though it also works well on Butter-Poached Halibut (page 214) or New Potato Salad with Fava Beans and Morels (page 149).

In a small bowl, stir together the lemon juice, shallot, and salt and let sit for 5 to 10 minutes to allow the sharp shallot flavor to mellow.

Place the crème fraîche in a small bowl and stir in the parsley, chives, and tarragon. Add the shallot mixture and the lemon zest and mix well. Season with the pepper, then taste and adjust with more salt and pepper if needed.

1 teaspoon lemon juice

1 teaspoon finely minced shallot

½ teaspoon salt

1 cup crème fraîche or sour cream (see page 370)

2 tablespoons finely minced flat-leaf parsley

1 tablespoon finely minced chives

2 teaspoons finely minced tarragon

¼ teaspoon lemon zest (see page 375)

¼ teaspoon freshly ground black pepper

Smoked Paprika and Espelette Crème Fraîche

MAKES ABOUT 1 CUP

Use this infused crème fraîche on anything you want to elevate with a mild smoky flavor, like Smoky Tomato Velouté with Parmesan Straws (page 97). Do not substitute plain paprika here, as it lacks the complex flavor of the smoked version. I prefer a Spanish smoked paprika, *pimentón de la Vera*, and in particular La Dalia brand (the sweet version, not hot).

Place the crème fraîche in a small bowl and stir in the salt, lemon juice, garlic, sugar, paprika, Espelette pepper, and 1 teaspoon hot sauce. Taste and adjust with more salt and hot sauce if needed.

1 cup crème fraîche or sour cream (see page 370)

½ teaspoon salt

1 teaspoon lemon juice

¼ teaspoon finely minced garlic

½ teaspoon sugar

1 teaspoon smoked sweet paprika

½ teaspoon Espelette pepper

1 to 2 teaspoons hot sauce of choice

Continued

Flavored Crème Fraîche

CONTINUED

Horseradish Crème Fraîche

MAKES ABOUT 1 CUP

This variation offers a punch of bright, spicy flavor to Pan-Seared Salmon (page 218) or Bone-In Rib Eyes (page 263).

In a small bowl, stir together the lemon juice, shallot, and salt and let sit for 5 to 10 minutes to allow the sharp shallot flavor to mellow.

Place the crème fraîche in a small bowl and stir in the parsley, chives, dill, and horseradish. Add the shallot mixture and the lemon zest and mix well. Season with the pepper, then taste and adjust with more salt and pepper if needed.

1¼ teaspoons lemon juice

1 teaspoon finely minced shallot

½ teaspoon salt

1 cup crème fraîche or sour cream (see page 370)

2 tablespoons finely minced flat-leaf parsley

1 tablespoon finely minced chives

2 teaspoons finely minced dill

2 tablespoons freshly grated horseradish, or 2 teaspoons jarred horseradish

¼ teaspoon lemon zest (see page 375)

¼ teaspoon freshly ground black pepper

Lemon Confit Crème Fraîche

MAKES ABOUT 1 CUP

Here, the already bright taste of crème fraîche is bumped up with the addition of lemon in two forms: fresh and confit.

In a small bowl, stir together the lemon juice, shallot, and salt and let sit for 5 to 10 minutes to allow the sharp shallot flavor to mellow.

Place the crème fraîche in a small bowl and stir in the shallot mixture, the lemon confit and confit oil, and the lemon zest. Taste and adjust with more salt if needed.

1 teaspoon lemon juice

1 teaspoon finely minced shallot

½ teaspoon salt

1 cup crème fraîche or sour cream (see page 370)

2 tablespoons minced lemon confit (page 343), with 1 tablespoon of its oil

¼ teaspoon lemon zest (see page 375)

Mint Crème Fraîche

MAKES ABOUT 1 CUP

A bright green color and refreshing flavors make this variation extra special. It matches well with roasted beets (see page 138) and is the perfect foil for lightly gamey Lamb Loin Chops (page 286).

In a small bowl, stir together the shallot and vinegar and let sit for 5 to 10 minutes to allow the sharp shallot flavor to mellow.

Finely chop the mint leaves. To get the mintiest flavor possible, crush the chopped mint with the salt into a rough paste in a mortar with a pestle, or sprinkle the chopped mint with the salt and make a mint paste by moving your knife back and forth across the cutting board, using the same method used for making the garlic paste.

Place the crème fraîche in a small bowl and stir in the shallot mixture, the mint paste, the garlic paste, and pepper. Taste and adjust the seasoning with more salt if needed.

2 teaspoons minced shallot

2 teaspoons red wine vinegar

2 cups loosely packed mint leaves

¼ teaspoon salt

1 cup crème fraîche or sour cream (see page 370)

¾ teaspoon garlic paste (page 344)

¼ teaspoon freshly ground black pepper

Tarragon Mousse

MAKES 1 CUP

Transforming a sauce with gelatin into a fluffy, distinctly flavored mousse is one of those little tricks that really elevates your presentation. It adds what one of my cooks, Mira, used to call a T.O.E., or "touch of elegance"—that extra something that makes a dish more special. Gelatin might seem intimidating to work with, but in fact it's remarkably simple.

I use this mousse mainly as a garnish for cauliflower velouté (see page 98). Plain crème fraîche was my usual garnish for this dish, but I didn't like how it sank and melted into the soup. A puff of light-as-air mousse that floats on the surface of the soup makes the dish more refined.

The same gelatin technique can be applied to any of the flavored crème fraîche recipes on the preceding pages. You can also flavor this mousse with a different herb, like finely chopped chives or flat-leaf parsley.

8 cups water, plus 1 tablespoon

2 tablespoons plus ½ teaspoon salt

4 cups ice cubes

½ cup packed tarragon leaves

1 cup crème fraîche or sour cream (see page 370)

¾ teaspoon powdered gelatin

⅛ teaspoon Tabasco sauce

½ teaspoon lemon zest (see page 375)

¼ teaspoon tarragon vinegar or white wine vinegar

½ teaspoon Dijon mustard

1/16 teaspoon sugar (optional)

2 tablespoons heavy cream

In a 2-quart saucepan, bring 4 cups of the water and 1 tablespoon of the salt to a boil. Set up a metal bowl with the remaining 4 cups of water, the ice cubes, and 1 tablespoon of the remaining salt. Have a fine-mesh strainer ready to go as soon as the salted water is boiling. Blanch the tarragon leaves (see page 375), cooking for about 5 seconds. Scoop out the leaves with the strainer and plunge them directly into the ice water to fully cool them. Remove the leaves from the ice water, roll them up in a kitchen towel, and squeeze out the excess liquid. Finely chop the blanched tarragon.

Place ½ cup of the crème fraîche in a food processor. Add the tarragon and purée for about 30 seconds, or until the tarragon is evenly dispersed. Add the remaining ½ cup crème fraîche and purée for 30 seconds to 1 minute, until the sauce is evenly blended and the tarragon is very fine.

In a small bowl, sprinkle the gelatin over the remaining 1 tablespoon water and let bloom for 5 to 10 minutes. Meanwhile, transfer the crème fraîche mixture to a metal mixing bowl. Add the Tabasco, lemon zest, vinegar, mustard, and the remaining ½ teaspoon salt and mix well. Taste and add sugar if needed.

Place your smallest saucepan (1 to 2 quarts) over medium-low heat and add the heavy cream. As soon as it is hot (don't let it burn!), remove the pan from the heat and drop the bloomed gelatin into the hot cream. Using a rubber spatula, stir quickly until no lumps of gelatin remain.

Using the spatula, scrape the cream mixture into the bowl holding the tarragon crème fraîche, being careful to get it all. Whisk until thoroughly combined. Pour the crème fraîche mixture into a container large enough so that there is about ¾ inch of headspace. Cover and refrigerate until fully set, about 3 hours, or for up to 4 days.

Just before using, whisk the mousse briefly to fluff it up. To serve, shape a quenelle (see page 377) of the mousse and place atop the dish you are garnishing.

Aioli and Variations

MAKES 1 CUP

Mastering homemade aioli is a great milestone in the kitchen. Making it requires patience, which is a good lesson for every cook to learn. Aioli is all about emulsification, or the coming together of two substances that do not normally combine smoothly. My silver bullet for making perfect aioli is to drape a Dutch oven or other big pot with a damp kitchen towel and place a metal bowl inside the pot. This arrangement holds the bowl steady while you whisk—like adding a third hand. To get the yolk moving properly, choose a bowl with a gradual curve and a small, flat bottom—the natural curvature of the bowl will encourage better motion with your whisk.

Work on a low surface (think kitchen table instead of the countertop—your arm will thank you later) and ready your *mise en place* before you start whisking. A stiff whisk will slow you down, while a flexible balloon whisk will get the job done in a few minutes. A squeeze bottle is ideal for adding the oil to the yolk slowly and carefully. If you don't have one, put the oil into a flexible plastic container—a take-out container or a leftover yogurt tub will do—so you can easily bend it into a little spout that will allow you to control the flow of the oil as you whisk.

The first time you make aioli, try doubling the recipe, as it's a bit easier to make with two eggs.

1 egg

½ cup extra-virgin olive oil

½ cup neutral oil (such as canola or grapeseed)

1½ teaspoons lemon juice mixed with 2 teaspoons room-temperature water

½ teaspoon garlic paste (page 344)

¼ to ½ teaspoon salt

Place the whole unshelled egg in a small heatproof bowl and pour in boiling water to cover. Let the egg sit, submerged, for 1 minute. (Coddling the egg this way begins to set the protein in the whites, helping the emulsification process and minimizing the bacteria on the shell.) Remove the egg from the water, crack it, separate the white from the yolk, place the yolk in the bowl in which you will be making the aioli, and discard the white.

Combine the olive oil and the neutral oil in a squeeze bottle or flexible plastic container (see the recipe introduction). Grip the whisk handle where it meets the wires, not at the top of the handle, and begin whisking the yolk with your dominant hand. When the yolk is broken up and smooth, start to very slowly—a drop or two at a time—add the mixed oils in a very fine stream while whisking constantly (see the photo, page 33). Stop pouring periodically while continuing to whisk to ensure proper emulsification. Keep your elbow glued to your waist as you whisk and let all of the motion come from your wrist. If your arm gets tired, it's fine to take a break for a few seconds, but make sure you've also stopped adding oil. You don't have to, nor do you want to, work fast—it's more important to whisk and pour consistently and slowly. If you do pour in too much oil at once, whisk very rapidly for a few seconds to combine.

Continued

Aioli and Variations

CONTINUED

I have found that 1 egg yolk can hold about ⅓ cup of oil before it hits its saturation point and starts to take on a slightly stringy or taffy-like appearance, usually after about 2 minutes of whisking. This is a critical point, and when it happens, use your fingertips to sprinkle about ½ teaspoon of the diluted lemon juice over the mixture to thin it out. Resume whisking and drizzling oil until the mixture becomes "tight" again, then add another scant 1 teaspoon diluted lemon juice and the garlic paste. Repeat until all of the oil and diluted lemon juice have been emulsified into the mixture. Finally, stir in the salt, starting with ¼ teaspoon and adding up to ½ teaspoon or as needed.

The aioli will keep in an airtight container in the refrigerator for up to 2 days.

Variations

In the following aioli variations, additional ingredients are mixed into the base recipe to create different flavor profiles. You may want to thin the aioli base slightly just before incorporating the ingredients, as sometimes adding an oily ingredient such as lemon confit to an already tight base can cause it to break. Thin the base with ½ to 1 teaspoon room-temperature water. Be sure to taste and add more salt as needed to the finished aioli.

Aioli Vert (see Fried Pork Rillettes photo, page 71): In a small bowl, combine 1 cup aioli, 1 teaspoon finely minced tarragon, 1 tablespoon finely minced chives, 2 tablespoons plus 2 teaspoons finely minced flat-leaf parsley, and ¼ teaspoon salt and mix well.

Mayonnaise: There's a time and place to use mayonnaise instead of aioli (on a fresh summer tomato sandwich, for example). Follow the aioli recipe, using 1 cup canola oil (instead of the oil mixture) and swapping ¾ teaspoon white wine vinegar and 2½ teaspoons water for the lemon juice and water. Omit the garlic paste and add ⅛ teaspoon sugar when you stir in the salt.

Fried Caper Rémoulade (see tomato and crab salad, page 125): Combine 1 cup aioli, 1 tablespoon plus 1 teaspoon finely minced cornichon, ½ teaspoon lemon zest (see page 375), 1 teaspoon lemon juice, 1 teaspoon finely minced chives, 2 teaspoons finely minced celery, ¼ teaspoon sugar, and ⅛ teaspoon freshly ground black pepper and mix well.

You'll need ¼ cup capers. If the capers are in brine, drain well and press gently between paper or cloth towels until totally dry. If the capers are salt packed, soak in warm water for about 10 minutes, then remove with a slotted spoon, allowing the salt crystals to fall to the bottom. Put the capers in a bowl of fresh water and let soak for 5 minutes more. Drain well and press gently between paper or cloth towels until totally dry. (I prefer salt-packed capers, which tend to be more mature, have a better flavor, and open up like flowers when fried.)

Pour 1½ cups canola oil into a 2-quart saucepan and heat to 350°F over high heat. Drop in the capers and cook for about 2 minutes, or until they open up into little flowers and begin to look crunchy. Using a slotted spoon, transfer to a paper towel and let cool completely, about 5 minutes. Stir the fried capers into the aioli just before serving or they will begin to soften.

Hollandaise

MAKES ¾ CUP

Making hollandaise is essentially the same process as making aioli (with warm butter instead of oil), so once you've mastered aioli (page 28), this will be a cinch. Don't let the length of this recipe intimidate you. Hollandaise is easy to make, but I have explained the process in detail so you know what to look, feel, and taste for when making it by hand.

The big difference between hollandaise and aioli is that here you need to temper the egg yolks with a little warm butter. Melt the butter and whisk it in *gradually*, as you do with the oil in aioli. Start with room-temperature eggs and use warm (but not hot) butter. If it's too hot, you'll break the hollandaise; if it's not warm enough, the sauce will be overly thick. Serve the sauce over warm or room-temperature dishes, because again, if the food is too hot, the sauce breaks, and if it is too cold, the sauce will congeal.

You can make plain hollandaise with lemon and spring herbs; you can add sherry vinegar, as we often do at Beast; or you can even fold in black garlic (see Variations, right) for a blast of umami. One of my favorite additions is pickled mustard seeds (see Variations, right); this version is shown served with the spring vegetable hash on page 203.

Place a small saucepan over medium-low heat. Add the butter and heat, swirling the pan occasionally, until the butter is completely melted and warm but not boiling or separated. Pour it into a clear liquid measuring cup or a bowl with a spout and set aside to cool slightly. (The butter should be warm, not hot, when you use it. If it's too hot, it will break the mixture; if it's too cold, the hollandaise will be too firm).

Fill a 2-quart saucepan one-quarter full with water, bring the water to a boil, and turn off the heat. Add the egg yolks to a small- to medium-size bowl that can rest inside the rim of the pot without touching the water. Ideally, you'll have a bowl with a gradual curve, as the natural curvature of the bowl will help you get a better motion with your whisk. On a countertop (rather than over the water), whisk the egg yolks vigorously for about 20 seconds, or until they begin to get foamy. As you whisk, try to keep the beaten yolks on the bottom of the bowl as much as possible, rather than splashing them on the sides, as any egg stuck to the side can overcook in the next step.

Place the bowl over the pan holding the hot water and continue to whisk, incorporating as much air as possible into the yolks and stopping and checking every 5 or 6 strokes, until the yolks are pale and have increased in volume, 1 to 2 minutes. Make sure the yolks are not beginning to scramble or cook. Take the bowl off the heat and check the temperature with your finger: it should feel warmer than body temperature but not hot. It's important to warm the yolks to nearly the same temperature as the melted butter, so the two ingredients emulsify properly.

Continued

10 tablespoons butter, cut into 1 tablespoon chunks

3 egg yolks (see page 377), at room temperature

¾ teaspoon lemon juice

½ teaspoon sherry vinegar

½ teaspoon salt

2½ to 3½ teaspoons warm water (not hot)

Variations

Pickled Mustard Seed Hollandaise: Whisk 1 tablespoon of drained pickled mustard seeds (page 350) into the finished hollandaise.

Black Garlic Hollandaise: Omit the salt. Following the directions for garlic paste on page 344, smash 3 cloves black garlic with ½ teaspoon salt and then whisk paste into the finished hollandaise. This regal-tasting hollandaise works equally well spooned over blanched and rewarmed asparagus (see page 144) as it does with a big steak and thick-cut fries in place of a traditional béarnaise.

Hollandaise

CONTINUED

Drape a Dutch oven or other big pot with a damp kitchen towel and place the bowl inside the pot to help stabilize it as you whisk. Very slowly—a drop or two at a time—add half of the melted butter into the yolks while whisking constantly; the mixture will gradually thicken. Stop pouring periodically while continuing to whisk to ensure proper emulsification. You don't have to, nor do you want to, work fast. It's more important to whisk and pour consistently and slowly to get an emulsified sauce. Be attentive to the butter's temperature throughout. You may have to move the bowl back and forth from the warm pot on the stove top to the cool countertop as you whisk to maintain the right texture.

Once half of the butter is fully incorporated, slowly drizzle in the lemon juice and vinegar, whisking at the same time, then whisk in the salt. Again working slowly, drizzle in the remaining butter while whisking constantly. Continue moving the hollandaise between the warm pot and cool countertop if needed to maintain the right emulsified texture. With a proper emulsification, there is no separation between ingredients. You should see one completely smooth and consistent substance with no beads of oil. In a broken emulsification, the surface isn't uniform; it looks a little scrambled and has oil droplets. Some milky white solids will have separated from the melted butter and fallen to the bottom of the measuring cup. You don't want these in the hollandaise, so incorporate all but the last 1 to 2 tablespoons of the butter into the eggs, then simply stop pouring and discard the solids.

Taste the sauce for salt, then thin the mixture by whisking in 2½ teaspoons warm water, or up to 3½ teaspoons if needed for a smooth and pourable consistency. Serve warm over warm or room-temperature dishes. If not serving right away, hold the hollandaise in a thermos (do not preheat the thermos with hot water) in a warm place for up to 2 hours. When you're ready to serve the hollandaise, you may need to very carefully warm and loosen the sauce if it has cooled too much and thickened. Use the same double-boiler method (see previous page) to warm the sauce over boiling water that has been removed from the heat. Whisk in about 1 teaspoon warm water to thin.

Demi-Glace

MAKES ABOUT 1 CUP

I cannot overstate the importance of knowing how to make demi-glace. This simple reduction of a well-made stock yields one of the most powerful ingredients in the kitchen. The only way to describe the taste is to call it the most highly concentrated essence of savory. It's a natural flavor enhancer and a little bit goes a long way.

Turning stock into demi-glace is fairly easy, but it does take time, patient observation, and skimming. At the restaurant, I like to call it babysitting. No one needs to stand there and watch the pot while it is reducing, but it is important to glance over and skim it every 10 to 15 minutes.

We make two batches of demi-glace a week at Beast, using 100 pounds of bones each time, because we serve it on so many things. A modest drizzle of warm demi-glace instantly heightens the flavor of any piece of meat, and once you have tasted it, you'll want to put it on just about everything, too.

In a pot, bring the stock to a gentle boil (or rolling simmer). The bubbles shouldn't be violent or hard; instead, the stock should look like it is rolling into itself over and over, like a swiftly moving river. Once that rolling motion has started, skim the stock every 10 to 15 minutes. The best way to do this is to keep a small (4- to 6-ounce) ladle near the stove—something that you leave in a visible place to remind you to skim continually. To ladle off the scum, fat, and proteins that gather, tilt the ladle at a 45-degree angle near the fat, pressing ever so slightly into the liquid and allowing the fats to "swim" into the ladle. It's important to skim slowly and carefully to avoid getting any of the precious stock into the fat mix that you will be discarding.

After 1 hour, if you have been diligently skimming, the stock should release fewer particles and less fat, so you can skim slightly less often. After about 1½ hours, the liquid should be much darker and starting to thicken. At this point, the stock should have reduced significantly, to about 1 quart. Transfer the liquid to a small 2-quart saucepan. Turn the heat down as low as possible (what a shame it would be to burn your liquid this close to the end!) and stir occasionally until the liquid is the consistency of a thin maple syrup and has reduced to about 1 cup, about 1 hour and 50 minutes more. Check the stock frequently to ensure you don't reduce it too much.

To test if the demi-glace is ready, spoon about ½ teaspoon onto a small plate. It should still be liquid, but when you drag your index finger through it, your finger should leave a trail. The demi-glace should not be sticky, and it should have a smooth mouthfeel and very rich taste. If you have accidentally reduced it too much, you can add 1 to 2 tablespoons of water or a little red wine reduction (see page 185).

Store in an airtight container in the refrigerator for up to 1 week or in the freezer for up to 3 months.

4 quarts homemade stock (page 346)

Demi-Glace Cream

MAKES 2 CUPS

Marrying pure demi-glace with rich heavy cream, as you do in this recipe, not only helps stretch the sauce but also creates the most refined version of gravy you'll ever encounter. It's great for adding umami, richness, and refinement to poultry dishes or Strip Loin Roast (page 269).

In a 4-quart saucepan, combine the cream and garlic and bring to a rolling simmer over medium-high heat. It's important to use a much bigger pot than the amount of cream you want to reduce, because as the cream heats, it bubbles up like crazy and has a tendency to boil over if the pot isn't big enough. Keep a small whisk handy so that when it bubbles, you can quickly stir it to keep it from spilling over the sides of the pan.

Once the cream has reached a rapid simmer, turn down the heat to medium-low and simmer very gently, stirring occasionally with the whisk, until the cream is reduced to 1 cup, 8 to 10 minutes. Remove the garlic cloves from the pan, discard, and set the cream aside in the pan.

Pour the sherry into a small saucepan and place over high heat until the sherry has reduced to 1 tablespoon, 2 to 3 minutes. Watch closely to ensure the sherry doesn't totally evaporate. Set the sherry reduction aside.

Return the pan with the reduced cream to low heat. When the cream is warm, whisk in the demi-glace and allow the mixture to heat slowly to a bare simmer, stirring occasionally. Add the sherry reduction and the pepper and stir to combine. Taste and add salt if needed.

The sauce can be made up to 2 hours in advance; gently reheat over low heat before serving. It will keep in an airtight container in the refrigerator for up to 1 week.

1½ cups heavy cream

4 cloves garlic

2 tablespoons dry sherry

¾ cup Demi-Glace (page 36), at room temperature

⅛ teaspoon freshly ground black pepper

Salt (optional)

Horseradish Gremolata

MAKES ABOUT ⅓ CUP

I consider this something of a dry *sauce verte* (see page 5), ideal for when you want to add freshness and brightness to a braised dish that already has a lot of liquid. This *gremolata* helps cut some of the richness of Balsamic Braised Short Ribs (page 273) and adds a touch of much-needed color, like a scattering of confetti, to an otherwise brown dish. As a bonus, the whole thing takes just a few minutes to make. It tastes best when assembled within a half hour of serving.

Fresh horseradish is dry when you grate it, and it has a pungency that's not as biting or as in your face as many jarred versions, which are usually puréed with vinegar, cream, and salt. Fresh horseradish tastes peppery and doesn't add unwanted liquid to what is meant to be a dry sauce.

This *gremolata* is intended to add balance to a dish, so it is important that it, too, tastes balanced, with brightness from the lemon, a vegetal quality from the parsley, and a little kick from the horseradish and garlic. If the garlic comes on too strong (wait for a minute after adding it before you taste the mixture, as the flavor of garlic can take at least a few seconds to bloom fully), add more parsley to tone it down a bit. Your knife skills really show here, so chop carefully and use a very sharp knife. Also, be sure the parsley is very dry before you chop it or it will bind together rather than remain distinct and fluffy (see page 376).

⅓ cup finely chopped flat-leaf parsley

1 tablespoon minced preserved lemon rind (from about ¼ lemon), or 1 tablespoon minced lemon confit (page 343)

1 teaspoon freshly grated horseradish

¼ teaspoon lemon zest (see page 375)

⅛ to ¼ clove garlic, grated on a fine-rasp Microplane grater (see page 374)

Combine all of the ingredients in a small bowl. Using your fingers, mix the ingredients until they are evenly distributed, 10 to 15 seconds. Taste and adjust with more horseradish if needed.

To use the gremolata, simply sprinkle it over the top of the dish just before serving. Use it all, or cover it with oil for another use, as it does not store well dry. It will keep in the refrigerator for up to 2 days.

Beurre Blanc

MAKES ABOUT 1 CUP

This is a classic sauce that's made up of ingredients you likely have on hand. It's delicious on everything, from steamed seafood to vegetables to chicken. Like some of the other sauces in this chapter, mastering this sauce takes patience and attentiveness to ensure that you whisk in all of the butter without breaking the sauce. And much like the soufflés on page 195, even if the sauce does break, it will still taste delicious.

The first few times you make this recipe, it's better to err on the side of your pan not being hot enough when whisking in the butter. Whisking over a flame allows you to make the sauce quickly, but you do run the risk of it breaking, so whisk mostly off the heat to begin with, and then rewarm the pan if necessary, rather than cook the sauce directly over the heat the entire time.

In an 8- to 10-inch nonreactive sauté pan, heat the shallots and wine over medium heat. Cook until you have a syrupy consistency and the wine has mostly evaporated, 10 to 15 minutes. Be careful not to reduce the wine too much; there should still be some liquid at the bottom of the pan.

Turn off the heat and add the butter, 1 cube at a time, whisking after each addition until thoroughly melted before adding the next cube. If the pan gets too cool to melt the butter, turn on the burner to the lowest possible setting and whisk in 1 or 2 cubes at a time. The goal here is to melt the butter without breaking it, so keep the temperature warm but not too hot, adjusting the heat as needed to keep the sauce smooth and evenly textured. It is also important to whisk constantly, just as you do when adding oil for aioli (see page 28). Whisk in the salt with the last cube of butter. Once all of the butter has been incorporated, the sauce should be silky smooth, warm to the touch, and fall in a thin but steady stream off the back of a spoon.

Strain the sauce through a fine-mesh strainer into a bowl to remove the shallots (see the photo, left). Serve the sauce immediately if possible, or hold it in a thermos (do not preheat the thermos with hot water) in a warm place for up to 1 hour.

¼ cup finely minced shallot

1½ cups dry white wine

16 tablespoons butter, cut into ¼-inch cubes

½ teaspoon salt

Variation

Beurre Rouge: Substitute red wine for the white wine and proceed as directed. This sauce complements steaks, poached eggs, and fattier fish like salmon.

Starters

The recipes in this chapter are versatile and will teach you a wide array of techniques. You can offer one or more of them to guests before the main event at a special-occasion dinner, or you can combine a few of them to make a meal. Most of the recipes require attention to detail, but they come together quickly, making them almost instantly gratifying.

Many of these dishes are served at Beast, and most of them are little bites that pack big flavors. Crème Fraîche Tarts (page 48) is an example of a genius foundational recipe: it is endlessly adaptable to nearly any kind of topping, making it a valuable tool in your repertoire. Chicken Liver Mousse (page 67), Fried Pork Rillettes (page 70), and Steak Tartare on Brioche with Quail Eggs (page 75) allow you to experiment with beginner-level charcuterie projects, with delicious results.

Although these recipes vary widely—some are rich and some are fresh, some are vegetarian and some are meat heavy—they all give you the opportunity to practice your knife skills and basic kitchen techniques, such as searing and emulsifying, to help you impress your dinner guests.

Crème Fraîche Tarts: Spring Pea Relish; Half-Dried Tomatoes and Strong Cheese; Butternut Squash Purée, Pancetta, and Crispy Fried Sage; Caramelized Onions with Anchovies and Olives ‖ 48

Burrata with Dandelion–Golden Raisin–Pistachio Pistou ‖ 55

Beet-Cured Salmon with Creamy Herbed Cucumbers ‖ 56

Figs with Foie Gras Mousse ‖ 60

Hazelnut and Wild Mushroom Pâté ‖ 64

Chicken Liver Mousse ‖ 67

Fried Pork Rillettes ‖ 70

Steak Tartare on Brioche with Quail Eggs ‖ 75

Coriander-Seared Tuna with Citrus and Fennel Salad ‖ 76

Baked Camembert with Armagnac Prunes, Mushrooms, and Thyme ‖ 79

Crème Fraîche Tarts

SERVES 6 TO 8

This is one of the most eye-opening recipes you'll ever learn, because once you know it, the possibilities for riffing on it are endless. Morgan Brownlow, my old chef and partner at clarklewis, taught me this dough. It's incredibly easy to make at home, even for less experienced cooks, and the results are particularly impressive, especially considering how little effort goes into it.

The key to success is to keep your ingredients cold and not to overmix them. Apart from that, this dough comes together in minutes. And once it's rolled out, you can top it with virtually anything—savory or sweet. It bakes up beautifully buttery and flaky and rises almost like puff pastry. I love that you can cut the dough into small pieces for tiny passed appetizers or use the whole batch for a full-size tart that's perfect for lunch with a simple salad.

MAKE THE DOUGH In a food processor, combine the flour, salt, and baking powder and process briefly to mix. Using the pulse function, add the butter, a few cubes at a time, pulsing 15 to 20 times until the butter is reduced to pea-size pieces. Work quickly to ensure the butter doesn't warm up too much. Add the crème fraîche directly from the refrigerator and pulse 4 to 6 times to incorporate. Then pulse another 4 to 6 times, until the dough begins to have a slightly uniform but pebbly texture and no dry flour remains.

Stretch a 2-foot-long sheet of plastic wrap across a clean work surface. Turn the dough out onto the plastic wrap. Gather all of the edges of the plastic wrap around the dough, press together, and form the dough into a ball. Tap the dough ball on the countertop to shape it into a rectangle about 6 by 10 inches, flattening the top surface at the end to create an even shape. Chill the dough in the refrigerator for at least 1 or for up to 24 hours.

Unwrap the dough and allow it to rest for no more than 15 to 20 minutes, just until it is slightly pliable. Lightly flour a clean work surface. Using a rolling pin, whack the dough several times across its surface to soften it. Pick up the dough, flour the work surface again ever so slightly, and return the dough to the surface.

Roll out the dough into a rectangle about 8 by 12 inches, with the long side parallel to the countertop's edge. Fold the rectangle in thirds, like a letter (see figures 7–9, page 333). The dough will look like a book: with a spine (the folded edge) on one side and the open edge on the other. Now rotate the "book" so the spine is facing your body, parallel to the countertop's edge. Roll the dough out again to an 8 by 12-inch rectangle. Fold the rectangle in thirds again. Rotate the "book" one more time so the spine is facing your body and roll out the dough a third time to a 9 by 15-inch rectangle that's about ¼ inch thick. Cut the rectangle lengthwise into three strips, each 3 by 15 inches. Line a baking sheet with parchment paper. Place the dough strips, not touching, on the prepared baking sheet and prick all over with a fork, leaving a ¼-inch boundary around the edge. Put the baking sheet with the dough into the freezer for about 15 minutes. Preheat the oven to 425°F.

Continued

DOUGH

2 cups all-purpose flour (see page 376)

2 teaspoons salt

2 teaspoons baking powder

16 tablespoons cold butter, cut into ½-inch cubes and refrigerated until needed

1 cup cold crème fraîche or sour cream (see page 370), refrigerated until needed

EGG WASH

1 egg

1 tablespoon heavy cream

From left: Half-Dried Tomatoes and Strong Cheese; Butternut Squash Purée, Pancetta, and Crispy Fried Sage; Spring Pea Relish; Caramelized Onions with Anchovies and Olives

Crème Fraîche Tarts

CONTINUED

MAKE THE EGG WASH In a small bowl, whisk together the egg and cream until well blended.

Remove the dough strips from the freezer and, using a pastry brush, brush each with egg wash, then bake for 10 minutes. Remove the pan from the oven, turn down the oven to 375°F, and wait for a few minutes for the temperature to adjust. Return the baking sheet to the oven and bake for 12 to 15 minutes more, until the pastry is rich golden brown. Carefully lift up the pastry with a metal spatula to ensure that the bottom is also toasted brown.

Top with one of the following combinations, all of which can be prepped while the dough is chilling in the refrigerator, and finish baking the tarts as directed in each recipe. The tarts will be fairly dark in color. Don't worry; the taste is far superior to an uncooked pastry.

Spring Pea Relish

Crème fraîche dough is a great vehicle for the tender sweetness of peas. Since peas are a lot of work to shuck, I let them take center stage when they're in season. I add cheese to this tart filling to introduce a rich, creamy element that balances the bright green vegetal quality of the peas.

8 ounces sheep's milk ricotta or fromage blanc

Spring Pea–Mint Relish (page 8)

Soften the cheese slightly by smashing it in a bowl with a spoon. Using the spoon and your fingers, spread the cheese along the parbaked pastry strips, dividing it evenly and leaving ¼ inch of pastry uncovered around the edges.

Return the tarts to the 375°F oven for 1 to 2 minutes, until the cheese is warm but not too runny. Keep a close eye on the tarts and remove them from the oven before the cheese turns to liquid. Spoon the relish on top of the warm tarts and cut crosswise into pieces. Serve immediately.

Half-Dried Tomatoes and Strong Cheese

This is one of my favorite ways to top these tarts: the tomatoes are bright and acidic and add a beautiful burst of color, while a funky cheese plays against the tender pastry. The whole thing gets balanced with a dose of herbaceous flavor from the thyme or savory in the half-dried tomatoes.

8 ounces cold strongly flavored soft cheese (such as Brie or Taleggio), sliced ⅛ inch thick

Half-dried tomatoes (page 350)

Arrange the cheese slices along the parbaked pastry strips, dividing them evenly and leaving ¼ inch of pastry uncovered around the edges. Spoon the tomatoes, cut side up, over the cheese and return the tarts to the 375°F oven for 3 to 5 minutes, until the pastry is very dark golden brown. Cut crosswise into pieces and serve immediately.

Butternut Squash Purée, Pancetta, and Crispy Fried Sage

In the fall, I love to mix the natural sweetness of winter squash with savory cured pork. The fried sage in this topping might seem like an unnecessary cheffy flourish, but frying sage is actually a great skill to master because the crisp leaves enhance the flavor of so many dishes, from pasta to stuffing to roasted vegetables. Here, you will use the sage-infused butter from frying the leaves, as well. When the leaves are ready, pour the butter from the hot pan into a small metal bowl to stop the cooking. Taste the sage butter. If it does not taste burned, you can blend it with the squash for the filling. However, if it tastes burned, use fresh butter instead. Weigh the squash pieces after you've peeled them to be sure you have just 1 pound; using more or less squash throws off the balance of the dish.

In a metal mixing bowl, toss the squash with the oil and salt, and then spread the squash in an even layer on a baking sheet. Roast in the 375°F oven until the squash is completely tender, 25 to 30 minutes.

Return the hot squash to the same bowl, add the garlic paste, and toss together until the squash is evenly flavored with the garlic. Pour the squash and garlic back onto the baking sheet and return the pan to the oven for another 5 minutes to cook the garlic.

Remove from the oven and transfer the squash and the sage butter to a food processor and purée until smooth, 30 to 45 seconds.

Place a 6- to 8-inch sauté pan over medium heat. When the pan is hot, add the pancetta, lower the heat to medium-low, and cook until golden brown and crispy, 3 to 4 minutes. Using tongs, transfer the pancetta to a paper towel to drain and cool.

Using a spoon and your fingers, spread the squash along the parbaked pastry strips, dividing it evenly and leaving ¼ inch of pastry uncovered around the edges. Return the tarts to the 375°F oven for 3 to 5 minutes, until the pastry is very dark golden brown and the squash is beginning to brown around the edges. Break the pancetta into 1- to 2-inch pieces and scatter them and the fried sage leaves over the tarts. Cut crosswise into pieces and serve immediately.

Continued

1 pound peeled and seeded butternut squash (from 1½-pound squash), cut into 1½- to 2-inch pieces

2 teaspoons extra-virgin olive oil

½ teaspoon plus ⅛ teaspoon salt

2 teaspoons garlic paste (page 344)

1 tablespoon melted sage butter (reserved from frying sage leaves, below) or butter (optional)

4 or 5 thin slices pancetta (about 1 ounce)

Fried sage leaves (see page 376)

Crème Fraîche Tarts

CONTINUED

Caramelized Onions with Anchovies and Olives

I first started making *pissaladière*, the Niçoise flatbread topped with caramelized onions, anchovies, and olives, when I began catering in 1999, and I've been playing around with the recipe ever since. The flavors are brilliant together: sweet onions; salty anchovies and olives; and crisp, flaky dough. This is still one of my favorite recipes.

In an 8- to 10-quart heavy pot or Dutch oven, heat the oil over medium-heat. (I don't like to caramelize onions in butter because they lose their translucent sheen when they cool.) Add the onions and ½ teaspoon of the salt and cook, stirring often, until the onions begin to turn translucent and become very soft, almost soupy, 20 to 25 minutes. (If the largest pot you own holds only 4 to 6 quarts, don't despair! Simply cook about two-thirds of the onions first, and when they have sweated, see page 377, down and lost much of their volume, add the last third of the onions to the pan and continue cooking. Caramelizing the onions in stages will, of course, increase your cooking time slightly.)

Turn down the heat to just below medium and stir only occasionally, allowing the onions to develop a fond, or crust, on the bottom of the pan. Every few minutes, scrape off the fond and stir it into the onions, then spread the onions evenly across the pan and allow a fond to form again. You want to be able to fully blend the frond back into the onions without darkening to black flecks. The onions should take on a lovely amber hue (see the photo, right). Stir more frequently at the end of caramelizing to ensure they don't burn. If the onions are sticking more than they should be or not picking up the fond when you scrape it, add a few tablespoons of water and continue scraping. After 25 to 35 minutes, the onions should be a deep caramel hue. Taste for salt and add another ¼ to ½ teaspoon if necessary. Be careful not to overseason, as the anchovies and olives are quite salty. Remove from the heat and allow the onions to cool completely.

Using a spoon and your fingers, spread a thin layer of onions along the parbaked pastry strips, leaving ¼ inch of pastry uncovered around the edges. (Use any leftover onions on a sandwich, in scrambled eggs, or with a cheese plate.) Sprinkle the anchovies and olives evenly over the onions. (Don't be tempted to add much more than the recipe calls for or the dish will be too salty.) Return the tarts to the 375°F oven for 3 to 5 minutes, until the onions are hot and beginning to brown around the edges and the flavors have melded. Garnish the tarts with the thyme. Cut crosswise into pieces and serve immediately.

¼ cup extra-virgin olive oil

6 large yellow onions, sliced into half-moons about 1/16 inch thick

¾ to 1 teaspoon salt

12 olive oil–packed anchovy fillets, cut into ½-inch pieces

2 ounces (¼ cup) Niçoise olives, pitted and halved

1½ tablespoons roughly chopped thyme

Burrata with Dandelion–Golden Raisin–Pistachio Pistou

SERVES 4

This *pistou* reminds me of leisurely meals in Sicily, where I first encountered flavors like these. French *pistou* is similar to Italian pesto, and this one in particular has a lot of complexity from the crunchy pistachios and soft, sweet raisins, plus bitterness from the dandelion greens.

Creamy *burrata* is a nice foil to the sharpness of the greens, but if you can't find a reliable source, a ripe French triple crème cheese will work instead. There are excellent *burratas* out there and some not-so-great ones, too, so it's worth tasting a few to find one that's very fresh. It should feel quite soft and taste incredibly rich and creamy. Carefully cut each cheese in half to serve four people.

You can skip the cheese entirely and serve this *pistou* with an oily fish like mackerel or swordfish, or with oil-packed sardines from a tin. It's also an easy sauce to stir into warm pasta or to use as a garnish on soup. At its simplest, this is a fabulous topping for warm, crusty bread.

Preheat the oven to 325°F. Spread the pistachios on a small baking sheet and bake until lightly toasted, 3 to 4 minutes. (Since pistachios have brown skins and a crisp texture, it can be hard to tell when they're toasted. Allow them to cool and taste one. You're looking for a very slightly toasted flavor and a still-green interior.) When the nuts are cool enough to handle, roughly chop and set aside.

Blanch and shock the dandelion greens as directed on page 375, leaving the greens in the boiling water for 30 to 45 seconds, until the stems are just tender and the leaves are bright green. When the greens have completely cooled in the ice water, pull them out of the water and squeeze dry with your hands. Chop finely and set aside.

Heat a 6- to 8-inch sauté pan over medium heat and add 2 tablespoons of the oil. When the oil is hot, add the shallot, lowering the heat slightly to prevent any color from forming. When the shallot is translucent, after 2 to 3 minutes, add the garlic, fennel pollen, chile flakes, salt, and pepper and stir to mix. Add the raisins and cook until they begin to expand, about 1 minute. Add the Marsala and cook off the liquid, about 1 minute. Add the dandelion greens and stir very briefly just to combine all the flavors, about 30 seconds. Transfer the mixture to a metal mixing bowl.

Add the chopped pistachios and 4 tablespoons of the remaining oil to the greens mixture and stir to combine. The mixture should have some pools of oil; add another splash of oil if necessary. The pistou can be stored, covered with thin layer of oil, in an airtight container in the refrigerator for up to 3 days. Before serving, leave it at room temperature for about 1 hour, until the olive oil is completely fluid.

To serve, top each piece of burrata with 3 or 4 tablespoons of pistou and spoon some of the excess olive oil around the edge of the burrata. Sprinkle lightly with flaky salt, drizzle with balsamic vinegar, and serve with toasted bread.

¼ cup raw, unsalted shelled pistachios

1 bunch dandelion greens

6 to 7 tablespoons extra-virgin olive oil

2 tablespoons finely minced shallot

2 cloves garlic, thinly sliced

½ teaspoon fennel pollen

¼ teaspoon red chile flakes

½ teaspoon salt

¼ teaspoon freshly ground black pepper

¼ cup golden raisins, soaked in just-boiled water for 20 minutes and drained

1 tablespoon sweet Marsala

2 fresh burrata cheeses, each 3 to 4 inches in diameter, halved

Flaky finishing salt, for serving

1 tablespoon 30-year aged balsamic vinegar (see page 370), optional

Rustic bread slices, toasted, for serving

Beet-Cured Salmon with Creamy Herbed Cucumbers

MAKES 2 POUNDS CURED SALMON; SERVES 4 TO 6, WITH LEFTOVER SALMON

Both sets of my parents had gardens when I was little, and at my dad and stepmother's house, we grew a lot of cucumbers. By August, the cucumbers would be going totally crazy, and we were at a loss for what to do with them. My stepmother Ronna's family is Norwegian, and she borrowed her grandmother's recipe for this light, creamy, and refreshing cucumber salad. It's best eaten very cold, after the cucumbers have chilled in the fridge for a few hours (but not overnight).

The salmon is an easy at-home curing project and it's less expensive than buying cured fish. You will need to plan ahead, however, as the fish must cure for 36 to 48 hours. The salmon can also be served without the salad, thinly sliced and accompanied by crackers (see page 366) or bagels and cream cheese.

Always buy the highest-quality wild-caught salmon available. Look for a thick, center-cut 2-pound fillet with the skin on. Do not buy two 1-pound pieces for this recipe, as you need a single 2-pound piece for the cure to work.

MAKE THE CURED SALMON Rinse the fillet under cold running water. Dry it with a paper towel, and then lay it on a piece of parchment paper. Remove the pin bones with culinary tweezers or with regular tweezers reserved for kitchen use. To locate pin bones, run your hand along the surface of the fish and feel for thin spikes. Angle your tweezers into the fish to avoid ripping the flesh, or use a small, sharp knife to cut the flesh back ever so slightly to expose the bone. Pull the tiny individual bones out in the direction they are running. Set the salmon aside.

Cover your cutting board with a layer of plastic wrap so it doesn't color from the beets as you grate them, and wear plastic gloves if you don't want to stain your hands red. Working over the plastic wrap, grate the raw beets on the biggest holes on a box grater. Gather up the grated beets in the plastic wrap and transfer them to a food processor.

Add the sugar, salt, juniper, and peppercorns to the processor. Using 15 to 20 long pulses, blend the ingredients until the mixture looks uniform and sandy. Transfer the beet mixture to a mixing bowl, add the lemon zest, lime zest, dill, and tarragon, and mix well with your hands.

Splash the aquavit across the flesh and the skin side of the salmon and smooth your hand across both surfaces to "rinse" the salmon with the liquor. Place the salmon, flesh side down, onto the top one-third of the parchment paper. Spread half of the beet-salt mixture evenly along the center of the parchment paper in a strip roughly the same size as the salmon fillet. Flip the salmon over, skin side down, on top of the beet mixture. Pack the remaining beet-salt mixture across the flesh side of the salmon. Fold the short side edges of the parchment in toward the salmon and then fold the bottom side over the top. Flip the fish over, creating a package of rubbed salmon.

Continued

CURED SALMON

1 (2-pound) center-cut skin-on salmon fillet, 1½ inches thick

1 large or 2 small red beets, unpeeled

2 cups granulated sugar

3 cups salt

10 juniper berries, toasted and very coarsely ground (see page 378)

1 teaspoon black peppercorns, toasted and very coarsely ground (see page 378)

2 tablespoons lemon zest (see page 375)

1 tablespoon lime zest (see page 375)

1 cup roughly chopped dill, stems included

⅓ cup roughly chopped tarragon

¼ cup aquavit or gin

CUCUMBER SALAD

2 English cucumbers

2 teaspoons very finely minced shallot

2 tablespoons white wine vinegar

1 teaspoon salt

½ teaspoon freshly ground black pepper

2 teaspoons sugar

2 tablespoons crème fraîche or sour cream (see page 370)

1½ teaspoons chopped dill

2 teaspoons chopped mint

1 tablespoon finely minced chives

Torn mint or celery leaves, for garnish

Beet-Cured Salmon with Creamy Herbed Cucumbers

CONTINUED

Wrap the entire salmon package in several layers of plastic wrap to seal it well. Lay the salmon on a rimmed baking sheet; use a baking sheet with at least ½-inch sides, as a lot of liquid will escape from the fish while it cures. Place another baking sheet on top and top the second sheet with any object or objects weighing a total of about 5 pounds, such as canned foods or a big pot.

Refrigerate the weighted baking sheets for 16 to 18 hours. After that time, flip the salmon over, then reweight it and refrigerate for another 16 to 18 hours. Open the salmon package and brush away the excess beet-salt mixture, reserving the mixture in case you find you need to continue curing the salmon for a few more hours. The salmon is ready when it springs back gently when you touch it. If it is hard, it is overcured; if it is too soft, it has not cured long enough. But the best way to know if it is ready is to cut into it and taste it. Rinse the salmon with water and thoroughly pat dry with paper towels.

Place the salmon on a cutting board. Lay your knife flat on the surface of the board and slice horizontally between the skin of the salmon and the flesh to separate the two. Do not remove all of the salmon from its skin; slice only about 2 inches deep. Cut a ¼-inch piece off the end of the skinless section of the salmon, slicing it on a sharp 45-degree angle. Taste an interior slice (not the end cut you just removed) for even seasoning. If the amount of seasoning is to your liking, continue slicing in paper-thin pieces. If the salmon isn't cured enough, repack it with the reserved beet-salt mix, rewrap it, reweight it, and cure for another 8 to 12 hours. If the salmon is too hard, place it in a bowl of fresh water and soak in the refrigerator for 4 to 6 hours, then drain and dry well. If it still tastes too salty to serve straight, fold it into cream cheese, eggs, or pasta. The salmon will keep, tightly wrapped, in the refrigerator for up to 1 week.

MAKE THE CUCUMBER SALAD Peel the cucumbers and halve lengthwise. Place them cut side up and, with a sharp spoon or melon baller, carefully scoop out and discard the seeds. Flip a cucumber half over onto its cut surface and cut ¼ inch off one end of the cucumber at a sharp 45-degree angle. At this same sharp bias, cut the entire cucumber half into ⅛-inch-thick slices. Repeat with the remaining halves.

In a bowl, combine the shallot, vinegar, salt, pepper, and sugar. Mix well to combine and let rest for 10 minutes to mellow some of the sharp taste of the shallot. Whisk in the crème fraîche; then wash your hands well, and add the cucumbers to the dressing and massage with your hands. Add the dill, mint, and chives and stir to combine. Cover and refrigerate for at least 2 hours or up to 4 hours before serving.

To serve, make sure the cucumber salad and the salmon have been refrigerated for a few hours so they are very cold. Use a slotted spoon to remove the cucumbers from their dressing. Place about ½ cup of the cucumbers in a nice tight pile in the middle of each plate. Arrange 4 or 5 thin salmon slices on the top of the cucumbers in a rosette shape, and set mint along the perimeter of the cucumbers as a garnish.

Figs with Foie Gras Mousse

SERVES 8 TO 12

I invented this recipe before Beast opened, when I was catering the wrap party for director Gus Van Sant's movie *Paranoid Park*, which was filmed in Portland. Many of the actors were French, and the party was held on Bastille Day, so I wanted to make something special for them.

I didn't have much experience cooking foie gras, so I called my friend and former sous chef Gabriel Rucker (now of Le Pigeon and Little Bird Bistro), who gave me the inspired advice to melt the foie a little bit before blending it into a mousse, a step that ultimately helps the mousse set properly. And I knew I wanted the dish to taste slightly like dessert, which is where the vanilla and figs come in. You can use any fig variety, as long as the fruits feel fairly soft and ripe. Drier varieties such as Black Mission are easier to caramelize, which you can do with a handheld torch (see page 373).

The mousse itself has become a signature dish at Beast: it is the filling in the foie gras bonbon that's been on our charcuterie plate since we opened.

Cut the foie gras into 1½-inch cubes and place them in a small square baking dish.

Using a paring knife, cut the vanilla bean in half along its length. Use the knife to flatten the pod gently against the countertop, and then scrape out the seeds with the blade. Add the vanilla seeds and half pod, the Calvados, curing salt, and salt to the foie gras. Gently toss the foie gras cubes, coating them evenly with the other ingredients. Let sit on the countertop for 15 to 20 minutes. Meanwhile, preheat the oven to 400°F.

Roast the seasoned foie gras for 2 to 3 minutes. The foie should feel slightly firm to the touch in the center and should have lost a little liquid (fat). Remove the foie from the oven and remove and discard the vanilla pod. Carefully transfer the contents of the baking dish to a strainer set over a small bowl. Place the strainer and bowl in the refrigerator for 30 to 45 minutes, until the foie is cold to the touch. The strained foie fat can be reserved for another use, such as spreading on toast.

Place the cold foie gras mixture in a food processor and, using short bursts, pulse 10 to 15 times, until the foie forms a smooth and uniform paste. Don't overprocess. Because the volume is small, the foie gras can overheat, which will cause the mousse to break. Scoop the foie gras paste into a fine-mesh strainer and push it through with a flexible rubber spatula or bowl scraper to remove any membrane.

Fill a disposable pastry bag fitted with a ¼-inch round tip (or a plastic bag with a ½-inch corner cut off) with the foie gras mousse and squeeze the mousse to the tip of bag. Line a baking sheet with a Silpat baking mat (see page 374) or parchment paper. Pipe out teardrop-shaped orbs of mousse (about the size of a Hershey's Kiss, with a base just larger than the size of a quarter) onto the prepared baking sheet. Place in the freezer to completely cool and harden, about 30 minutes.

Continued

8 ounces foie gras

½ vanilla bean

1 teaspoon Calvados

⅛ teaspoon pink curing salt no. 1 (see page 371)

¾ teaspoon salt

8 ripe figs

4 teaspoons sugar

Figs with Foie Gras Mousse

CONTINUED

Trim off the stem from each fig, then cut the figs in half lengthwise. Cut a ⅟₁₆-inch-thick slice off the rounded side of each fig half so it will sit flat. Place the fig halves, cut sides up, on a baking sheet with no parchment or lining of any kind. Sprinkle each fig with ⅛ teaspoon sugar, and then toast with a handheld torch until the sugar melts and forms a thin, hard crust on the surface of the fig, about 5 seconds per fig. Sprinkle another ⅛ teaspoon sugar on top of the initial sugar layer and repeat torching until the sugar is bubbling and completely melted, forming an even (not thick) crust of crunchy, melted sugar. Let cool completely, about 10 minutes.

Remove the baking sheet of foie gras mousse from the freezer. Using an offset spatula, gently slide each teardrop of mousse off the baking sheet and onto a fig half. Before serving, allow the piped foie gras to temper until firm but no longer frozen, 15 to 20 minutes.

Hazelnut and Wild Mushroom Pâté

MAKES 1½ CUPS

This pâté was one of the first recipes I successfully adjusted on my own. My stepmother clipped the original recipe from a newspaper, probably in the late 1980s, and I revisited it around the time of my first cooking job in college. Its base was hazelnuts and mushrooms, which is inherently a great combination, but with a few small adjustments, I improved on the original. All I did was trust my instincts and play around a bit. Today, I make a version of that same pâté with a few more tweaks.

In Oregon, chanterelles are in season at the same time as hazelnuts, so this starter is a particularly lovely expression of where I'm from. I usually serve this rich dish as an appetizer, but because it has a meaty flavor from the nuts and mushrooms, it works nicely as part of a vegetarian main dish, as well. You can also serve this versatile pâté with my buttery Homemade Ritz Crackers (page 365), spread it on a crusty baguette, use it as a topping for a savory dough (like Crème Fraîche Tarts on page 48), or serve it with a cheese plate (page 329).

Preheat the oven to 350°F. Clean the mushrooms (see Note, page 160). Cut or tear into evenly sized pieces about ½ inch thick. Divide the mushrooms into two equal batches.

Spread the hazelnuts on a small baking sheet and toast in the oven for 6 minutes. Carefully shake the baking sheet to turn the nuts over, then toast for 2 to 4 minutes longer. To test if the nuts are ready, cut one in half; it should be a light golden color and toasted all the way through.

In a large black steel pan, heat 1 tablespoon of the butter over medium heat. Add the shallot and cook, stirring frequently, until translucent, 1 to 2 minutes. Add the garlic paste and ¼ teaspoon of the salt and cook, stirring frequently, until the garlic no longer smells raw, about 1 minute. Transfer the shallot mixture to a plate and set aside. Wash and thoroughly dry the pan.

In the same large black steel pan, heat 2 tablespoons of the remaining butter over medium heat until melted. Add half of the mushrooms, ½ teaspoon of the salt, and ¼ teaspoon of the pepper and stir briefly to combine. Sauté, moving the mushrooms around constantly, for 4 to 5 minutes, until they start to color on their edges and the moisture they release evaporates. All of the mushrooms should be soft and tender, with no spongy quality or rawness to them. (Note that the mushrooms may seem overseasoned when you taste them on their own, but the pâté will taste balanced because the hazelnuts aren't seasoned.) If the mushrooms have not begun to brown at the edges, turn up the heat slightly and continue to cook for another minute or two.

Transfer the mushrooms to a plate and set aside. Wipe out the pan and repeat using 2 tablespoons of the remaining butter, the second batch of mushrooms, and the remaining ½ teaspoon of salt and ¼ teaspoon of pepper. When the second batch is

Continued

1 pound wild mushrooms (such as chanterelles or porcini)

⅓ cup hazelnuts (see Note, below)

9 tablespoons butter

1 cup finely minced shallot

2 teaspoons garlic paste (page 344)

1¼ teaspoon salt

½ teaspoon freshly ground black pepper

1 tablespoon dry Marsala

1 tablespoons tawny port

1 teaspoon aged sherry vinegar (see page 370)

1¾ teaspoons 10-year aged balsamic vinegar (see page 370)

1/16 teaspoon cayenne pepper

1/16 teaspoon freshly grated nutmeg

¼ teaspoon lemon zest (see page 375)

NOTE It's best to buy raw hazelnuts and toast them yourself. But if the freshness is assured, pre-toasted unsalted nuts are acceptable. If you're toasting the nuts at home, rub the just-toasted nuts between two kitchen towels to remove the papery skin covering each nut. Don't worry if tiny bits of skin remain.

Hazelnut and Wild Mushroom Pâté

CONTINUED

cooked, add the first batch back to the pan along with the shallot mixture and warm until all of the mushrooms are heated through. Add the Marsala and port, allow the mixture to absorb them for 20 to 30 seconds, and then turn off the heat. Set aside to cool.

In a small saucepan, melt the remaining 4 tablespoons butter over medium-low heat. Add the sherry and balsamic vinegars and remove the pan from the heat.

Place the hazelnuts in a food processor and pulse until they have the texture of coarse meal, about 7 bursts. Add the mushroom mixture, the cayenne, nutmeg, and lemon zest and, with the machine running, slowly pour in the melted butter mixture. Taste for seasoning and adjust if necessary.

Put the pâté into a ramekin and smooth the surface. Serve at room temperature. Leftover pâté can be refrigerated, tightly covered, for up to 5 days. Bring it to room temperature before serving.

Chicken Liver Mousse

MAKES 2 CUPS

We started serving chicken liver mousse at Beast within a week of opening, and it's now one of our signature charcuterie items. The exact formula has been played with a lot over the years, as I've experimented with different liquors. I have also tried out various vehicles to serve it with, but my favorite is buttery, flaky Homemade Ritz Crackers (page 365).

You can bake the mousse in essentially any type of vessel (a 1½-quart terrine mold or glass loaf pan works well). You must allow at least ¾-inch headroom, however, as the mousse rises slightly as it bakes. Once the mousse has been in the oven for 15 minutes, keep an eye on the temperature because the size and depth of the vessel will affect cooking time. For the water bath, which will allow the mousse to cook gently, you will need a deep roasting pan, hotel pan (see page 373), or other large ovenproof pan or dish for holding the terrine mold or loaf pan (the water must come at least halfway up the sides of the smaller dish).

Combine the chicken livers and buttermilk in a small bowl, cover, and soak overnight in the refrigerator to pull out any blood and impurities.

The next day, rinse and dry the livers, then trim off any large veins or discolored parts. Toss the livers with the salt, curing salt, and pepper, coating evenly, and set aside.

Put the Madeira, port, bourbon, amaretto, shallot, thyme, garlic, and bacon in a 1- to 2-quart saucepan. Place the pan over medium-low heat and cook until the liquid has reduced to about 2 tablespoons, 20 to 25 minutes. Let cool to room temperature.

Remove and discard the thyme sprig from the cooled shallot-bacon mixture, then transfer the mixture to a blender and add the livers. Blend until the mixture is very smooth, about 1½ minutes.

Preheat the oven to 300°F. For this next step, it is important that all of the ingredients are truly at room temperature (except for the cream, which should be cold). Anything that isn't will prevent emulsification, which means you'll end up with a splotchy, unappealing spread. With the machine running, add the egg and blend until fully incorporated, about 30 seconds. Then slowly add the pieces of butter, one at a time, until they are fully incorporated and the mixture is totally emulsified, 1 to 2 minutes. In the last few seconds of blending, pour in the cream. Test the mousse by spreading a small amount across a plate with the back of the spoon. If it is properly emulsified, the mixture will look smooth and uniform, and if not, you'll see separate pieces of fat and protein. Keep in mind that you will also be passing the mousse through a fine-mesh strainer, so don't worry about a few specks of membrane or bacon.

If the mixture is not emulsified properly, there is a fix: Scrape it into the bowl of a stand mixer fitted with the whisk attachment. Wrap the bowl with a hot kitchen towel

Continued

8 ounces chicken livers

1 cup cultured full-fat buttermilk

½ teaspoon salt

⅛ teaspoon pink curing salt no. 1 (see page 371)

⅛ teaspoon freshly ground black pepper

2 tablespoons Madeira

2 tablespoons port

1 tablespoon bourbon

¾ teaspoon amaretto

¼ cup thinly sliced shallot

1 thyme sprig

1 clove garlic, thinly sliced

1 cup diced bacon, in small pieces (about 4 ounces)

1 egg, at room temperature

14 tablespoons unsalted butter, sliced into 1-inch pieces, very soft

1 tablespoon cold heavy cream

Chicken Liver Mousse

CONTINUED

and turn on the mixer to high speed. The towel will warm everything to the same temperature, and the mixture will emulsify.

Pour the liver mixture into a fine-mesh strainer and push it through with a bowl scraper or the back of a large serving spoon to strain out anything that didn't blend completely. Pour the mousse mixture into a 1½-quart terrine mold or glass loaf pan. To prevent a skin from forming on the top of the mousse during baking, cut a piece of parchment paper slightly larger than the top dimension of the mold or pan, place the parchment over the top, and gently tuck in the edges.

Place the terrine mold or loaf pan into a deep roasting pan or hotel pan and fill the larger pan halfway with hot water (the water should come at least halfway up the sides of the mold). Cover the whole thing with aluminum foil to create a steam bath for cooking the mousse.

Bake until a thermometer inserted into the center of the mousse reads 150°F. This can take anywhere from 15 to 30 minutes, depending on the size of the mold. Remove the roasting pan from the oven, and then remove the mold from the water bath. Pull back the parchment and allow the mousse to cool to room temperature. Once it has cooled completely, wrap the mousse still in its container securely with plastic wrap. Refrigerate for at least 8 hours or for up to 1 week.

Serve the mousse chilled, directly from the vessel in which it was baked or spooned into a serving bowl. Exposure to oxygen will cause discoloration, so put out only as much as people will eat in one sitting and scoop the rest into tightly sealed containers. If you plan to serve the mousse in the container in which it was baked, after it has chilled, scrape off the slightly oxidized top layer to reveal the pale pink mousse underneath.

Fried Pork Rillettes

MAKES 25 (1-INCH) BALLS

Rillettes are an impressive entry-level charcuterie project. Making a batch is mostly a passive affair and the finished product is versatile. I started making rillettes because I often cook pork shoulder at Beast and was looking for a way to use up any scraps. The fact that they keep for a long time is an added bonus. If you're not planning on eating them within a few days, simply pour some of the reserved duck fat (you'll have plenty) on top of the meat to "seal" it; you can then keep the pan, tightly wrapped, in the refrigerator for up to a month.

Once the rillettes have chilled, they are ready to eat. You could simply spread them on toast with orange marmalade and be more than happy. However, at Beast we developed this recipe for fried rillettes as a way to add some texture to our charcuterie plate. Serve these with Savory Tomato Confiture (page 11), Smoked Paprika and Espelette Crème Fraîche (page 22), or any of the aioli variations (pages 28–31; shown on facing page with Aioli Vert, page 31), and Quick Pickles (see page 349).

Cut the pork shoulder and bacon into 1½-inch cubes. Place in a large, heavy Dutch oven, add the salt, curing salt, pepper, and nutmeg, and toss to mix evenly. Add the onion, garlic, and bay leaves and mix well.

In a small pot over medium-low heat, carefully warm the duck fat just until melted. Do not allow it to come to a boil. If you pour duck fat that is too hot onto the pork, the fat will flash-fry the meat, giving it a hard exterior. Pour the melted duck fat over the meat mixture, submerging the meat completely.

Cover the Dutch oven, place over very low heat, and cook for about 2½ hours, checking often to make sure the bubbles are tiny and infrequent, until you can smash the shoulder meat easily between two fingers. Remove from the heat and let stand until cool enough to handle, about 1 hour. Pour the contents of the pot into a fine-mesh strainer placed over a bowl. Remove and discard the bay leaves. Reserve the duck fat.

Transfer the drained meat to a stand mixer fitted with the paddle attachment and mix on the lowest speed for about 3 minutes, or until uniformly mixed. With the machine running, drizzle in ⅓ cup of the reserved duck fat and mix for about 1 minute, or until homogenous. Reserve the remaining fat for another use. It will keep in an airtight container in the refrigerator for up to 1 week or in the freezer for up to 3 months.

Pack the meat mixture into a 1½-quart terrine mold or loaf pan and refrigerate for at least 12 hours or for up to 3 days.

Line two baking sheets with parchment paper. Use a melon baller or spoon to scoop up 1- to 1½-inch balls of the chilled rillettes. Roll each ball lightly between your palms and place on one of the prepared baking sheets.

Continued

1 pound boneless fatty pork shoulder

3 ounces slab bacon

1 teaspoon salt

⅛ teaspoon pink curing salt no. 1 (see page 371)

⅛ teaspoon freshly ground black pepper

⅛ teaspoon freshly grated nutmeg

⅔ cup coarsely chopped yellow onion

4 cloves garlic, smashed with the flat side of a knife blade

2 fresh or 4 dried bay leaves

4½ cups rendered duck fat

½ cup all-purpose flour (see page 376)

3 eggs

2¼ cups panko (or finely ground homemade bread crumbs, see page 363)

1½ quarts canola oil

Fried Pork Rillettes

CONTINUED

Set up a breading station with 3 bowls. Place the flour in the first bowl. In the second bowl, beat the eggs until blended. Place the panko in the third bowl. One at a time, dip the rillette balls in the flour, coating evenly; and then in the egg, allowing the excess to drip off; and finally roll in the panko, again coating evenly. Set the breaded rillettes on the second prepared baking sheet. You can do this step up to 24 hours in advance and hold the breaded rillettes on the baking sheet, wrapped in plastic wrap, in the refrigerator until ready to fry. You can also freeze the rillette balls on the baking sheet for up to 1 week, and then defrost them in the refrigerator for 24 hours before frying.

To fry the rillettes, pour the oil into a large, heavy Dutch oven and heat to 350°F over high heat. Use a clip-on digital thermometer (see page 374) to ensure the oil doesn't overheat. Line a baking sheet with paper towels to absorb excess oil from the fried rillettes.

When the oil is ready, add as many rillette balls as will fit without crowding the pot (about 1 dozen). The temperature of the oil will drop when you add them, so keep your heat on high and be careful that it doesn't exceed 375°F. Fry the rillettes, turning them gently using a spider (see page 374), until deeply golden on all sides, 2 to 3 minutes. Use the spider to transfer the rillettes to the prepared baking sheet.

Serve immediately (with Aioli Vert, page 31), or keep in a low (200°F) oven for up to 30 minutes while you fry the remaining batch(es).

Steak Tartare on Brioche with Quail Eggs

MAKES 12 APPETIZER-SIZE TOASTS

There's a lot of steak tartare in this world, and there are many chefs who put all sorts of creative things in their tartare, often to delicious effect. I am not one of them. This tartare is classic, and I like it for its simplicity. Start this dish one day before you want to serve it to allow enough time to freeze the meat completely. Freezing makes it possible to slice the meat into perfectly clean, neat cubes without any mushing or tearing.

A final note: Buy a few more quail eggs than you plan to serve, as the yolks in one or two will inevitably break before serving. Quail eggs can be found at many Asian markets (and sometimes even at local farmers' markets).

6 ounces beef tenderloin (preferably grass-fed)

¾ teaspoon finely minced shallot

1½ teaspoons rinsed and finely minced capers

1½ teaspoons finely minced cornichons

1½ teaspoons finely minced chives

3 slices quick brioche (page 362), each ⅓ inch thick

3 tablespoons butter, melted

12 quail eggs (plus a few extra for insurance)

¼ rounded teaspoon salt

¼ teaspoon freshly ground black pepper

1½ teaspoons extra-virgin olive oil

Freshly cracked black pepper, for serving

Trim the meat of any excess fat or sinew. Wrap the whole 6-ounce piece tightly in plastic wrap and place in the freezer overnight, until fully frozen.

Remove the meat from the freezer and let sit at room temperature for 20 to 25 minutes, until it is still frozen but can be sliced through cleanly with a knife. To cut it into a fine mince, slice the whole piece across the grain into ⅛-inch-thick slices. Stack the slices and cut the stack lengthwise into ⅛-inch-wide strips (julienne). Finally, cut the strips crosswise into little squares (mince). The pieces should be very small and uniform by the time you're done. You have to work quickly, as the meat will warm up and become soft, making precise knife cuts more difficult.

Place the meat in a small mixing bowl, add the shallot, capers, cornichons, and chives, and stir to mix evenly. Cover with plastic wrap and refrigerate until ready to serve.

About 45 minutes before serving, preheat the oven to 400°F. As soon as the oven is ready, cut off the crust from each brioche slice and cut each slice into four same-size squares. Using a pastry brush, generously coat both sides of the brioche squares with the butter and arrange the squares on a baking sheet. Bake for 7 to 8 minutes, turning the squares once at the midway point, until evenly browned. Let cool.

Just before serving, crack all of the quail eggs into a small bowl. Remove the beef from the refrigerator, add the salt, ground pepper, and oil, and mix vigorously with a spoon. Taste for seasoning and adjust if necessary.

To serve, arrange the brioche toasts on a tray. Divide the meat into twelve ½-ounce portions (one per toast). Using your hands, form a small mound of meat on top of each toast and push your thumb in the center to form a well for the quail egg. Be sure to push deeply enough to create a definitive hollow for the yolk, as you don't want it sliding off.

Using your hands, carefully remove a yolk from the bowl of quail eggs, gently shake off any excess egg whites, and slide the yolk into the hollow on the beef mound. Repeat with remaining toasts. Finish with a pinch of cracked black pepper on top of each toast. Transfer to a serving platter and serve immediately.

Coriander-Seared Tuna with Citrus and Fennel Salad

SERVES 6 AS AN APPETIZER OR 3 AS A LIGHT MAIN COURSE

This is a classic example of three ingredients that work really well together. The recipe is so simple that every ingredient really needs to shine. I only make this dish during the winter, when citrus is at its best. When shopping for tuna, be specific: The term *sushi grade* isn't regulated, so ask your fishmonger for #1 grade ahi (yellowfin or bigeye) tuna, which is the tuna industry's highest ranking. Make sure it's shiny, firm, and lacking any fishy smell. Ask the fishmonger to cut a log about 4 inches long and 2½ inches wide from the tuna loin. If this isn't possible, you may need to cut smaller pieces from a larger steak, as described below.

Trim the tuna as needed to remove any bloodline, sinew, or skin. The tuna steak, viewed from the top, resembles a pear shape. Cut off the "pointy end" of the pear and then cut the remaining piece in half, so you end up with 3 same-size triangular pieces. Place the tuna on paper towels to dry while you assemble the salad.

Remove the green tops from the fennel bulb and save the fronds for the garnish. Cut the bulb in half lengthwise. Set a mandoline to create slices about as thick as a quarter. Slice each fennel half crosswise on the mandoline, stopping before you hit the base ends. Discard the ends.

Supreme the citrus fruits (see page 375). Place the citrus segments in a strainer placed over a small bowl. Give the leftover "core" of each citrus a quick squeeze over the segments to collect any extra juice.

In a small bowl, whisk together 2 tablespoons of the collected citrus juice, the cider vinegar, the shallot, ¼ teaspoon each of the salt and pepper, the olive oil, and the champagne vinegar to make a vinaigrette. Set aside.

In a separate mixing bowl, combine the coriander, ½ teaspoon of the salt, and the remaining ½ teaspoon pepper. Season the outer sides (the long sides of the log) of each piece of tuna with some of the spice mixture.

In a bowl, pour half of the vinaigrette on the fennel and the parsley and toss to coat. Taste and add an extra pinch of salt if needed. Set aside.

Heat a black steel pan over high heat until very hot. Add the canola oil and heat until the oil is rippling but not smoking. Add the tuna pieces spiced side down and cook, pressing once to ensure an even sear, for about 20 seconds on each side. Remove the tuna from the pan and set aside.

On each plate, arrange a portion of the fennel and parsley mixture and garnish with a fennel frond. Put a few segments of each type of citrus to the side of the fennel mixture and pour some of the remaining vinaigrette on top of the citrus. Slice each piece of tuna in half and place the halves, with the raw interior facing up, to the side of the salads. Serve immediately.

1½ pounds center-cut ahi tuna

1 fennel bulb

1 large or 2 small Valencia oranges

1 grapefruit

1 tablespoon cider vinegar

1 teaspoon finely minced shallot

1 teaspoon salt

¾ teaspoon freshly ground black pepper

2 tablespoons extra-virgin olive oil

¼ teaspoon champagne vinegar

1 teaspoon coriander seeds, toasted and ground (see page 378)

¼ cup loosely packed flat-leaf parsley leaves

2 tablespoons canola or grapeseed oil, for cooking the fish

Baked Camembert with Armagnac Prunes, Mushrooms, and Thyme

SERVES 4 TO 6

One Christmas, I wanted to make two kinds of baked Camembert—one sweet and one savory—but I had never actually baked Camembert before. For the savory one, I sweated (see page 377) some mushrooms with fresh herbs and shallots, and for the sweet, I paired the cheese with poached prunes. Unfortunately, I didn't have two free pans because I was making so many other things for the holiday meal, so I put both cheeses in one large pan, thinking I could still serve them separately.

They ended up melting and morphing into a single dish—a very happy accident, indeed. I set the whole thing out on the table with a baguette for people to rip into, and everyone went nuts for the dish. I know it might sound surprising, but the combination of earthy, sweet, and savory flavors all mixed together really works. Sometimes cooking is just like that. It's important to stay calm and realize that mistakes can lead to great things.

Preheat the oven to 400°F.

In a large black steel pan, warm the butter and oil over medium-high heat. Add the shallot and cook just until translucent, 1 to 2 minutes. Add the mushrooms, salt, and pepper and sauté, moving the mushrooms around, for 7 to 10 minutes, until they begin to color on their edges and the moisture they release evaporates. All of the mushrooms should be soft and tender, with no spongy quality or rawness to them. Turn the heat up at the end of cooking to evaporate any additional mushroom moisture and brown the edges very slightly. Add the thyme and prunes and sauté for an additional minute. Remove the pan from the heat and allow the mixture to cool slightly, about 5 minutes.

Unwrap the Camembert and place in a small baking dish. Place the prune and mushroom mixture all around and slightly on top of the cheese and bake for 5 to 10 minutes, until the cheese is warmed through, softened, and beginning to melt; you will see some cheese oozing out. Serve immediately.

2 tablespoons butter

1 teaspoon extra-virgin olive oil

½ cup diced shallot

2 cups thinly sliced cremini or button mushrooms

½ teaspoon salt

¼ teaspoon freshly ground black pepper

2 teaspoons thyme leaves

¾ cup Armagnac-poached prunes (page 369), roughly chopped into ½-inch pieces

1 (8- to 10-ounce) wheel Camembert or other double-crème, French-style cheese, such as Brie

NOTE The time it takes for the cheese to reach the correct texture depends largely on how ripe it is at the time you purchase it. The ideal final consistency is oozing and melted but not liquefied.

Soups

Soups should be elegant—they are the purest expression of seasonality. I treat the soup course as seriously as I treat any main dish, and I spend a lot of time considering how to best capture and celebrate the ingredient being showcased.

That said, soup is a relatively low-risk way to experiment with a new flavor or ingredient. Most of the recipes in this chapter are simple and inexpensive to make (with some exceptions, like the Classic French Onion Soup on page 102) and can be tweaked to use the odds and ends in your refrigerator.

There are a few things to keep in mind when making soup that will help turn it into a showstopper. If preparing a velouté, or creamy soup, you must cook the vegetables until you can squish them very easily, so they will purée smoothly. An overly thick creamed soup is unappealing, and to achieve a perfectly smooth, fine consistency, the vegetable itself must be perfectly fine and smooth before it's blended. Secondly, of course, you'll need a blender—the more powerful, the better. The Vitamix I use at the restaurant and at home gets the job done in seconds, but a strong blender and a chinois (see page 373) will get yours close enough. And finally, when you need to thin a soup with water or dairy, it will increase in volume and thus will require more seasoning. Taste often and season accordingly.

Most of these soups are not meant to be served as large portions; I usually serve six to eight ounces per person as part of a larger meal or alongside a salad and some toasted bread for a light lunch. It might be worth investing in a few small, shallow bowls if you find yourself making soup often, as I do.

Finally, a note on warming and chilling soup bowls: If your oven is free, heat it to 200°F, place the soup bowls inside, and warm them for about 20 minutes before serving. (If you need to cool the bowls down slightly, remove them from the oven, spread the bowls apart, and wait for a few minutes.) Alternatively, boil water on the stove top and pour some into each soup bowl. Wait for about 3 minutes before discarding the water and drying the bowls. Warming the bowls buys you a little bit of time to finish garnishing yet still serve the soup at the optimal temperature. Conversely, if you're making a chilled soup and refrigerator space isn't an obstacle, chill your bowls for up to an hour before serving.

Asparagus Velouté with Walnut-Parsley Pistou

SERVES 4 TO 6

Asparagus is the star of spring, and this is a refined way to present it. The spears are so vegetal that combining them with dairy softens their green flavor. This makes a lovely first course in a multicourse meal, but it's also really delicious paired with a simple salad for lunch. The base of this velouté can be made up to 24 hours in advance, but make the spinach "dye" the same day and add it at the very end, after the base has been thoroughly reheated, to preserve the bright green color.

I like to garnish this soup with Walnut-Parsley Pistou because the savoriness from the nuts and Parmesan mixed with the brightness of the parsley enhance the flavor and texture. Top each bowl with a float of lemon-pressed olive oil to add an extra layer of sophistication.

1 bunch spinach

1 pound asparagus (about 1 bunch), ends snapped off at natural breaking point, tips of 4 to 6 spears reserved and remaining stalks cut into ¼-inch-thick slices

4 tablespoons butter

3 cups finely diced yellow onion

4 cloves garlic, thinly sliced

1¾ teaspoons salt

½ teaspoon freshly ground black pepper

2 cups whole milk, plus up to 1 cup more if needed to thin

1 cup heavy cream

4 to 12 tablespoons Walnut–Parsley Pistou (page 6), for garnish

Lemon-pressed olive oil (see page 371), for garnish (optional)

Wash the spinach well (see page 378), then blanch and shock it as directed on page 375. Reserve the shocking water. Blanch and shock the reserved asparagus tips, cooking until bright green and al dente, 1 to 2 minutes or so. Cut the tips in half lengthwise and set aside.

Add the spinach and ¾ cup of the shocking water to a blender and blend on high speed until the mixture is very smooth and uniform, about 1 minute. Stop and scrape down the sides of the blender with a rubber spatula as needed. This purée will be used as a natural "dye" to restore the green color lost by cooking the asparagus. Measure out ¼ cup and set aside to use for the soup. Freeze the remainder in an ice-cube tray for future use.

In a 4-quart saucepan, melt the butter over medium heat. Add the onions and sweat (see page 377) for 6 to 7 minutes, until translucent. Add the garlic and sweat for an additional 2 minutes. Add the asparagus, salt, and pepper and cook until the asparagus is bright green, about 5 minutes.

Add the milk and the cream and turn down the heat to medium-low. Allow the mixture to come to a simmer, about 5 minutes. Keep the liquid at a very gentle bubble and cook the asparagus, stirring occasionally, until it is completely soft and can be easily squished between two fingers, about 25 minutes. I cannot overstate the importance of cooking the asparagus to complete tenderness at this stage to ensure a perfectly smooth purée. Remove the pan from the heat.

Carefully add half of the hot soup to the blender. Remove the plastic insert from the lid of the blender and replace it with a kitchen towel to allow some steam to escape. Purée the soup, starting on low speed until just blended, about 30 seconds, and then turning to high speed and continuing until completely smooth, about 1 minute. If you have not used a high-powered blender, strain the soup through a chinois

Continued

Asparagus Velouté with Walnut-Parsley Pistou
CONTINUED

(see page 373) into a clean saucepan. If you have used a high-powered blender, pour the purée directly into the saucepan. Repeat with the remaining half of the soup.

Warm the soup bowls (see page 83). Set the saucepan of soup over medium heat and stir constantly to avoid scorching the bottom. As soon as the soup is hot, and just before serving, add the ¼ cup spinach dye and stir to mix. (Add the spinach dye as close to serving as possible, as its color will fade as it heats up.) To test the consistency of the soup, pour some soup from a spoon; it should pour easily in a steady stream. If it doesn't, thin it slightly with the additional 1 cup milk. Be careful not to overthin the soup or the garnishes will sink to the bottom of the bowl. Taste and adjust the seasoning as necessary.

To serve, transfer the soup to a pitcher (pouring from a pitcher is a lot neater than ladling). Divide the soup evenly among the warmed bowls. If necessary, stir 1 to 2 tablespoons olive oil into the pistou to "loosen" it to a spoonable consistency, and then spoon 1 to 2 tablespoons pistou on top of each bowl. Place 2 of the sliced asparagus tips, cut side up, on top of the pistou. Drizzle the lemon-pressed olive oil on top and serve immediately.

Chilled Cucumber and Yogurt Soup with Crab

SERVES 4 TO 6

Chilled soups are one of summer's great pleasures. This is a very refreshing soup, and one of the lightest recipes in the book. Oftentimes, chilled cucumber-yogurt soup is only a purée, but the finely diced cucumber in this one adds an element of texture that makes for a more refined presentation, and it's a good excuse to practice your knife skills.

Cucumbers are extremely abundant in the summer, and this is a delicious way to use up quite a few of them. I like Persian cucumbers because they're extra crunchy, have thin skin and very few seeds, and boast a strong cucumber flavor. If you can't find Persians, buy 3 or 4 English cucumbers instead.

When it comes to crab, get whatever is freshest and in season near you. Here in Portland, that's usually Dungeness, but any type of crab will work well as long as it's very fresh. Buy the already cooked version from your fishmonger. The sweet flavor of the crabmeat balances the bright, vegetal cucumber.

This soup tastes better when it's had time to chill in the refrigerator to allow its flavors to develop; try to make it at least 4 hours in advance, or up to overnight, and serve it very cold. Serve this soup in shallow bowls, so the crab doesn't get lost beneath the surface. If you don't have shallow bowls, you may want to increase the amount of crab.

MAKE THE SOUP In a small saucepan, heat the oil over medium heat. Add the onion and 1 teaspoon of the salt and cook, stirring frequently, until the onion turns translucent but takes on no color (lower your heat if necessary), 6 to 7 minutes. Set aside to cool.

Roughly chop 3 of the cucumbers and add them and the water to a blender. Blend on high speed until smooth, about 45 seconds. Strain the purée through a fine-mesh strainer lined with cheesecloth to remove any solids. This should yield about 2 cups cucumber juice; set aside.

Add the cooked onion, yogurt, and garlic paste to the blender (there's no need to rinse it after making the juice) and blend on high speed until smooth, about 1 minute. In a mixing bowl, whisk together the puréed onion-yogurt mixture and the cucumber juice. You should have about 4 cups.

Finely dice the remaining 3 cucumbers into small, even cubes (about ¼ inch). Stir the cubes into the yogurt-cucumber purée. Season with the lemon zest, Tabasco, the remaining ½ teaspoon salt, and the sugar. You shouldn't really be able to taste the lemon or hot sauce; they should blend seamlessly into the soup for balance. Cover the soup and refrigerate for at least 4 hours or up to overnight.

Continued

SOUP

3 tablespoons extra-virgin olive oil

1½ cups very finely diced sweet onion

1½ teaspoons salt

6 large Persian cucumbers, unpeeled

1 cup water

1 cup whole-milk plain yogurt

½ teaspoon garlic paste (page 344)

¼ teaspoon lemon zest (see page 375)

⅛ teaspoon Tabasco sauce

½ teaspoon sugar

CRAB SALAD

6 ounces fresh-cooked crabmeat, picked over for shell fragments

3 tablespoons aioli (page 28)

1½ teaspoons lemon juice

1 teaspoon finely minced chives

¼ teaspoon finely chopped dill

¼ teaspoon finely chopped tarragon

¼ teaspoon freshly ground black pepper

¼ teaspoon salt

Nasturtium petals, for garnish (optional)

Chervil leaves for garnish (optional)

Chopped chives, for garnish (optional)

Chilled Cucumber and Yogurt Soup with Crab

CONTINUED

MAKE THE CRAB SALAD In a small mixing bowl, gently stir together the crab, aioli, lemon juice, chives, dill, tarragon, and pepper. Taste before adding the salt, as the saltiness of crab varies. The crab salad can be refrigerated, covered, for 1 day.

To serve, chill the soup bowls in the refrigerator for at least 1 hour before serving. Evenly divide the soup among the bowls. Place a small mound of crab salad in the middle of each bowl. Garnish with a few nasturtium petals, chervil leaves, or chopped chives.

Chilled Tomato-Cucumber Soup with Bread and Almonds

SERVES 6 TO 8

This is one of my favorite soups at Beast. It's similar to gazpacho but has more layers of flavor and texture. It has a savory note from the onion and garlic, a bright acidity from the chopped tomatoes, sweetness from the cherry tomatoes, and crunch from the cucumbers and toasted bread, not to mention from the addictive almonds on top. It is very much a seasonal soup that showcases summer produce at its best, so it's not worth making when wonderful tomatoes are not available. Grab whatever large ones look best for the soup base and select the sweetest cherry tomatoes you can. I like Sungolds, which offer a juicy-sweet pop of texture.

This soup tastes best when it's had time to chill in the refrigerator long enough to allow its flavors to develop. Try to make it at least a few hours in advance, or preferably up to overnight, and serve it in chilled bowls.

MAKE THE SOUP Remove the core and make a small X in the blossom end of each large tomato, pressing your knife gently through the skin. Working in batches of 3 or 4 tomatoes to avoid crowding the pan, blanch and shock the large tomatoes (see page 375), cooking just until the skin begins to curl back slightly at the X, 45 to 60 seconds. Wait for the water to come back to a full rolling boil before adding the next batch.

Remove the tomatoes from the shocking water and, using your fingers, peel off the skins and set the tomatoes on a cutting board. Once all of the tomatoes have been peeled, cut them into quarters or sixths and, using your fingertips, push out the seeds into a strainer placed over a bowl to catch all of the tomato juice. Discard the seeds but reserve the liquid. Roughly chop the tomatoes and combine them in a large bowl with the liquid. You should have about 6 cups.

Repeat the X cut, blanching, shocking, and peeling with the cherry tomatoes but leave them whole. You should have about 1½ cups peeled cherry tomatoes. Set aside in a bowl.

In a saucepan, warm 3 tablespoons of the olive oil over medium heat. Add the onion and cook, stirring frequently, until it turns translucent but takes on no color, 6 to 7 minutes. Add the garlic and cook for another 1 to 2 minutes, until fragrant and translucent. Season with 1½ teaspoons of the salt and ½ teaspoon of the pepper, then remove from the heat and let cool to room temperature.

Roughly chop 2 of the Persian cucumbers (or ½ of the English cucumber) and add to a blender with the water. Blend on high speed until smooth, 45 to 60 seconds. Strain the purée through a cheesecloth-lined strainer to remove any solids. This should yield 1 generous cup juice.

Continued

SOUP

5 pounds large tomatoes

1 pint cherry tomatoes

½ cup extra-virgin olive oil

1½ cups finely diced sweet onion

4 large cloves garlic, thinly sliced

4 teaspoons plus ¼ teaspoon salt

1¼ teaspoons freshly ground black pepper

3 small Persian cucumbers, or 1 English cucumber

¾ cup water

1¼ teaspoons aged sherry vinegar (see page 370)

1 teaspoon minced shallot

¼ teaspoon lemon zest (see page 375)

¼ teaspoon Tabasco sauce

½ teaspoon sugar

¼ cup roughly chopped basil

½ cup roughly chopped Marcona almonds, for garnish

3 to 4 teaspoons lemon-pressed olive oil (see page 371) or high-quality extra-virgin olive oil, for garnish

Basil leaves, for garnish (optional)

TOASTED BREAD

10 ounces rustic bread (about ½ large artisanal loaf)

2 tablespoons melted butter

2 tablespoons extra-virgin olive oil

¼ teaspoon salt

⅛ teaspoon freshly ground black pepper

NOTE If you aren't planning to serve all of the soup, remove only what you need and add the appropriate amount of toasted bread. Without the bread mixed in, the soup keeps wonderfully for up to 5 days.

Chilled Tomato-Cucumber Soup with Bread and Almonds

CONTINUED

Finely dice the remaining cucumber and add it to the bowl holding the cherry tomatoes. Season with ¾ teaspoon of the vinegar, the shallot, the lemon zest, 1 tablespoon of the olive oil, and ¼ teaspoon each of the salt and pepper and mix gently.

Add the cucumber juice and the onion mixture to the bowl holding the chopped tomatoes. Season with the remaining 2½ teaspoons salt, ½ teaspoon pepper, and ½ teaspoon vinegar and with the Tabasco and sugar and mix gently. Cover and refrigerate both bowls for at least 2 hours or up to overnight to allow the flavors to blend.

One hour before serving, remove the bowls from the refrigerator.

MAKE THE TOASTED BREAD Preheat the oven 350°F. Cut the crust off the bread and tear the bread into ½-inch pieces. This should yield about 5 cups. Place in a bowl, drizzle with the butter and oil, and toss to coat evenly. Add the salt and pepper and toss again. Line a baking sheet with parchment paper and spread the bread across it.

Bake for 15 to 20 minutes, until the bread is pale golden brown. Let cool completely, about 30 minutes.

Just before serving, mix the cherry tomato mixture into the chopped tomato–cucumber juice mixture. Add the remaining ¼ cup olive oil and stir to mix. Add the basil, toss in the bread, mix well, and check for seasoning. Ladle immediately into chilled bowls and sprinkle with the almonds. Drizzle each serving with ½ teaspoon lemon-pressed oil, garnish with fresh basil leaves, and serve right away.

Celery Velouté with Bacon-Brioche Croutons

SERVES 4 TO 6

This velouté was born out of the big pile of celery stalks we were left with one day at Beast after making a salad that used only the hearts. If you always picture celery in its raw, astringent state, think again. Celery has a natural salinity (this is why nitrate-free meats are often cured using celery salt as a color preservative) and a natural acidity. When it combines with the sweetness of onion and the richness of dairy, it creates its own flavor balance. Although this recipe feels like spring, celery is thankfully available year-round, and it's inexpensive, too.

I like to garnish soup with croutons—it's a classic combo for a reason. Brioche is a good choice for making croutons because it's so buttery, and the smoky, savory hint of bacon in these croutons contrasts beautifully with the light, clean flavor of the celery.

MAKE THE VELOUTÉ In a small saucepan, bring 4 cups of the water and 1 tablespoon of the salt to a boil. Set up a bowl with the remaining 4 cups water, the ice cubes, and 1 tablespoon of the salt. When the water reaches a full rolling boil, add the parsley and cook for 30 seconds, until bright green and pliable. Using a spider (see page 374), transfer the parsley to the ice water and submerge to shock, which stops the cooking and preserves the color. Scoop out the parsley and reserve ¼ cup of the shocking water.

Add the parsley and the ¼ cup reserved shocking water to a blender and blend on high speed until the parsley is very smooth and uniform, about 1 minute. Stop to scrape down the sides of the blender with a rubber spatula as needed. Pour the liquid through a fine-mesh strainer to remove any coarse bits. This purée will be used as a natural "dye" to restore the green color lost by long cooking the celery. Set the parsley dye aside.

In a 4-quart saucepan, melt the butter over medium heat. Add the onion and sweat (see page 377) until translucent, 6 to 7 minutes. Add the garlic and sweat for an additional 2 minutes. Add the celery, the remaining 2 teaspoons salt, and the pepper and sweat until the celery is tender, about 20 minutes.

Add the milk and the cream and turn down the heat to medium-low. Allow the mixture to come to a simmer, about 5 minutes. Keep the liquid at a gentle bubble and cook the celery, stirring occasionally, until it is completely soft and can be easily squished between two fingers, about 40 minutes. I cannot overstate the importance of cooking the celery to complete tenderness at this stage to ensure a perfectly smooth purée.

MAKE THE CROUTONS Preheat the oven to 350°F. Place the brioche cubes in a mixing bowl. In a cast-iron or other heavy ovenproof skillet, cook the bacon over medium-low heat for about 3 minutes, until most of the fat has rendered but the bacon hasn't

Continued

VELOUTÉ

8 cups water

2 teaspoons plus 2 tablespoons salt

4 cups ice cubes

1 cup packed flat-leaf parsley leaves

4 tablespoons butter

2 cups finely diced yellow onion

2 tablespoons thinly sliced garlic

3 cups very thinly sliced celery (about ¹⁄₁₆ inch thick), pale inner leaves reserved

½ teaspoon freshly ground black pepper

2½ cups whole milk, plus up to 1 cup more if needed to thin

1 cup heavy cream

⅛ teaspoon Tabasco sauce

Lemon-pressed olive oil (see page 371), for garnish (optional)

CROUTONS

2 cups cubed quick brioche (page 362), challah, or other egg-enriched bread, in ¼-inch cubes

⅓ cup finely diced bacon (from about 3 thick slices)

1 tablespoon butter

¼ teaspoon salt

¼ teaspoon freshly ground black pepper

Celery Velouté with Bacon-Brioche Croutons

CONTINUED

gotten too brown or crispy. Turn off the heat, add the butter to the pan, and swirl the pan until the butter is fully melted. Pour the bacon with the fat into the mixing bowl with the brioche, sprinkle with the salt and pepper, and toss to coat evenly. Spread the croutons across a baking sheet.

Bake the croutons, stirring every 2 to 3 minutes, until golden brown, 8 to 10 minutes. (Note that brioche will toast up a slightly darker color than some other types of bread because of its sugar and egg content.) The croutons can be made up to 2 hours in advance and rewarmed in the oven just before serving.

When the celery is ready, remove the pan from the heat. Carefully add half of the hot soup to a blender. Remove the plastic insert from the lid of the blender and replace with a kitchen towel to allow some steam to escape. Purée the soup, starting on low speed until just blended, about 30 seconds, and then turning to high speed until completely smooth, about 1 minute. If you have not used a high-powered blender, strain the soup through a chinois (see page 373) into a clean saucepan. If you have used a high-powered blender, pour the purée directly into the saucepan. Repeat with the remaining half of the soup.

Warm the soup bowls (see page 83). Set the saucepan of soup over medium heat and stir constantly to avoid scorching the bottom. As soon as the soup is hot, and just before serving, add ¼ cup of the parsley dye and stir to mix. (Add the parsley dye as close to serving as possible as its color will fade as it heats up.) To test the consistency of the soup, pour some soup from a spoon; it should pour easily in a steady stream. If it doesn't, thin it slightly with the additional 1 cup milk. Be careful not to overthin the soup, however, or the garnishes will sink to the bottom of the bowl. Season with the Tabasco and taste and adjust with salt if necessary.

To serve, transfer the soup to a pitcher (pouring from a pitcher is a lot neater than ladling). Divide the soup evenly among the warmed bowls, then divide the croutons among the bowls, placing them in the center. Drizzle lemon-pressed oil on top and garnish each serving with a few reserved celery leaves. Serve immediately.

Smoky Tomato Velouté with Parmesan Straws

SERVES 4 TO 6

One of the first soups I made at Beast, this smoky tomato velouté is the favorite of our longtime server, Lisa. She's been with me since the very beginning, and we've made many soups over the years, so if this is her favorite, it must be special. I published a similar recipe in *Food & Wine* magazine when I received its Best New Chef award in 2009, though since then I've added smoked onions, which amps up the flavor in a more complex way.

Smoking onions at home is easy; you can do it indoors on your stove top (open your windows) or outside on a gas or charcoal grill (I've included directions for both). The great thing about this technique is that you can use it to smoke virtually anything, from bacon to mushrooms to duck breasts.

In a 4-quart saucepan, heat the olive oil over medium-low heat. Add the smoked onions and cook for 8 to 10 minutes, until lightly caramelized. Add the garlic, tomato paste, salt, sugar, and paprika and cook, stirring frequently to avoid scorching, until the oil begins to separate from the mixture, about 5 more minutes. Add the tomatoes, lower the heat slightly, and simmer until they darken a bit, about 15 minutes. Add the water and simmer gently for 20 minutes. Remove the pan from the heat.

Carefully add half of the hot soup to a blender along with half of the milk and cream. Remove the plastic insert from the lid of the blender and replace it with a kitchen towel to allow some steam to escape. Purée the soup, starting on low speed until just blended, about 30 seconds, and then turning to high speed until completely smooth, about 1 minute. If you have not used a high-powered blender, strain the soup through a chinois (see page 373) into a clean saucepan. If you have used a high-powered blender, pour the purée directly into the saucepan. Repeat with the remaining half of the soup and the remaining milk and cream, adding the blended soup to the saucepan. To test the consistency of the soup, pour some soup from a spoon; it should pour easily in a steady stream. If it doesn't, thin it slightly with the additional 1 cup milk.

Set the saucepan of soup over low heat and season it with the fish sauce, Tabasco, and lemon zest. Taste and adjust the seasoning as necessary.

To serve, transfer the soup to a pitcher (pouring from a pitcher is a lot neater than ladling). Divide the soup among teacups, top each cup with a drizzle of lemon-pressed oil, and lay a Parmesan straw across one side.

3 tablespoons extra-virgin olive oil

2 cups roughly chopped smoked onions (see page 377)

3 cloves garlic, thinly sliced

3 rounded tablespoons tomato paste, preferably Italian

2¼ teaspoons salt

2 tablespoons sugar

1 teaspoon smoked paprika

2½ cups chopped canned tomatoes (see page 371 and Note, below), drained

2½ cups water

2 cups whole milk, plus up to 1 cup more if needed to thin

½ cup heavy cream

½ teaspoon fish sauce (see page 370)

⅛ teaspoon Tabasco sauce

¼ teaspoon lemon zest (see page 375)

4 to 6 Parmesan Straws (page 337), for garnish (optional)

Lemon-pressed olive oil (see page 371), for garnish (optional)

NOTE You can also make this velouté with in-season fresh tomatoes. It is an ideal way to use up tomatoes with blemishes. Just remember to core, blanch and shock, then peel and chop the tomatoes before beginning the recipe (see Chilled Tomato-Cucumber Soup with Bread and Almonds, page 90).

Cauliflower Velouté with Trout Roe and Tarragon Mousse

SERVES 4 TO 6

This was the first smooth, creamy soup I learned to make. Cauliflower cooks quickly, so the gratification is even more immediate with this recipe compared to the other (relatively fast) soups in this chapter. This is a delicate soup—bone white and very refined, despite being inexpensive to make.

Make the tarragon mousse a few hours ahead to give it time to set in the fridge, then give it a quick fluff before you float it like a cloud atop the velouté. If you can't find trout roe, salmon roe or *tobiko* (flying fish roe) work just as well.

In a 4-quart saucepan, melt the butter over low heat. Add the onion and sauté until translucent, 6 to 7 minutes. Make sure the onion does not take on any color. Add the garlic and continue to sauté for 4 minutes, until fragrant and no longer raw. Like the onion, the garlic should not take on any color. If the onion and garlic color, they will turn the entire soup an unappetizing shade of beige (so watch carefully and start over if necessary).

Add the cauliflower, salt, and water, cover, and cook until the cauliflower is completely soft and falling apart, about 30 minutes. Stir frequently and lower the heat as needed to avoid scorching the soup. The cauliflower is done when you remove one of the largest pieces and it gives easily when you push down on it with your finger. I cannot overstate the importance of cooking the cauliflower to complete tenderness at this stage to make a perfectly smooth purée.

Remove the pan from the heat. Carefully add half of the hot soup to a blender along with half of the cream and milk. Remove the plastic insert from the lid of the blender and replace with a kitchen towel to allow some steam to escape. Purée the soup, starting on low speed until just blended, about 30 seconds, and then turning to high speed until completely smooth, about 1 minute. If you have not used a high-powered blender, strain the soup through a chinois (see page 373) into a clean saucepan. If you have used a high-powered blender, pour the purée directly into the saucepan. Repeat with the remaining half of the soup and the remaining cream and milk, adding the blended soup to the saucepan. Stir in the verjus. To test the consistency of the soup, pour some soup from a spoon; it should pour easily in a steady stream. If it doesn't, thin it slightly with the additional 1 cup milk. But be careful not to overthin the soup or the garnishes will sink to the bottom of the bowl. Taste the soup for seasoning and adjust if necessary.

Warm the soup bowls (see page 83). Set the saucepan of soup over low heat, and whisk constantly to prevent scorching. When the soup is piping hot, taste again and adjust the salt, acidity, and consistency one more time. If the soup needs a little acid for balance, add a couple of drops of vinegar or a little lemon zest.

To serve, transfer the soup to a pitcher (pouring from a pitcher is a lot neater than ladling). Divide the soup evenly among the warmed bowls. Place a quenelle (see page 377) of the mousse in the center of each bowl. Top with some of the roe, a sprig of tarragon, and a few drops of herb oil and serve immediately.

4 tablespoons butter

2 cups finely diced yellow onion

1 clove garlic, thinly sliced

1 pound cauliflower (from 2 small or 1 medium head), florets separated and sliced into ¼-inch-thick pieces

2 teaspoons salt

1 cup water

¾ cup heavy cream

1¾ cups whole milk, plus up to 1 cup more if needed to thin

1 tablespoon verjus

White wine vinegar or lemon zest (see page 375), for balance, if needed

½ cup Tarragon Mousse (page 27), for garnish

1 ounce trout roe, for garnish

4 to 6 small tarragon sprigs, for garnish (optional)

Herb oil (page 345), for garnish (optional)

Cabbage Velouté with Lemon Confit Crème Fraîche and Herb Oil

SERVES 4 TO 6

I know cabbage velouté isn't the sexiest-sounding soup, but trust me when I say this recipe will change the way you think about this cruciferous vegetable. When you cook cabbage with cream and butter, it loses all of its cabbagey aroma and takes on a sweet, subtle flavor that reminds me of a classic vichyssoise made of leeks, potatoes, and cream. This soup looks and tastes very refined. I like to serve this dish before something hearty, like Fennel-Brined Pork Loin (page 247).

In a 4-quart saucepan, melt the butter over low heat. Add the onion and 1 teaspoon of the salt and sweat (see page 377) the onion until translucent, 6 to 7 minutes. Don't allow the onion to take on any color. Add the garlic paste and continue to sauté for 5 minutes, until fragrant and no longer raw. Like the onion, the garlic should not take on any color. If the onion and garlic color, they will turn the entire soup an unappetizing shade of beige.

Add the cabbage and the water, cover, and cook over medium-low heat, stirring occasionally until the cabbage begins to become translucent, about 10 minutes. Add the remaining ½ teaspoon salt, stir to combine, and turn down the heat to low. Cover and simmer gently until the cabbage has completely softened, about 40 minutes. Remove the pan from the heat.

Carefully add half of the hot soup to a blender along with half of the milk, cream, and crème fraîche. Remove the plastic insert from the lid of the blender and replace with a kitchen towel to allow some steam to escape. Purée the soup, starting on low speed until just blended, about 30 seconds, and then turning to high speed until completely smooth, about 1 minute. If you have not used a high-powered blender, strain the soup through a chinois (see page 373) into a clean saucepan. If you have used a high-powered blender, pour the purée directly into the saucepan. Repeat with the remaining half of the soup and the remaining milk, cream, and crème fraîche, adding the blended soup to the saucepan. To test the consistency of the soup, pour some soup from a spoon; it should pour easily in a steady stream. If it doesn't, thin it slightly with the additional 1 cup milk. Be careful not to overthin the soup or the garnishes will sink to the bottom of the bowl.

Season the soup with the lemon zest and Tabasco for balance, then taste and adjust further as necessary. You shouldn't really taste the lemon zest or the hot sauce. They should blend seamlessly into the soup.

To serve, test the consistency of the crème fraîche by pouring some soup into a ramekin and topping it with a spoonful of the crème fraîche. If the crème fraîche sinks, thin it with a tablespoon or more of heavy cream, until it floats on the soup. Once the crème fraîche has reached the correct consistency, warm the soup bowls (see page 83) and gently reheat the soup over medium-low heat until hot. Divide the velouté among the warmed bowls. Place a dollop of the crème fraîche in the center of each bowl and dot a few drops of herb oil on top. Drag a toothpick or the tip of a sharp knife through the oil droplets to create the design in the photograph and sprinkle with diced lemon confit. Serve immediately.

4 tablespoons butter

2 cups finely diced yellow onion

1½ teaspoons salt

1 teaspoon garlic paste (page 344)

4 cups sliced green cabbage, in ⅛-inch-wide ribbons

1½ cups water

1½ cups whole milk, plus up to 1 cup more if needed to thin

½ cup heavy cream

¼ cup crème fraîche (see page 370)

¼ teaspoon lemon zest (see page 375)

⅛ teaspoon Tabasco sauce

4 tablespoons Lemon Confit Crème Fraîche (page 25), at room temperature, for garnish

1 to 2 teaspoons herb oil (page 345), for garnish

10 strips diced lemon confit (page 343), for garnish (optional)

Classic French Onion Soup

SERVES 6 TO 8

This soup is pure umami flavor at its finest, and it's probably the most popular soup at Beast. Rich and salty, hearty and cheesy, when French onion soup is done correctly, the flavors are perfectly balanced. The star here is the onion, showcased at its deeply caramelized peak. (I always use yellow onions for caramelizing; sweet onions taste great but contain too much water to brown well.)

I love to make French onion soup with some of the leftover liquid from making a braise, such as Balsamic Braised Short Ribs (page 273). Braising liquid has a lovely meaty richness and acidity from the wine that complements the stock and onions; it does increase the salt level, so be aware of that when seasoning this soup. You can replace up to 2 cups of the stock with leftover braising liquid from another recipe.

Making this soup takes a bit of effort. You should make the stock, which takes two (mostly passive) days to prepare. And deeply caramelizing onions takes time, as well. For this reason, I don't recommend halving this recipe, even if you don't plan to eat all of it at once. The soup freezes well, so make a big batch and save some for later. You'll be glad you did.

In an 8- to 10-quart heavy pot or Dutch oven, heat the oil over medium heat. (I don't like to caramelize onions in butter because they lose their translucent sheen when they cool.) Add the onions and 1¼ teaspoons of the salt and stir often until the onions begin to turn translucent and become very soft, almost soupy, 20 to 25 minutes. (If the largest pot you own holds only 4 to 6 quarts, don't despair! Simply cook about two-thirds of the onions first, and when they have sweated down and lost much of their volume, add the last third of the onions to the pan and continue cooking. Caramelizing the onions in stages will, of course, increase your cooking time slightly.)

Turn the heat to just below medium and stir only occasionally, allowing the onions to develop a fond, or crust, on the bottom of the pan. Every few minutes, scrape off the fond and stir it into the onions, then spread the onions evenly across the pan and allow a fond to form again. You want the fond to exist but not to get so dark that it cannot be fully blended back into the onions, leaving you with little black flecks. The onions should take on a lovely amber hue, but don't let them get too dark. Stir more frequently at the end of caramelizing to ensure they don't burn. The onions should be a deep caramel hue after 25 to 35 minutes.

Continue cooking the onions and scraping often. After about 45 minutes, add the sherry and balsamic vinegar and allow them to cook down. After about 1 hour, the onions should be just about done. When finished, they should be a deep caramel brown that is nearly the same color as the broth, not a blond "wood" shade (see the

Continued

2 tablespoons extra-virgin olive oil

8 large yellow onions, quartered lengthwise and sliced into half-moons ⅛ inch thick

2½ teaspoons salt

¼ cup dry sherry

2 teaspoons 30-year aged balsamic vinegar (see page 370)

2½ quarts homemade stock (page 346) or other high-quality stock

¼ teaspoon fish sauce (see page 370)

⅛ teaspoon Tabasco sauce

Freshly ground black pepper

6 to 8 baguette slices, each ¼ inch thick

2 tablespoons butter, melted

1 clove garlic

1¼ pounds Gruyère cheese, grated

Classic French Onion Soup

CONTINUED

photo, page 53). Taste for salt and add the remaining 1¼ teaspoons of salt if necessary (the onions should be well seasoned); if you'll be using braising liquid, season with less salt.

Add the stock to the pot and turn down the heat to low. Gently simmer the stock and onions for 15 to 20 minutes, until the flavors have melded. Add the fish sauce and Tabasco, a few turns of the pepper mill, and adjust for salt as needed.

Preheat the oven to 350°F. Lay the baguette slices on a baking sheet and brush one side of each slice with the melted butter. Toast in the oven until light golden brown, 5 to 7 minutes. Remove the toasts, rub lightly with the garlic clove, and turn the oven to broil.

Arrange broiler-proof bowls on a baking sheet and ladle the soup into the bowls, filling them nearly to the top. Float 1 baguette slice on top of each bowl. Sprinkle the Gruyère on top of the baguette slices, dividing it evenly. It will seem like a giant mountain of cheese, but if you use any less, it won't form a delicious crust over the top. Place the bowls under the broiler for 5 to 7 minutes, until the cheese is browned and bubbly. Serve immediately and be sure to warn guests that the liquid is very hot.

Consommé

SERVES 6 TO 8

If you're starting this recipe with reserved stock from a previous cooking session, it won't take more than a few hours to complete. But if you're starting from scratch, this consommé will take several days.

After you've mastered making stock, sharpen your skills further by making consommé, which I sometimes call bone tea. It's artful and refined, and when you are able to turn a cloudy liquid into something clear, you'll feel incredibly accomplished. I know, because I was mystified by consommé for years. I looked up recipes, watched videos, and researched old cookbooks, but nothing was instructive enough. That's why this recipe is so detailed. I want to demystify the entire process.

Consommé is achieved by building a "raft" out of mirepoix, egg whites, ground meat, and aromatics. As you slowly heat the stock and raft, the egg whites start to coagulate, attracting proteins and fats and acting like a built-in fine-mesh strainer to clarify the cloudy stock into a crystal-clear, ultra-flavorful liquid. If you can't purchase ground chicken thigh, substitute the leanest ground beef possible to reinforce the deep, meaty flavor lost through clarification.

I serve this elegant consommé with thinly sliced truffles or matsutake mushrooms when I can, and I drink it from a favorite teacup like the prize it is. If you don't want to use mushrooms, a garnish of perfectly *brunoise*-cut (finely diced) carrots, celery, and potato cooked separately in seasoned water is another lovely option (see the photo, page 109).

MAKE THE CONSOMMÉ Carefully crack the eggs into a large metal mixing bowl. Pull out and discard the yolks or save them for another use (see page 377). Lightly whisk the whites for no more than 10 seconds (or about 25 turns of the whisk), until just barely frothy. Add the onion, carrot, celery, tomato, thyme, parsley, chicken, and salt and mix well using a wooden spoon or a stiff whisk.

Remove the stock from the refrigerator and turn it upside down into the mixing bowl. Mix very well until a somewhat lumpy but uniform paste forms. Between the gelatinous stock, egg whites, and ground meat, the contents of the bowl will not look appetizing (it will resemble a very wet meat loaf), but the finished product will be beautiful.

Transfer the mixture to a small stockpot (or large saucepan) no more than 9 inches across. If the pot is too wide, the raft will be weak and break apart, ruining the consommé. Place over very low heat (I use a diffuser; see page 373) and cook, stirring slowly in a figure-eight pattern with a spatula or flat-bottomed wooden spoon (see the chart on page 107). Be sure to stir along the entire bottom of the pan so no egg white bits get stuck anywhere. Eventually the egg whites, meat, and aromatics should form one semisolid mass in the middle of the pot. The entire clarification process takes about 1 hour.

Continued

CONSOMMÉ

4 eggs

½ cup finely diced yellow onion

¼ cup finely diced peeled carrot

¼ cup finely diced celery

½ plum tomato, finely diced

2 thyme sprigs, chopped

1 teaspoon chopped flat-leaf parsley

12 ounces ground chicken thigh

2 teaspoons salt

2½ quarts homemade stock (page 346) or other high-quality stock, refrigerated until needed

Consommé

CONTINUED

During the last 15 minutes of simmering, set a strainer on top of a 2-quart saucepan. Line the strainer with a clean linen napkin or paper towel. At the 1-hour mark, turn off the heat under the consommé. Hold a ladle on the raft's edge and very slowly tilt the stockpot over the saucepan so the liquid pours through the strainer. When done, the raft will be on the bottom of the stockpot. Tilt the pot very slightly to get whatever leftover stock you can into the saucepan. Discard the raft.

You can choose to leave the consommé as is, especially if you want a simple, impressive clear broth to start a meal (served in a beautiful teacup). Or you can garnish it with blanched and shocked English peas, finely sliced matsutake mushrooms, or shaved truffles.

Continued

Clarification Process

0 minutes: Set the pot over low heat and begin very gently stirring in a figure-eight pattern.

5 minutes: Small particles begin to float to the surface.

8 minutes: A tiny bit of white foam forms on the surface.

12 minutes: Some egg strands (ribbons) begin to form.

16 minutes: Small oil bubbles begin to break on the surface.

22 minutes: Start taking small breaks from stirring and watch for liquid at the edge of the pot to simmer.

24 minutes: Steam begins to rise.

27 minutes: Raft starts to stick together and move as one entity. Stop stirring. An important note: If the liquid simmers or moves too much, the fragile raft will break. But there should be some tiny bubbles consistently forming from this point. Keep a close eye on the temperature and adjust if necessary.

30 minutes: A small amount of foam forms at the edge of the pot.

35 minutes: The edge of the raft should be firm. Very gently tap the edge with your finger to test.

36 minutes: First bubbles form in the center of the pot. Gently run your spatula around the edge of the pot, encouraging the raft to move away from the edges and toward the center.

Very gently poke a small hole in the center of the raft to allow the liquid to simmer through (see the photo, right).

40 minutes: The liquid should be at a consistent gentle simmer. When you peek around the edges of the raft, the liquid should look clear.

45 minutes: The middle of the raft should feel firm.

45 to 60 minutes: Simmer over very low heat and assemble the equipment for straining.

Consommé

CONTINUED

MAKE THE GARNISH Slice off the sides of the potato, carrots, and celery stalks to transform them from rounded vegetables into squared-off ones. Slice each vegetable into rectangular slabs ¼ inch thick. Stack the slabs and cut them into ¼-inch-wide strips. Slice the strips crosswise into a *brunoise*, or small uniform squares (about ⅛ inch). Put the cut potato in a small bowl of water to prevent browning until ready to use.

In a saucepan, bring 4 cups of the water and 1 tablespoon of the salt to a boil. Set up a metal mixing bowl with the remaining 4 cups water, the ice cubes, and the remaining 1½ tablespoons salt. Add the carrots to the boiling water and cook until al dente, 30 to 60 seconds. Using a spider (see page 374) or slotted spoon, transfer the carrots to the ice water to stop the cooking. When fully cooled, transfer them to a kitchen towel to drain. Cook, shock, and drain the peas and celery in the same way. Drain the potato of its soaking water, add to the boiling water, and cook until tender but still firm, 1½ to 2 minutes. Shock the potato in the ice water and transfer to the kitchen towel. Let the veggies come to room temperature.

To serve, divide the vegetables evenly among the consommé cups. Heat the consommé over medium heat and pour it into a teapot or other beautiful pouring vessel. Bring the cups with the vegetables to the table and pour the hot consommé into the cups. Garnish with the chervil and serve immediately.

GARNISH

1 Yukon Gold potato, peeled

2 large carrots, peeled

2 celery stalks

8 cups water

2½ tablespoons salt

4 cups ice cubes

¼ cup shelled English peas

24 tiny chervil leaves, or 2 teaspoons minced edible blossoms (such as chive flowers or calendula petals), optional

Salads

In my mind, a meal isn't complete without a salad. Salads add freshness, acid balance, and texture. From the time I was a little girl, picking lettuce and pulling carrots from a backyard garden, salads have been a particularly meaningful part of my table.

The recipes in this chapter are all about showcasing the purity of fresh ingredients and combining things in a complementary way. A salad is the place to let local produce shine and to showcase your very best ingredients. There's nowhere to hide subpar produce in a salad. Take care to wash and prep your salad ingredients properly, as described on page 378.

Constructing a proper salad is about more than just tossing all of the ingredients together in a bowl. The most important element in any salad is the acid balance, which acts as a palate cleanser in a meal full of rich flavors. To understand acid balance, you must understand your ingredients. For example, some greens are hearty, such as fall arugula; others are very tender, such as the first spring greens. The more tender they are, the higher the acid should be in the dressing, so you can use less dressing overall and still achieve the desired flavor without weighing down fragile greens with excess oil. Heartier or more structured greens, by contrast, need a creamier dressing, while more bitter greens do well with dressings that have a certain restrained sweetness. I often add a tiny pinch of sugar to my salad dressing for balance. If you taste the sugar, you've added too much, but when done right, it subtly enhances the flavor of the dressing.

It's a good idea to test your vinaigrette on the particular greens you plan to use by whisking the dressing thoroughly and dipping a piece of your greens into the mixture (rather than attempting to taste the vinaigrette on its own). Also, any time you're making a tossed salad, toss it with your (clean) hands rather than tongs or spoons to ensure even dressing distribution and to avoid bruising the fragile ingredients. Seasoning salads with flaky finishing salt and pepper is a great opportunity to practice the aerial salting method described on page 375.

Mom's Simple Salad

SERVES 4 TO 6 (BUT CAN BE EASILY HALVED OR DOUBLED)

This is one of the most important recipes in this book, and it's hardly a recipe at all. It is the salad that my mom made almost every night of my childhood. She used red leaf or butter lettuce and topped it with green onions, celery, carrots, tomatoes, and anything else that was ready in our little backyard garden. The dressing uses cheap red wine vinegar and olive oil; I've made it with good vinegar and it just doesn't taste the way I remember. I can trace my obsession with balance directly back to this salad. It's perfect next to the soufflés my mom and I made when I was growing up—the salad is fresh, crunchy, and acidic; the soufflé is eggy, fluffy, and mild. I liked to alternate bites to keep my palate interested. To this day, I would never not have a salad on the table for my family. A meal without it just doesn't seem complete.

MAKE THE DRESSING Combine the oil, vinegar, lemon juice, salt, and pepper in a small glass jar or plastic container with a tight-fitting lid and shake vigorously.

MAKE THE SALAD Trim off and discard about 1 inch from the root end of the head of lettuce. Separate the leaves, then wash and dry the lettuce (see page 378).

In a chilled metal mixing bowl, combine the lettuce and the prepared vegetables. Just before dressing the salad, sprinkle the greens and vegetables with the salt and pepper. Tilt the dressing container at a 45-degree angle, mix the dressing well with a large spoon, and ladle a few spoonfuls, making sure to get an even amount of vinegar and oil, along the perimeter of the salad. Mix in from the sides, gently tossing the whole thing with your hands. Taste for acidity and add a squeeze of juice from the lemon wedges and more salt and pepper if necessary—finishing with proper seasoning is the key to a great salad. Garnish with the flowers and serve immediately.

DRESSING

6 tablespoons extra-virgin olive oil

2 tablespoons plus 1½ teaspoons inexpensive red wine vinegar

2 teaspoons lemon juice

½ teaspoon salt

¼ teaspoon freshly ground black pepper

SALAD

1 head red leaf lettuce

1 or 2 carrots, peeled and sliced into bite-size pieces

1 or 2 celery stalks, sliced into bite-size pieces

¼ small red cabbage, thinly sliced

2 green onions, green and light green parts only, thinly sliced

2 small radishes, thinly sliced

1 small or ½ large tomato, cut into bite-size wedges

⅛ teaspoon salt

⅛ teaspoon freshly ground black pepper

2 lemon wedges, seeded (see page 375)

Edible flowers, for garnish (optional)

Bread Salad with Asparagus, Pickled Rhubarb, and Flat-Leaf Parsley

SERVES 8

I remember having an epiphany about raw asparagus at clarklewis, when I tried a salad of raw asparagus tossed with just lemon juice, olive oil, and shaved Parmesan cheese. It was beyond good! Who would have thought that raw asparagus could taste so incredible?

I knew when I opened Beast that I wanted to introduce more people to raw asparagus. Bread salad is an old staple of mine, so when asparagus comes into season in the spring, I like to combine the two. I love bread salad because it's not quite a starch and not quite a salad, and because it's a perfect accompaniment to almost any protein.

This is a rustic bread salad with a lot of rough edges, so try to find a mature and hearty arugula as opposed to the baby variety. It's often sold in bunches and the leaves are slightly waxier. If you're lucky enough to find arugula that's sprouting in the spring, use that, as it's very spicy and intense, and a perfect foil to the rhubarb.

MAKE THE PICKLED RHUBARB Cut a 1-foot square of cheesecloth and fold it over once. Place the coriander seeds, fennel seeds, and black peppercorns on the cloth, gently roll it lengthwise into a small sachet, and tie both ends with kitchen twine (like a wrapped candy).

In a nonreactive saucepan, combine the water, vinegar, lemon peel, bay leaves, salt, and the spice sachet and bring to a boil over high heat. Turn down the heat to medium-low and simmer for 5 minutes, then add the sugar. Return the mixture to a full rolling boil, stirring to dissolve the sugar. Add the rhubarb and cook for 30 seconds, until the mixture is close to simmering again and small bubbles are forming.

Pour the rhubarb and pickling liquid into a heatproof glass or ceramic bowl, making sure the rhubarb is fully submerged (if necessary, top it with a piece of parchment paper and a heavy plate to keep it submerged). Let the rhubarb cool to room temperature (about 1 hour), then refrigerate it, covered, for up to 2 weeks. Remove the rhubarb from the pickling liquid with a slotted spoon as needed; reserve the liquid for future pickling projects or use it in another vinaigrette.

MAKE THE TOASTED BREAD Preheat the oven to 325°F. Line a baking sheet with parchment paper. Cut the crust off the bread and tear the loaf into rustic 1-inch pieces. They don't have to be uniform. In a small saucepan, warm the butter, oil, salt, and pepper over medium-low heat until the butter is melted. Put the bread in a mixing bowl and drizzle the butter-oil mixture over it. Toss the bread until it absorbs all of the fat; it will be more or less soaked through with butter and oil. Spread the bread across the prepared baking sheet.

Continued

PICKLED RHUBARB

1 tablespoon toasted coriander seeds (see page 378)

1 teaspoon toasted fennel seeds (see page 378)

½ teaspoon toasted black peppercorns (see page 378)

½ cup water

⅔ cup white wine vinegar

Peel from ½ lemon (see page 375)

2 fresh or 4 dried bay leaves

2 teaspoons salt

2 cups sugar

About 1 pound rhubarb, sliced on the bias ¼ inch thick (about the thickness of four quarters)

TOASTED BREAD

10 to 12 ounces artisanal bread, such as levain or sourdough (about ½ large loaf)

2 tablespoons butter

2 tablespoons extra-virgin olive oil

¼ teaspoon salt

⅛ teaspoon freshly ground black pepper

VINAIGRETTE

2 tablespoons finely minced shallot

3 tablespoons aged sherry vinegar (see page 370)

1 tablespoon 10-year aged balsamic vinegar (see page 370)

½ teaspoon salt

¼ teaspoon freshly ground black pepper

¼ cup extra-virgin olive oil

SALAD

1 pound asparagus (preferably with thick stalks)

6 ounces arugula (see recipe introduction)

3 ounces Parmigiano-Reggiano cheese, shaved with a vegetable peeler

½ cup mint leaves

½ cup flat-leaf parsley leaves

¼ teaspoon flaky finishing salt

⅛ teaspoon freshly ground black pepper

Bread Salad with Asparagus, Pickled Rhubarb, and Flat-Leaf Parsley

CONTINUED

Bake the bread pieces, stirring every 2 to 3 minutes, until golden brown on the outside but still slightly soft on the inside when pressed, 5 to 8 minutes. Allow the bread to cool for about 10 minutes while you assemble the rest of the ingredients.

MAKE THE VINAIGRETTE Place the shallot in a mixing bowl, cover with the vinegars, add the salt and pepper, and whisk lightly. Let sit for about 10 minutes to soften the sharp bite of the raw shallot, then slowly drizzle in the oil while whisking.

MAKE THE SALAD Snap off the tough ends of the asparagus by bending each stalk until the asparagus naturally breaks. Cut each stalk on a very sharp bias into pieces about the thickness of two quarters.

Wash and dry the arugula (see page 378).

In a large mixing bowl or serving bowl, combine the toasted bread and the asparagus and toss with ¼ cup of the vinaigrette. Let sit for 4 to 5 minutes so the bread and asparagus soften slightly. Add the rhubarb and the cheese to the bread and asparagus mixture, followed by the mint, parsley, finishing salt, and pepper. Toss to combine. Add the arugula, along with 1 to 2 more tablespoons of the vinaigrette to taste, and toss gently. Serve immediately.

Little Gem Lettuces with Creamy Pistachio Vinaigrette

SERVES 4

I like to think of this as an updated version of the classic iceberg wedge salad. The Little Gem lettuces, which are served halved, are ideally shaped for holding the dressing. More tender lettuces can't stand up to a heavy dressing like this one, but Little Gems have a tight, small core that won't wilt under a creamy topping.

The dressing is a great recipe to try after you've mastered Aioli (page 28), because its base includes ⅓ cup aioli (if you haven't yet tried the aioli, this will give you an excuse to practice). This creamy vinaigrette has a subtle nutty flavor that's enhanced and refined with the addition of a splash of pistachio oil, if you have it (it's not mandatory). You can also thicken the dressing with an additional ½ cup finely chopped toasted pistachios and use it as a dip for crudités.

MAKE THE VINAIGRETTE Preheat the oven to 325°F. Place the shallot in a small mixing bowl, cover with the vinegar, add ½ teaspoon of the salt, and set aside to macerate for about 10 minutes. This helps to soften the sharp bite of raw shallot.

Spread the pistachios on a small baking sheet and bake until lightly toasted, 3 to 4 minutes. Since pistachios have brown skins and a crisp texture, it can be hard to tell when they're toasted. If you are not sure, allow them to cool and then taste one. You're looking for an only slightly toasted flavor and a green interior. They won't be crunchy until they cool. Roughly chop the pistachios and divide them into two batches of ½ cup and ¼ cup. Set them aside.

In a small mixing bowl, whisk together the macerated shallot and its liquid, the remaining ¾ teaspoon salt, the lemon zest and juice, the aioli, the pistachio oil, and the crème fraîche. Add the minced herbs and whisk again. Taste for balance and season with pepper and sugar if necessary.

MAKE THE SALAD Trim off the very end of the base of each lettuce but leave the head intact. Cut each lettuce in half vertically and submerge the halves in water to clean thoroughly. Drain on paper towels and spin out any remaining water in a salad spinner.

Set a mandoline (see page 373) blade to create slices about the thickness of a dime. Arrange a small bowl of ice water next to your cutting board. Slice the radishes on the mandoline and place the slices in the ice water. About 5 minutes before serving, remove the radishes from the water and dry well in a salad spinner.

Stir ½ cup of the chopped pistachios into the vinaigrette. To serve family-style, put about ⅔ cup of the vinaigrette on a serving plate and arrange the lettuce halves on the top. Spoon the remainder of the vinaigrette over the top of the lettuce. Top with the radish slices, the remaining chopped pistachios, a sprinkle of finishing salt, and some pepper.

VINAIGRETTE

3 teaspoons minced shallot

1 tablespoon plus 2 teaspoons white wine vinegar

1¼ teaspoons salt

¾ cup raw, unsalted shelled pistachios

½ teaspoon lemon zest (see page 375)

1¼ teaspoons lemon juice

⅓ cup aioli (page 28)

3 tablespoons pistachio oil (optional)

⅓ cup crème fraîche or sour cream (see page 370)

1½ teaspoons minced tarragon

3 teaspoons minced chives

3 teaspoons minced chervil or flat-leaf parsley

¾ teaspoon freshly ground black pepper

¼ teaspoon sugar

SALAD

2 large or 4 small heads Little Gem lettuce

2 radishes

Flaky finishing salt

Freshly ground black pepper

Variation

Use 2 heads butter lettuce instead of Little Gem. Prepare the heads as directed, peeling off and discarding the outer leaves until just the pale green centers remain; the heads should be the size of a large fist. Cut each lettuce in half vertically, and follow the instructions at left to compose the salad.

Arugula with Cherries, Shaved Sheep's Milk Cheese, and Sherry Vinaigrette

SERVES 4 TO 6

I like using arugula in the summer when it's just starting to sprout and beginning to go through its flowering stage; this is when it's at its most spicy and hearty flavor. Arugula is the perfect balance for sweet summer cherries. If you can find more than one kind of cherry, buy a mix, as it will help to brighten the color of the salad. Sheep's milk cheese is an interesting departure from the more common shaved Parmesan on a salad and it pairs well with the cherries.

If you have a well-aged balsamic on the shelf, this is one of the best places to use it. Even just a tiny drizzle before serving will elevate this salad.

MAKE THE VINAIGRETTE Place the shallot in a small glass jar or plastic container with a tight-fitting lid. Cover with all three vinegars, the salt, and the pepper. Pour in the oil, cover tightly, shake vigorously, and set aside.

MAKE THE SALAD Wash and dry the arugula (see page 378). Using a vegetable peeler, shave 1-inch-wide strips of cheese. To avoid browning, pit the cherries and cut them in half immediately before assembling the salad. Discoloration happens especially quickly if you're using lighter-colored cherries.

In a chilled metal mixing bowl, combine the arugula, half of the cheese, and the cherries. Just before dressing, sprinkle the greens with the salt and pepper. Tilt the dressing container at a 45-degree angle, mix the dressing well with a large spoon, and ladle 3 tablespoons of the dressing, making sure to get an even amount of vinegar and oil, along the perimeter of the salad. Mix in from the sides, gently tossing the whole thing with your hands. Taste for seasoning and add more vinegar if necessary.

Arrange the salad on individual plates, sprinkle with the remaining cheese, and drizzle with 30-year balsamic. Serve immediately.

VINAIGRETTE

1 teaspoon finely minced shallot

2 tablespoons aged sherry vinegar (see page 370)

1 teaspoon 10-year aged balsamic vinegar (see page 370)

1½ teaspoons 30-year aged balsamic vinegar, plus more for drizzling

¼ teaspoon salt

⅛ teaspoon freshly ground black pepper

¼ cup extra-virgin olive oil

SALAD

6 ounces arugula

2 ounces aged sheep's milk cheese (such as Manchego or Pecorino)

8 ounces sweet cherries

⅛ teaspoon salt

⅛ teaspoon freshly ground black pepper

Tomatoes with Crab, Sungold Tomato French Dressing, and Fried Caper Rémoulade

SERVES 4

This dish is an homage to my southern grandmother, who often made a supper out of ripe tomatoes she grew in her yard and creamy mayonnaise. To this day, these are two of my favorite ingredients to combine. My grandparents loved seafood, too, and they hosted big crab boils in their yard, so this salad is a kind of mash-up of those memories. It's also no secret that my nickname is the Condiment Queen, and this recipe shows why: it features two sauces that come together in a beautiful way.

Make this salad in the summer when sugary Sungold cherry tomatoes are in season—they yield a sweet dressing that plays well with the bright, acidic heirloom tomatoes. The rémoulade is basically glorified tartar sauce, but the fried capers add an unexpected element of crunch if you fold them in at the last second. Although the finished dish is saucy and perhaps a bit messy, it still somehow tastes refreshing, like summer on a plate.

MAKE THE DRESSING In a small saucepan, heat 2 tablespoons of the olive oil over medium-high heat. Add the tomatoes and cook until they begin to burst, about 1 minute. Be attentive to splattering. Add the garlic, ½ teaspoon of the salt, and the pepper. Cook until the garlic is soft and translucent, about 1 minute. Add the honey and watch for it to make large bubbles, 15 to 20 seconds. Add the vinegar and remove from the heat.

Transfer the tomato mixture to a blender and blend on high speed for 20 to 30 seconds, until smooth. Pass the mixture through a fine-mesh strainer set over a bowl to remove any solids.

Whisk the remaining 2 tablespoons oil and the remaining ¼ teaspoon salt into the tomato purée. Taste for salt and adjust if necessary. Set the dressing aside.

MAKE THE SALAD Slice the heirloom tomatoes about ¼ inch thick and sprinkle the slices with the salt and pepper. Put 1 tablespoon of the dressing in the center of each of four small salad plates. Evenly divide the tomato slices and place them on top of each pool of dressing. Spoon 1½ tablespoons of the rémoulade in the center of the tomatoes slices, and arrange the crabmeat on top, dividing it evenly. Garnish with the chive batons and edible flowers, sprinkle with pepper, and serve immediately.

DRESSING

4 tablespoons extra-virgin olive oil

1 cup Sungold cherry tomatoes

1 rounded tablespoon sliced garlic

¾ teaspoon salt

¼ teaspoon freshly ground black pepper

1 tablespoon honey (preferably local and wild; see page 370)

1 tablespoon white wine vinegar

SALAD

2 large heirloom tomatoes

¼ teaspoon salt

⅛ teaspoon freshly ground black pepper

⅓ cup Fried Caper Rémoulade (page 31)

4 ounces fresh-cooked crabmeat, picked over for shell fragments

Chive batons, for garnish

Edible flowers, for garnish (optional)

Freshly ground black pepper

Melon with Radicchio, Crispy Prosciutto, and Caramelized Honey–Black Pepper Vinaigrette

SERVES 8

I like working with chicories, especially in the fall, and I'm forever trying to convince people they're not unpalatably bitter. If you soak radicchio (or escarole, for that matter) in ice water for an hour before using, it removes some of the bitterness. Just be sure to dry the leaves well or the dressing won't stick.

Sharply flavored greens need the right dressing to offset their natural bite: either something creamy or something bright and just slightly sweet. This dressing goes for the latter. Honey is, of course, sweet, but caramelizing it brings out rich, deep undertones, and the pepper helps balance out the sweetness. All vinaigrettes should be balanced, but this one has a particularly lovely sweet-and-sour effect that nicely amplifies the other flavors in the dish.

Buy your prosciutto sliced thinly to order if you can, though the packaged sliced prosciutto at many grocery stores will do in a pinch. Cook it until it starts to get smoky. You may think it's burning, but it's not. Prosciutto doesn't get crispy right away. It must cool down in order to harden, so keep an eye on the baking sheet and take it out when the fat on the edges is golden brown.

Any melon will work in this dish except watermelon—it's great to use a variety of heirloom melons (Charentais, a small French varietal of cantaloupe, is one of my favorites). To check a melon for ripeness, gently press the navel end (where the blossom was), and then take a sniff. It should give slightly and emit a floral fragrance.

VINAIGRETTE

2 tablespoons honey (preferably local and wild; see page 370)

2 teaspoons finely minced shallot

¼ cup white wine vinegar

¾ teaspoon salt

1 teaspoon Dijon mustard

½ teaspoon freshly ground black pepper

½ cup extra-virgin olive oil

SALAD

4 cups ice cubes

8 cups water

1 large head radicchio

1 bunch flat-leaf parsley

½ small cantaloupe

8 very thin slices prosciutto

2 ounces Parmigiano-Reggiano cheese

Flaky finishing salt

Freshly ground black pepper

MAKE THE VINAIGRETTE Heat the honey in a small saucepan over medium-high heat until it bubbles, thickens slightly, and turns a shade darker, about 1 minute. Remove immediately from the heat. Be careful not to overcook the honey.

In a mixing bowl, whisk together the shallot, vinegar, salt, mustard, and pepper. Allow this mixture to stand for 5 minutes, then whisk in the honey and the oil. If the honey seizes up when you stir it in, put the entire mixture back into the saucepan used to cook the honey. Set the pan over medium heat and stir to dissolve. When the dressing has cooled, check for seasoning (dip a piece of radicchio into the dressing) and adjust as needed.

MAKE THE SALAD Fill a large bowl with the ice and water. Quarter the radicchio lengthwise and remove the core. Tear the radicchio quarters into roughly 2-inch pieces. Soak the radicchio in the ice water for 1 hour.

Pick the leaves from the parsley bunch and add them to the ice water. Drain the radicchio and parsley and dry them thoroughly in a salad spinner. Wrap them in a paper towel or kitchen towel, place inside a plastic bag, and set aside in the refrigerator.

Continued

Melon with Radicchio, Crispy Prosciutto, and Caramelized Honey–Black Pepper Vinaigrette

CONTINUED

Peel and seed the melon. Slice it into ¼-inch-thick half-moons. Set aside on a plate or in a bowl in the refrigerator (uncovered is fine).

Preheat the oven to 350°F. Line a baking sheet with a Silpat baking mat (see page 374) or parchment paper. Lay the prosciutto slices in a single layer on the prepared baking sheet. Bake for 5 minutes or until the fat is golden brown. If it isn't ready, return the baking sheet to the oven, but check every minute to ensure the prosciutto doesn't burn. You should expect light smoking. The prosciutto will crisp up once it has cooled to room temperature.

Put the chilled radicchio and parsley in a metal mixing bowl. Using a large-holed Microplane grater, grate the Parmigiano-Reggiano into the mixture. Season lightly with flaky finishing salt and pepper. Pour ¼ cup of the vinaigrette around the perimeter of the salad and mix in from the sides with your hands, tossing well. Taste the greens for acidity and sweetness and add more vinaigrette to taste. Arrange 3 or 4 melon slices in an overlapping pattern on each plate. Cover with the radicchio-parsley mixture and top with 1 piece crispy prosciutto. Spoon a generous teaspoon of vinaigrette over the melon slices and top with a little finishing salt and pepper. Serve immediately.

Escarole Caesar

SERVES 6 TO 8

This salad is a marriage of many recipes. I got the original dressing recipe from a former cook at Portland's now-closed Zefiro restaurant, who probably borrowed it from Zuni Café in San Francisco, and I've changed it slightly over the years. The idea to use escarole came from my friend and former business partner Tommy Habetz, who worked at Lupa under Mario Batali. I like bitter greens but recognize that they can sometimes taste *too* bitter, which is why this is such a great recipe: the cheese, lemon, and anchovy help balance the whole thing out.

The dressing has a similar method to making aioli (see page 28 for the proper whisking technique), but it's more forgiving. Since this dressing uses a whole egg, rather than just yolks, it won't emulsify to the same thickness as an aioli, so to achieve a nice creamy texture, you will need to pour the olive oil in a slow, steady stream while you quickly whisk. The dressing won't come together fully until you add the cheese, and when you do, you'll want to use it on everything.

The dressing will keep in the refrigerator for a few days if you make it ahead of time, but it's important to let it come to room temperature before adding it to your salad. Because it's so fatty, the dressing solidifies when chilled, and trying to toss cold dressing with fresh greens is like trying to dress a salad with butter—not an enjoyable experience.

Everyone has his or her favorite Caesar. Add more garlic, anchovy, or lemon as you like, but remember that flavors bloom as they sit, so make one final seasoning adjustment just before serving.

MAKE THE DRESSING Place the whole unshelled egg in a small heatproof bowl and pour in boiling water to cover. Let the egg sit, submerged, for 1 minute. (Coddling the egg this way minimizes bacteria on the shell and helps the emulsification process.) Remove the egg from the water, crack it into a mixing bowl, and begin whisking with your dominant hand. When the yolk is broken up and smooth, slowly start drizzling in the oil while you whisk. You don't have to work fast; it's more important to whisk and pour consistently. When you've added about 2 tablespoons of the oil, add the mustard, and then continue to drizzle in the rest of the oil while whisking, until the mixture is totally emulsified, about 5 minutes.

Add the anchovy paste, garlic paste, lemon juice, salt, pepper, Parmigiano-Reggiano, Tabasco, and fish sauce and whisk to combine. Taste and adjust the seasoning if necessary.

MAKE THE CROUTONS Preheat the oven to 325°F. Slice the baguette as thinly as possible, about ⅛ inch or the width of two quarters. As I cut, I smash it down with my nonslicing hand. Try to make the slices as even as possible so they will all take the same time to cook. Put the bread slices in a mixing bowl.

Continued

DRESSING

1 egg

1 cup extra-virgin olive oil

¼ teaspoon Dijon mustard

2 teaspoons anchovy paste
(from 4 to 5 fillets; see page 370)

1¼ teaspoons garlic paste
(page 344)

3 tablespoons plus 1 teaspoon
lemon juice

¾ teaspoon salt

½ teaspoon freshly ground black pepper

1 cup ground Parmigiano-Reggiano
cheese (see page 376)

⅛ teaspoon Tabasco sauce

⅛ teaspoon fish sauce (see page 370)
or Worcestershire sauce

CROUTONS

¼ loaf day-old baguette

2 tablespoons butter

2 tablespoons extra-virgin olive oil

⅛ teaspoon salt

⅛ teaspoon freshly ground black pepper

SALAD

2 heads flat-leaf escarole, or
3 romaine hearts

½ lemon, seeded (see page 375),
optional

2 ounces Parmigiano-Reggiano cheese,
grated on a large-holed Microplane
grater (see page 374) or shaved with a
vegetable peeler, for garnish (optional)

Anchovy fillets, for garnish (optional)

Flat-leaf parsley leaves, for garnish
(optional)

Escarole Caesar

CONTINUED

In a small saucepan, warm the butter and oil over medium-low heat until the butter is melted. Pour the warm butter-oil mixture around the perimeter of the mixing bowl holding the bread. Using your hands, toss the bread to coat it evenly with the fat, then season the bread with the salt and pepper. Spread the bread evenly on a baking sheet.

Toast the bread, rotating the pan frequently. Check the croutons after 5 minutes, then set a timer for 1 minute and rotate the pan and check the croutons every minute for another 4 to 5 minutes, until the croutons are light golden brown. Remove any fully toasted slices as they are ready.

MAKE THE SALAD Trim off the very end of the base of each escarole and discard the dark outer leaves (or use them in the quick-sautéed greens on page 163). Cut or tear the remaining pale green leaves into 3-inch pieces. If using romaine, trim off the very end of the base of each lettuce but leave the head intact. Slice the heads crosswise into three pieces, creating 2- to 3-inch pieces. Wash the greens and dry extremely well (see page 378) to ensure you don't dilute the dressing with excess moisture.

In a large mixing bowl, toss the cooled croutons with ½ cup of the dressing and let sit for 5 minutes. Place the escarole on top of the croutons and spoon a generous amount of dressing—about ⅓ cup—over the greens. It's better to be heavy-handed with this dressing than too light. Toss with your hands to combine well. Taste and adjust the seasoning. You may wish to squeeze the lemon half over the top of the salad for a burst of freshness, especially if you made the dressing ahead of time. Garnish with a dusting of Parmigiano-Reggiano, the anchovy fillets, and/or the parsley. Serve immediately.

Mixed Chicories with Grapes, Candied Walnuts, and Aged Balsamic Vinaigrette

SERVES 8

This salad is similar to one that fellow chef Morgan Brownlow used to make at clarklewis. He learned the dish from chef Paul Bertolli at Oliveto in Oakland. Morgan's version had pancetta in it, but I wanted to make a vegetarian version. Adding a little extra sweetness by candying the nuts and adding grapes is a nice foil for the powerful chicories. This is a fall salad, ideal for when grapes are in season. Use a local variety if possible, though everyday seedless red table grapes will work, too. The choice of bitter greens is flexible, as well. It's okay to skip the endive or swap in baby kale, if that's what you have on hand.

This salad feeds a crowd, but all of these greens can be stored for up to a week if well washed, dried thoroughly, and kept in a resealable plastic bag (squeeze out all of the excess air) with a paper towel inside to soak up any extra moisture. You can also toss the greens with a different dressing a few days later if you so choose, like the Caramelized Honey–Black Pepper Vinaigrette on page 126.

MAKE THE SALAD Fill a large bowl with cold water and a few ice cubes to keep the greens crisp. Pick the arugula, discarding the stems, and add the leaves to the water. Cut the radicchio lengthwise into quarters and remove the core. Tear the radicchio into bite-size pieces and add to the water. Trim the base from the endive, separate the leaves, and slice them in half lengthwise; add to the water. Trim and discard the outer leaves from the escarole, leaving only the creamy, pale white interior. Tear that into pieces and add to the water, as well. Let the greens soak for about 30 minutes to extract some of their bitterness, then dry in a salad spinner and pat gently with paper or cloth towels. Make sure the greens are very dry or the dressing will not adhere to them properly.

MAKE THE VINAIGRETTE In a small mixing bowl, whisk together the shallot, sherry vinegar, balsamic vinegar, salt, and pepper. Slowly drizzle in the oil while whisking until blended. Just before serving, pour the vinaigrette into a small glass jar or plastic container with a tight-fitting lid and shake well to recombine.

Place the greens in a large chilled metal mixing bowl and sprinkle them with the finishing salt and pepper. Shake the vinaigrette well, then drizzle three-fourths of it around the perimeter of the salad. Mix in the vinaigrette from the sides, tossing the whole thing with your hands. Scatter the grapes across the top, followed by the candied walnuts (crush them up in your hands a little if you like) and the Parmigiano-Reggiano. Gently toss together and serve immediately.

SALAD

1 bunch arugula

1 head radicchio

1 Belgian endive

1 head flat-leaf escarole

⅛ teaspoon flaky finishing salt

⅛ teaspoon freshly ground black pepper

1½ cups seedless grapes (preferably organic), halved

1 cup candied walnuts (see page 351), roughly chopped

3 ounces Parmigiano-Reggiano cheese, grated on a large-holed Microplane grater (see page 374) or shaved with a vegetable peeler (about 1 cup)

VINAIGRETTE

1 tablespoon finely minced shallot

2 tablespoons aged sherry vinegar (see page 370)

2 tablespoons 10-year aged balsamic vinegar (see page 370 and Note, below)

¼ teaspoon salt

⅛ teaspoon freshly ground black pepper

⅓ cup extra-virgin olive oil

NOTE It's important to use balsamic vinegar that's been aged; it really takes this salad to the next level.

Kale with Quick-Pickled Apple, Gruyère Crisps, and Creamy Dijon Vinaigrette

SERVES 6 TO 8

I was a little worried about including a kale salad in this book because they were very trendy for a while, and I don't want the book to seem dated. But this is a magical version of kale salad. It has so much of what other kale salads are often missing: crisp cheese for texture, a creamy dressing for richness, and a serious kick from a strong Dijon mustard. Don't use something like Grey Poupon here. Look for a brand that has some real heat, like Edmond Fallot.

The availability of apples changes constantly throughout the year, so taste a few different varieties to find ones that are very tart and crisp.

My favorite part of this recipe is the Gruyère crisps, which are reminiscent of the crunchy bits that ooze out of a grilled cheese sandwich. The crisps are easy to make (you'll need a Silpat baking mat; see page 374), versatile, and are a nice gluten-free alternative to croutons—and they're a totally addictive snack on their own.

MAKE THE GRUYÈRE CRISPS Preheat the oven to 325°F. Line a baking sheet with a Silpat baking mat. Using a fine-holed Microplane grater, grate the Gruyère and spread it across the prepared baking sheet as evenly as possible. Bake until the cheese is melted and is a light golden straw color, 20 to 25 minutes. The cheese won't be crispy until it has fully cooled, so be patient before tasting. If it is undercooked, it won't be crispy enough; if it is overcooked, it will taste bitter. Once the cheese has cooled completely, use your hands to break it into 3- to 4-inch pieces. The crisps can be made up to 5 hours ahead of time and set aside, uncovered. (Any leftover crisps can be stored in an airtight container at room temperature for 1 or 2 days.)

MAKE THE QUICK-PICKLED APPLE Place the shallot in a mixing bowl, cover with the vinegar, add the salt, and set aside to macerate for about 5 minutes. This helps to soften the sharp bite of raw shallot. Whisk in the oil and lemon juice.

Quarter and core the apple and slice each quarter crosswise about ⅛ inch thick, or the thickness of two quarters. Toss to coat in the shallot dressing, and then allow the apple to sit in the dressing for about 30 minutes so the flavors can meld.

MAKE THE VINAIGRETTE Place the shallot in a small mixing bowl, cover with the vinegar, and allow to sit for 10 minutes. Add the salt, pepper, sugar, crème fraîche, mustard, and lemon juice and whisk to combine. Slowly drizzle in the oil while whisking to combine. Set aside at room temperature.

MAKE THE SALAD Cut or tear the kale into 1- to 2-inch pieces. In a large chilled metal mixing bowl, season the kale with the finishing salt and pepper. Add about two-thirds of the vinaigrette and toss to coat evenly. Add half of the Gruyère crisps and all of the pickled apple and toss gently to combine. Taste for acidity and salt, and adjust as needed. Sprinkle a handful more cheese crisps on top to garnish. Serve immediately.

GRUYÈRE CRISPS

7 ounces cave-aged Gruyère cheese (see Note, below)

QUICK-PICKLED APPLE

2 teaspoons finely minced shallot

2 teaspoons cider vinegar

⅛ teaspoon salt

2 teaspoons extra-virgin olive oil

2 teaspoons lemon juice

1 tart, crisp apple

VINAIGRETTE

2 tablespoons finely minced shallot

3 tablespoons cider vinegar

¾ teaspoon salt

¼ teaspoon freshly ground black pepper

½ teaspoon sugar

3 tablespoons crème fraîche or sour cream (see page 370)

2 teaspoons strong Dijon mustard (such as Edmond Fallot)

1 tablespoon lemon juice

⅓ cup extra-virgin olive oil

SALAD

1 to 1½ bunches Lacinato or Red Russian kale, washed and dried (see page 378), stems removed

¼ teaspoon flaky finishing salt

¼ teaspoon freshly ground black pepper

NOTE It's important to purchase cave-aged Gruyère cheese, which is drier than regular Gruyère, to achieve the proper texture for the crisps. If you can't find cave-aged Gruyère, use Parmigiano-Reggiano that you grind yourself (see page 376). Note that Parmigiano-Reggiano may take less time to crisp.

Roasted Beets and Pink Grapefruit with Frisée and Mint Crème Fraîche

SERVES 4

I like to break this salad out in the dead of winter, when it provides a vibrant pop of color to an otherwise drab season. Not only is it beautiful, it's also fresh and light, which helps balance out some of the heavy, hearty dishes we tend to crave when temperatures drop.

One of the questions I get asked most frequently is how I roast beets. Roasting beets is easy, but there are a few things that can make them better. For starters, pay attention when they're in the oven and add more water to the bottom of the roasting pan if the pan begins to dry out. Beets are done when they feel slightly and evenly resistant all the way through. The outer edge of the vegetable will cook faster, so make sure you test all the way through to the center. If they feel light or fluffy and offer no resistance, they're probably overcooked. Begin checking beets after about 40 minutes in the oven, using the pointy end of a metal or a wooden skewer. Beets of different sizes cook at different rates, so start checking the small ones first. Beets of different colors can cook at different rates, too, so check them all if you're roasting a variety. Finally, I prefer to buy beets with their tops on for the same reason I prefer to buy carrots with their tops: even if I'm not using them, greens guarantee freshness.

To make this salad more substantial, add a second citrus, like blood orange, trimmed of the rind and sliced into wheels. This dish is great for showing off winter's gorgeous citrus and beet colors.

MAKE THE BEETS Preheat the oven to 400°F. Scrub the beets well with a brush and remove the greens. (If the greens look healthy—they are similar in texture and flavor to Swiss chard—wash them well and save for another use.)

In a small rectangular roasting pan or a loaf pan, toss together the garlic, orange peel, thyme, bay leaves, and peppercorns. Rub the beets all over with ¼ cup of the oil and sprinkle with the salt. Add the beets to the pan and roll the beets around in the garlic-citrus mixture, seasoning them evenly. Fill the pan ½ inch with water.

Cover the pan with aluminum foil and roast until the beets are slightly and evenly resistant throughout, 40 to 60 minutes. Beets of different colors can cook at different rates, so be sure to test all types you're roasting.

Uncover the pan and let the beets cool until they can be comfortably handled, 15 to 20 minutes. While the beets are still warm, carefully peel them: hold a beet in one hand and, with your other hand, gently rub and peel off the skin with a paper towel. Wear plastic gloves if you don't want your hands stained.

Continued

BEETS

3 golf-ball- to tennis-ball-size beets in assorted colors (red, yellow, candy-stripe) with tops intact

1 head garlic, halved crosswise

3 (½-inch-wide) strips orange peel (see page 375)

2 thyme sprigs

4 fresh or 8 dried bay leaves

2 teaspoons black peppercorns

¼ cup plus 3 teaspoons extra-virgin olive oil

1½ tablespoons salt

1½ teaspoons red wine vinegar

VINAIGRETTE

2 teaspoons minced shallot

1 tablespoon red wine vinegar

2 teaspoons extra-virgin olive oil

¼ teaspoon salt

¼ teaspoon freshly ground black pepper

SALAD

2 red grapefruits, such as Rio Red or Star Ruby

2 heads baby frisée

1 cup Mint Crème Fraîche (page 25)

16 to 20 mint leaves, for garnish

Flaky finishing salt

Roasted Beets and Pink Grapefruit with
Frisée and Mint Crème Fraîche

CONTINUED

Cut a thin slice off the top and bottom of the red beet, then slice it into ¼-inch-thick disks. Cut the other 2 beets into wedges about ¾ inch wide. Keep the cut beets separated by color, placing them in small bowls or plastic containers. Add ½ teaspoon of the vinegar and 1 teaspoon of the remaining oil to each container and toss to coat the beets evenly. Allow the beets to marinate for at least 30 minutes at room temperature, or up to overnight, covered, in the refrigerator. If marinating overnight, remove the beets from the refrigerator at least 1½ hours before serving so they come to room temperature and the oil isn't congealed.

MAKE THE VINAIGRETTE In a small container or jar with a tight-fitting lid, combine the shallot, vinegar, oil, salt, and pepper and shake vigorously. Set the vinaigrette aside.

MAKE THE SALAD Supreme the grapefruits (see page 375). Place the citrus segments in a strainer set over a small bowl and set aside.

Strip the mature outer leaves off the frisée until you reach the creamy, pale green and white center leaves. Trim off the frizzy tips so they won't poke the mouths of your guests. Wash thoroughly and dry well with a salad spinner (see page 378) and set in a mixing bowl in the refrigerator until ready to serve.

To serve, dress the frisée with half of the vinaigrette and taste. Add more vinaigrette if necessary. On each of four small plates, pour a full spoonful of the crème fraîche, then use the back of the spoon to swoop it into a gentle curve in a single stroke. Arrange the beets and grapefruit on top of the crème fraîche, and tuck the frisée in neat tufts. Garnish each plate with 4 or 5 mint leaves and a sprinkle of flaky finishing salt. Serve immediately.

Vegetables

Vegetables deserve the same attention and care as meat, if not more. It's entirely possible—and even easy—to make a beautiful, satisfying meal consisting solely of vegetables. I was a vegetarian for seven years, so I speak from experience. To this day, vegetables are the way to my heart.

There's a lot to learn in this chapter, both philosophically and technically. Vegetables are, by their very nature, an ephemeral pleasure because they're of the moment seasonally. And they demand attention while they cook. It's easy enough to put a piece of meat in the oven and cook it to the right temperature, but vegetables require some finesse.

A lot of little things go into cooking a great vegetable dish: proper selection and cleaning of the produce itself, careful knife work, constant tasting for flavor and texture. Your reward is a canvas on which you, the cook, can be the most expressive. Vegetables give you perhaps the best chance to show off your skills.

The recipes in this chapter should not be thought of as only side dishes. Each of them does appear alongside a protein later in the book, but everything here can also stand alone. These are important recipes that highlight basic cooking techniques. You'll learn how to blanch and shock asparagus, how caramelizing carrots and Brussels sprouts helps bring out their umami-like qualities, why long cooking is a brilliant way to approach summer produce, and more.

Asparagus with Black Garlic Hollandaise

SERVES 6 TO 8

Asparagus arrives in the Pacific Northwest at that sweet transitional spot between spring and summer, and it's a very nostalgic flavor for me. The amount of time it takes to cook asparagus depends on how thick the stalks are. Skinny stalks might take a minute and thick ones may take 2 to 2½ minutes. Pull one out as they cook to test if they are ready. I like the texture to have lost its raw snap and be slightly al dente, rather than soft throughout. And remember to reheat the asparagus lightly before serving it with the hollandaise. Warm hollandaise and cold food don't mix.

Keep the hollandaise warm while you cook the asparagus. Snap off the ends of the asparagus by bending the stalks until the asparagus naturally breaks. This natural break point is the place where the tender stalk meets the more fibrous woody end. Discard the woody ends (and eliminate the need to peel the asparagus). Trim the ends slightly if you want an even cut. Blanch and shock the asparagus (see page 375), cooking until bright green and al dente, 1 to 2 minutes or so, depending on the thickness of the stalks. Reserve the blanching water in the pot.

Just before serving, reheat the asparagus so the hollandaise doesn't seize up on it: turn the heat back on under the blanching water and dunk the asparagus in the barely simmering water for 30 seconds to 1 minute. Dry the spears on a clean kitchen towel.

To serve, arrange the asparagus stalks, with the tips all facing the same direction, on a serving plate and spoon the warm hollandaise over the top. Garnish with the fried garlic chips and serve immediately.

¾ cup Black Garlic Hollandaise (page 32)

2 pounds asparagus (about 2 bunches)

½ cup fried garlic chips (page 353)

NOTE Sort the asparagus by size and blanch small, medium, and large stalks separately to ensure even cooking.

Spring Pea Risotto

SERVES 8

There's a small window of time during the spring when fresh English peas are available. This bright, pretty risotto is the perfect dish to showcase them in all of their sweet glory, especially since you have to shell each pod individually. (In a pinch, this dish can be made with frozen petite peas, though with far inferior results.) The chopped herbs add another vibrant pop of green to this seasonal dish, which is substantial enough to stand on its own and also works beautifully to accompany Herbed Leg of Lamb (page 281). Be careful when adding the tarragon, as using any more than called for will overpower the dish. A lot of risotto recipes call for stock, but I like to use lightly seasoned water instead because I find that stock adds a meaty element you don't necessarily want in this vegetable-forward preparation.

I feel strongly that risotto should be plated individually, not served family-style, because it needs to be eaten immediately. When people share food, there's always a moment of hesitation over who's going to dig in first, and in the meantime, your risotto is going downhill, absorbing liquid and thickening up by the second. A proper risotto is rich and ever so slightly al dente.

In a 4-quart saucepan, bring 2 quarts of the water and 2½ tablespoons of the salt to a boil. Set up a metal mixing bowl with 1 quart of the water, the ice cubes, and 1 tablespoon of the salt. Add 1½ cups of the English peas to the boiling water and cook for 3 to 4 minutes, until the peas are completely tender. (Reserve the remaining 1½ cups uncooked peas to use later in the recipe.) Remove the peas from the water with a slotted spoon or spider (see page 374) and transfer to the ice water for 1 minute to cool. Reserve the cooking water.

Once the peas have cooled slightly, drain them, transfer to a blender, and purée until completely smooth, adding a few tablespoons of the cooking water to get the mixture to blend to a totally smooth consistency. Set the purée aside.

In a large pot over high heat, bring the remaining 3 quarts water and 1 tablespoon plus 1 teaspoon of the salt to a boil, then reduce the heat until the water is simmering. This is the liquid you'll slowly ladle into the rice. Be careful to keep this pot over the very lowest heat so you don't reduce the water too much and end up with a very salty risotto.

In a large, deep pot, such as an enameled Dutch oven, melt the butter over medium-high heat. When it starts to bubble and sizzle, add the rice (don't rinse it first; you want as much starch as possible to make a creamy risotto) and stir it frequently until it is a slightly golden toasted color but no dark spots have developed, 1 to 2 minutes.

Continued

6 quarts water

4½ tablespoons plus 1 teaspoon salt, plus ¼ to ¾ teaspoon for finishing

4 cups ice cubes

3 cups shelled English peas (from about 4 pounds)

3 tablespoons butter

1½ cups Carnaroli or Arborio rice

½ cup finely minced shallot

½ cup dry white wine

1½ cups sliced stemmed sugar snap peas, on sharp bias ¼ inch thick

3 tablespoons crème fraîche or sour cream (see page 370)

3 tablespoons ground Parmigiano-Reggiano cheese (see page 376)

1 teaspoon lemon zest (see page 375)

½ teaspoon finely minced tarragon

1 tablespoon minced chives

Freshly ground black pepper

NOTE If you're planning to serve the risotto with other dishes that need to be prepped and/or cooked, stop cooking the risotto when the grains of rice are still quite firm at the center but are not powdery, about 20 minutes after your first addition of water. Spread the parcooked risotto across a baking sheet so it will cool quickly and set the baking sheet aside at room temperature. The risotto will take 15 to 20 minutes to finish cooking from this point. When you return to cooking the risotto, heat an additional tablespoon of butter in the pan before adding the cooled risotto. You may need to add a few additional tablespoons of the hot seasoned water to loosen up the risotto before you continue to cook.

Spring Pea Risotto

CONTINUED

Add the shallot and cook until translucent, 30 seconds to 1 minute. Add the wine and stir frequently until absorbed, about 1 minute. Turn down the heat to medium and add ½ cup of the seasoned water. Cook, stirring very well and nearly constantly, until all of the liquid is absorbed. Add another ½ cup seasoned water and again stir until absorbed. With each addition of water, stir and wait until nearly all of the liquid is absorbed before adding the next ½ cup water. Repeat seven more times, which should take about 20 minutes total. At this point, the rice should still be very al dente when you bite into a grain but should not have a powdery interior. Continue adding the warm seasoned water, ½ cup at a time and stirring constantly, until the rice is tender but not too soft, another 4 or 5 additions and about 10 minutes.

Add the reserved uncooked English peas followed by 1 or 2 more additions of seasoned water and cook, stirring constantly, until the peas are just tender, 3 to 5 minutes. When the rice is still al dente but not undercooked and feels very close to a texture you'd want to eat a whole bowl of, add the pea purée, the snap peas, crème fraîche, Parmigiano-Reggiano, and lemon zest. Stir to combine. Add the tarragon and chives. The grains should be just tender but not mushy and the rice should have a consistency like that of a very thick soup or stew, nothing like "rice" as you know it. Add enough water to make the consistency more soupy than you want it because the grains continue to absorb liquid and the risotto tightens up as you serve it. Finally, taste and adjust the seasoning—you may need to add ¼ to ¾ teaspoon salt—and serve immediately, sprinkled with pepper.

New Potato Salad with Fava Beans and Morels

SERVES 4 TO 6

The season that gets me most excited about cooking is spring, when limited-edition produce first appears. In Oregon, the first new potatoes are dug at the same time we begin seeing morels and fava beans, and the combination of the three is absolutely lovely. The blush-colored potatoes that start the season barely have any skin at all, and they cook quickly into fluffy, soft clouds. This recipe will work with any kind of potato, but the first ones of the season are worth seeking out if you're making this in the spring.

This dish is a beautiful way to use morels and fava beans when they're briefly available, but it's also delicious with just the spring onions and fennel. It's the perfect recipe to use up all sorts of odds and ends: young garlic from the farmers' market and leftover lemon confit (page 343) are two smart additions. This is a quick side dish for a weeknight dinner of roasted Pan-Seared Pork Chops (page 244)—the combination of vinegar and rich pork recalls classic German cuisine.

MAKE THE POTATOES In a 4-quart saucepan, combine the potatoes, water, and salt and bring to a boil over high heat. Lower the heat slightly to a low boil and cook for 10 to 12 minutes for very fresh new potatoes and up to 18 to 20 minutes for larger or storage potatoes, until you can pierce a sharp skewer through the center of the potato without resistance. Be careful about checking too frequently with the skewer, as too many holes can cause the potato (especially young potatoes) to fall apart in the water. It's okay if they're very tender, or even beginning to fall apart after they are fully cooked. It's better to have an overcooked potato than one that's underdone, and the softness of the potato will help the vinaigrette soak in better. (Fingerlings usually don't fall apart, but all potatoes are different, so paying close attention is key here.)

Remove the pan from the heat. If the potatoes are beginning to fall apart, drain them right away. Otherwise, let the potatoes sit in the cooking liquid for 5 minutes to absorb salt and soften just a bit more, then drain. Cut the potatoes into rustic 1- to 2-inch pieces and set aside.

MAKE THE VINAIGRETTE In a small saucepan, warm the oil, vinegar, sugar, salt, and pepper over medium heat and whisk until the sugar has completely dissolved, 1 to 2 minutes. Remove from the heat.

MAKE THE FENNEL SALAD In a mixing bowl, toss the warm vinaigrette with the fennel and spring onion and let marinate for 15 minutes.

Continued

POTATOES

1½ pounds new or fingerling potatoes

6 cups water

3 tablespoons salt

VINAIGRETTE

⅓ cup extra-virgin olive oil

⅓ cup red wine vinegar

¾ teaspoon sugar

1 teaspoon salt

¼ teaspoon freshly ground black pepper

FENNEL SALAD

½ fennel bulb, thinly sliced, plus about 1 cup loosely packed fronds, for garnish (optional)

½ small spring onion, thinly sliced, or 2 green onions, white and pale green parts, thinly sliced

1½ cups shelled fava beans or English peas (see Notes, page 150)

Mint or basil leaves, for garnish (optional)

Minced lemon confit (page 343), for garnish (optional)

MORELS

½ tablespoon extra-virgin olive oil

1 pound morels, cleaned (see Note, page 150), large ones cut into ½-inch pieces or small ones halved

¼ teaspoon salt

⅛ teaspoon freshly ground black pepper

1 tablespoon butter

New Potato Salad with Fava Beans and Morels

CONTINUED

MAKE THE MORELS In a large sauté pan, heat the oil over medium-high heat, add the morels, and season with the salt and pepper. If the pan is not large enough to avoid crowding the mushrooms, cook them in two batches. Cook, stirring occasionally, until the mushrooms release their liquid and begin to caramelize slightly, about 15 minutes. Add the butter, swirl the pan for 20 seconds, and then transfer the mushrooms to a small bowl and set aside to cool slightly.

To serve, in a serving bowl, gently toss together the potatoes, fennel salad, and about three-fourths of the vinaigrette. Add the warm morels and toss again. Taste and add more vinaigrette if necessary. Add the fava beans just before serving to avoid discoloration from contact with the acids in the vinaigrette. Garnish with the fennel fronds, mint, and lemon confit. Serve immediately.

TO SHELL FRESH FAVA BEANS, tear off the stem end of the pod and squeeze the beans out of the pod one at a time. Blanch and shock the fava beans (see page 375), adding the beans to the boiling water in large handfuls. Cook for 1 to 2 minutes, then immediately transfer to the ice water. Repeat until all of the beans have been blanched and shocked. Remove the outer skin from each blanched bean to reveal the tender, vibrant green bean inside.

TO SHELL ENGLISH PEAS, remove them from their pods the same way you remove favas from their pods. For this recipe, blanch (see page 375) the shelled peas for 1 minute before shocking.

TO CLEAN MORELS, fill a large bowl with 8 cups of water and 2 tablespoons salt. Add the morels and let soak for 10 minutes, periodically swishing them about, then drain and dry thoroughly with a salad spinner. The salt helps extract dirt from the hard-to-reach crannies and has the added benefit of lightly seasoning the mushrooms before you cook them.

Crispy Baby Artichokes

SERVES 4 TO 6

One of my favorite vendors at the Portland Farmers' Market is Denoble Farms, which has incredible artichokes that start their run in the late spring or early summer. When I shop there, I hear the matriarch of the family, Patreece, describe again and again how to handle and cook baby artichokes because they're a little mysterious. They're very different from the big artichokes that you cook and peel leaves from one by one. With baby artichokes, you can eat almost the whole thing.

If you get baby artichokes when they're small enough, they might not yet have developed a choke. A little bit later in the season, they'll probably have some small, fine hairs forming on the inside that you'll need to clean out using the method below. Baby artichokes are, in a word, delightful, boasting both a grassy quality and a gentle sweetness.

These crispy artichokes are beautiful to eat on their own, but I especially like to pair them with rich and toasty Hazelnut Romesco (page 14) and, for a full meal, Fennel-Brined Pork Loin (page 247), which has its own natural sweetness. If you're planning on serving these artichokes as a main course, make a few more than called for here.

8 quarts cold water

2 lemons

24 to 30 baby artichokes, each about 2 inches in diameter

1 cup white wine

¾ cup salt

2 thyme sprigs

1 fresh or 2 dried bay leaves

6 cloves garlic

Peel of 2 lemons (see page 375)

4 tablespoons extra-virgin olive oil

Hazelnut Romesco (page 14), optional

Herb salad (page 353), for garnish (optional)

To prep the artichokes, pour 4 quarts of the water into a large bowl. Halve the lemons, squeeze their juice into the water, and then add the spent lemons to the bowl. Swirl to combine.

Working with 1 artichoke at a time, remove the tough outer leaves until only the pale interior leaves are visible. Peel off one more layer of outer leaves than you think is necessary; this will ensure that only the most tender inner leaves are left, so the whole artichoke is edible (and not stringy). Using a sharp paring knife, cut off the end of the stem, then trim the stem and base (the area to which the leaves are attached), paring off the outer layers until no green fibers are visible. Immediately submerge the pared artichoke in the lemon water to prevent oxidation. Working carefully but quickly is imperative.

Repeat with the remaining artichokes. When all of the stems and bases have been trimmed, working one at a time, pull the artichokes out of the lemon water and cut off about ¾ inch from the apex of the leaves, leaving only an inch or so of the leaves' pale base. Return each artichoke to the lemon water immediately after trimming.

Once all of the apexes have been trimmed, pull an artichoke out of the water and cut it in half lengthwise. If there is a choke (the fuzzy part that becomes the thistle), with the tip of the knife, carefully cut it out of each half, being careful not to remove any leaves. Using your fingers, remove all bits of choke and any interior leaves with sharp spikes (some baby artichokes will not have spiky leaves). Place the trimmed artichoke halves back in the lemon water and repeat with the remaining artichokes.

Continued

Crispy Baby Artichokes

CONTINUED

Line a baking sheet with a kitchen towel. To parcook the artichokes, pour the remaining 4 quarts water into an 8-quart pot, place over high heat, add the wine, salt, thyme, bay leaf, garlic, and lemon peel, and bring to a boil, stirring to dissolve the salt. Place 1 artichoke half into the boiling water and cook for 3 minutes. Using a slotted spoon or spider (see page 374), transfer the artichoke to the prepared baking sheet, then taste it for doneness and seasoning. The artichoke should be tender but not soft because you'll be cooking it further before serving. If 3 minutes was the right amount of time (this can vary according to the size of the artichokes), divide the artichokes into four batches and repeat the cooking process until all of the artichokes are cooked and drained. This can be done up to 4 hours in advance.

To finish the artichokes, divide the artichokes into four batches again. Heat a black steel pan over medium-high heat until hot. Add 1 tablespoon of the oil and heat until the surface is rippling but not smoking and place a batch of artichokes in a single layer, cut sides down, in the pan. Be careful not to crowd the artichokes or they won't brown properly. Weight the artichokes down with a heatproof plate that fits inside the pan. Check the artichokes frequently, using tongs and a kitchen towel to remove the plate. When the cut sides of the artichokes are golden brown, after 4 to 5 minutes, transfer them to a plate and repeat with the remaining batches and oil.

Place all of the artichokes in the black steel pan and cook over medium heat for about 1 minute just until heated through. Serve the artichokes with a dollop of the romesco and garnished with the herb salad.

Long-Cooked Green Beans

SERVES 4 TO 6

Long cooking vegetables is something of a lost art, probably because so many people associate it with a mushy result. But it is actually a delicious method of cooking vegetables such as green beans, broccoli, or summer squash, particularly mature specimens that have lingered until the end of their season.

Long cooking calls for a very low temperature and lots of olive oil to bring out all of the natural sweetness of the vegetable. Your vegetables are done when they're so soft they are nearly impossible to lift from the oil, and they are an earthy shade of green. That's when they're at their tastiest and sweetest. This is a rich side dish and should be served with something simple, like Seared Duck Breasts (page 229) or Lamb Loin Chops (page 286).

I cannot overstate the importance of keeping the oil over very low heat; too high and you'll fry the vegetables. If you have a high-powered stove, invest in a diffuser (see page 373) to temper the heat. If the flame on your stove top goes out at the lowest setting, transfer the pot to a low oven (250°F) instead. Because the oil never gets hot enough to break down or denature, you can store it in an airtight container in the freezer for up to 3 months and use it again for long-cooking vegetables.

Warm the oil in a 6- to 8-quart Dutch oven or other heavy pot over very low heat for about 5 minutes. Add the garlic and allow it to soften, 2 to 3 minutes. Add the green beans and salt and cook, tossing frequently, until the color along the edges of the beans begins to brighten, 5 to 7 minutes. The beans should be almost (but not quite) submerged in the oil; add a splash more oil if necessary.

Cover the pot with a tight-fitting lid and cook until the beans are very tender and nearly (but not quite) falling apart, about 1 hour. Check frequently to make sure the oil temperature is low enough to cook the beans very slowly. Using tongs or a slotted spoon, gently remove beans from the oil and serve immediately.

2 cups extra-virgin olive oil

5 cloves garlic, smashed with the flat side of a knife blade

1¾ pounds green beans, trimmed

1 teaspoon salt

Variations

Long-Cooked Zucchini: Cut 1½ pounds zucchini (about 4) in half crosswise. Cut each half lengthwise into 4 to 6 spears. Proceed as directed for the beans, but cook the zucchini uncovered for 30 to 35 minutes. Remove the zucchini spears from the oil gently, as they will be very soft.

Long-Cooked Broccoli: Cut 1½ pounds broccoli (about 2 heads) into 2- to 3-inch-long florets, each about ½ inch wide. Proceed as directed for the beans, cooking the broccoli covered for 55 to 60 minutes. Check the broccoli frequently and gently move the florets around to ensure they're fully covered by the oil. When the broccoli is ready, carefully remove it from the oil with a slotted spoon. Broccoli tends to break apart easily when cooked this way, so if you plan to store the oil, pour it through a fine-mesh strainer placed over a bowl to filter it. The tiny bits you capture in the strainer are my favorite; I like to sop them up with a piece of bread.

Fresh Corn and Summer Vegetable Succotash

SERVES 6 TO 8

Succotash reminds me of my southern grandmother, who seemed to cook some version of beans and corn nearly every night. This recipe is simple and captures the flavors of summer at their peak. The bright colors in this dish are gorgeous together. If you can find summer savory, grab it (or grow it!), chop ½ teaspoon, and toss it in at the end.

The keys to this recipe are proper *mise en place* and timing. Roast your pepper and blanch and shock (see page 375) your green beans first and have everything else prepped and ready to go before you start cooking. To keep each color distinct, add each ingredient to the pan separately and allow it to cook for 1 to 2 minutes before adding the next ingredient. That keeps each element looking vibrant and remaining texturally distinct.

I often serve this succotash with Sherry-Glazed Pork Belly (page 251) because the freshness of the vegetables works well alongside the richness of the pork belly. But this is a versatile side.

I must confess that I first tested this recipe in the winter, when not all of the fresh produce was available, and I was pleasantly surprised at how well it worked with frozen corn and jarred roasted *piquillo* peppers from Spain. So if you're really homesick for a summery dish in the off-season, even a less-than-farm-fresh succotash will hit the spot.

1 red bell pepper, or 2 jarred roasted Spanish piquillo peppers

2 teaspoons extra-virgin olive oil

4 ounces green beans

3 tablespoons butter, at room temperature

1 large shallot, finely diced

2 cloves garlic, thinly sliced

2½ cups fresh corn kernels, or one 10-ounce bag frozen corn kernels

1 (14-ounce) can cannellini beans, rinsed and drained

½ cup cherry tomatoes, halved

¾ teaspoon salt

¼ teaspoon freshly ground black pepper

½ teaspoon chopped summer savory (optional)

If using the bell pepper, preheat the broiler. Place the pepper on a small baking sheet and brush it with the oil. Roast, turning the pepper every 2 to 3 minutes as it colors, until all of the skin is blackened and begins to separate from the flesh, about 15 minutes. Transfer the pepper to a small bowl, cover tightly with plastic wrap, and allow to sit for at least 15 minutes, or until cool enough to handle. (The longer it steams, the easier it will be to peel off the skin.) When cool, lay the pepper on a cutting board, pull out the stem from the top and discard, scrape the inside clean of any seeds, and then flip the pepper over and peel the skin off the outside. Cut the pepper into large dice and set aside. If using piquillo peppers, cut into large dice and set aside.

Trim the green beans and slice each bean into quarters on a sharp bias. Blanch and shock the beans (see page 375), cooking them for about 2 minutes.

In a sauté pan, heat the butter over medium-high heat until lightly browned around the edges of the pan, 1 to 2 minutes. Add the shallot and cook, stirring occasionally, for about 1 minute. Add the garlic and cook for about 30 seconds. Add the corn and cook, stirring occasionally, for about 2 minutes. Add the cannellini beans and cook, stirring occasionally, for about 1 minute. Add the green beans and cook, stirring occasionally, for about 1 minute. Add the roasted bell pepper and the cherry tomatoes and cook, stirring occasionally, for about 1 minute. All the ingredients should be heated through and each should retain its color and texture.

Season with the salt, pepper, and savory and serve immediately.

Pan-Seared Wild Mushrooms with Parsley and Parmesan

SERVES 4 TO 6

This is a classic, simple way to prepare mushrooms. There's not a lot to this dish, but its success lies in cooking the mushrooms correctly—that is, allowing them to release their moisture fully and develop some light caramelization. I like to use sherry vinegar to bring out the natural earthy flavor of the mushrooms at the end. It's like squeezing a lemon over the top, but a little more refined. I get wild mushrooms from the farmers' market in the early fall in my part of the country, but you can often find unusual varieties of cultivated mushrooms (such as oyster and maitake) in grocery stores year-round, too.

Tear or cut any large mushrooms into quarters and the rest in half. Leave the smallest ones whole. Divide the wild mushrooms into four batches.

Heat a black steel pan over high heat until very hot. Add 1 tablespoon of the oil and heat until the surface is rippling but not smoking. Add a batch of mushrooms, ½ to ¾ teaspoon salt (depending on how dry your mushrooms are; dry mushrooms may need slightly more salt), and ¼ teaspoon of the pepper. Be careful not to crowd the pan or you won't get that all-important sear. Lower the heat to medium-high, add a garlic clove, and sauté the mushrooms, moving them around, for 7 to 8 minutes, until they are beginning to color on the edges and the moisture they release evaporates. Add a thyme sprig in the final minute of cooking. All of the mushrooms should be soft and tender with no spongy quality or rawness to them. Add 1 tablespoon of the butter and cook for another 1 to 2 minutes. Transfer the mushrooms to a mixing bowl. Pick out the thyme sprig and the garlic and discard. Wipe the pan out with a paper towel and repeat with the remaining oil, mushrooms, salt, pepper, garlic, thyme, and butter, cooking in three batches.

When all of the mushrooms have been cooked, toss them all into a stainless-steel pan and rewarm over medium heat. Drizzle with the vinegar and sprinkle with the parsley. Let cool until barely warm, add the Parmigiano-Reggiano and toss so the cheese melts slightly but still tastes distinct. Serve immediately.

2 pounds wild mushrooms (such as chanterelle or porcini), cleaned (see Note, below)

4 tablespoons extra-virgin olive oil

2 to 3 teaspoons salt

1 teaspoon freshly ground black pepper

4 cloves garlic, smashed with the flat side of a knife blade

4 thyme sprigs

4 tablespoons butter

1½ teaspoons aged sherry vinegar (see page 370)

½ cup roughly chopped flat-leaf parsley

1½ ounces Parmigiano-Reggiano cheese, shaved with a vegetable peeler

NOTE To clean wild mushrooms such as chanterelles or porcini, cut off the bottom end of the stem if dirt is present. Using a soft cloth or napkin, wipe the surface of the mushroom and then brush it with a stiff-bristled brush if necessary to remove any dirt. Peel the stem with a paring knife and gently scrape off any remaining dirt.

Quick-Sautéed Greens with Garlic, Lemon Confit, and Chile Flakes

SERVES 6

I try to eat greens almost every day, and this is my go-to method for preparing them. It's dead simple, and it works for all kinds. Greens have seasons, so you should touch and taste a variety of them at the market to find the ones you like best. Spinach, for example, is beautiful in the late spring and early summer, while kale usually tastes best after the first frost. Rabe is also lovely, and there's so much more than just broccoli rabe out there: watch for Brussels rabe and kale rabe, too. The ones with sprouts on top taste sweetest.

Pay attention to the texture and heartiness of your greens because both affect cooking time. If you're mixing more than one type of green, don't just throw them all in at once. Start with the heartiest selection, which will take the longest to cook. Save the more delicate leaves for the very end, so they don't overcook and form tight clumps. The concept of cooking something al dente doesn't just apply to pasta: your cooked greens should still have some texture without being tough or fibrous.

Keep an eye on your garlic to ensure it doesn't burn, and have a little water on hand to sprinkle over the greens if they're too dry when they hit the pan or if they start to stick to the bottom.

Strip the hard rib from each kale leaf (and any other greens that have one), discard or, in the case of chard, save the ribs for quick pickling (see quick pickles, page 349). Tear the greens into 3-inch pieces.

In a 10- to 12-inch sauté pan or enameled Dutch oven, heat the oil over medium-high heat. Add the garlic paste and chile flakes and stir for about 20 seconds. Make sure the garlic doesn't brown or take on any color. Add the hardiest greens (if using the above combination, it will be the kales) and then the water to keep the garlic from burning. Cook, stirring occasionally, for about 2 minutes, until the greens have softened slightly and collapsed in volume.

Push the kale to the side of the pan, add the chard or spinach, and cook, stirring occasionally, for another 2 to 3 minutes, until completely wilted and tender. Sprinkle the lemon confit and salt across the greens and stir to combine. Serve immediately, with lemon wedges on the side for squeezing over the greens.

1 bunch (about 8 ounces) Lacinato kale or Red Russian kale, thoroughly washed (no need to dry)

1 bunch (about 8 ounces) Swiss chard or spinach, thoroughly washed (no need to dry)

1 tablespoon extra-virgin olive oil

½ teaspoon garlic paste (page 344)

¼ teaspoon red chile flakes

2 to 3 teaspoons water

2 tablespoons minced lemon confit (page 343), or zest of ½ lemon (see page 375)

Scant ½ teaspoon salt

6 lemon wedges, seeded (see page 375), for serving (optional)

Variation

Mustard greens and spinach are another lovely combination to sauté quickly; the spinach helps soften the sharp taste of the mustard greens. Proceed as directed, cooking the mustard greens first and adding the spinach during the final 30 seconds of cooking.

Fennel Gratin

SERVES 6 TO 8

When fennel is cooked, it takes on a mild, delicate flavor that's distinct from the flavor of raw fennel. And because fennel is available year-round, this is a great recipe to have on hand. Use this cheesy gratin base with other vegetables, too, such as potatoes or Belgian endive.

This is a rich, comforting dish that pairs well with something simple and rustic, like Fig and Red Wine–Braised Lamb Shanks (page 289). It's also an elegant dish to prepare and serve family-style in a pretty casserole or portioned into individual gratin dishes. If your fennel bulbs are large, plan on serving about a half bulb per person, and if they are small, plan on a whole bulb per person.

MAKE THE FENNEL Chop 3 tablespoons of fennel fronds and set them aside for later use. If you're using large fennel bulbs, cut them lengthwise into quarters; if you're using small bulbs, cut them lengthwise in half. Leave the base fully attached in both instances. Turn the fennel pieces cut side up and season with the salt and pepper (this is a great time to practice the aerial salting method described on page 375).

Heat your largest sauté pan over medium-high heat. Add the oil and butter, and then working in batches to avoid overcrowding, add the fennel cut side down and sear until deep chestnut brown, 2 to 3 minutes. If the fennel is quartered, flip the pieces to sear the other cut surface for an additional 2 to 3 minutes. Transfer the fennel to a large Dutch oven.

Add the stock and wine to the Dutch oven, place over low heat, cover, and simmer until the fennel is fork-tender but not mushy, 20 to 25 minutes. If there is any liquid remaining in the pot, drain it off. Place the fennel in a 9 by 13-inch baking dish and set aside.

MAKE THE CHEESE SAUCE In a saucepan over medium heat, melt the butter and whisk in the flour. Whisk for about 1 minute, then add the garlic paste. Whisk until the flour begins to take on a pale gold color, 2 to 3 minutes. At this point, you will have removed any raw flour taste from your sauce. You don't want too much color, however, as the flour will taste bitter if it gets overly toasted. You want a shade between off-white and not quite beige when you stop whisking.

Gradually whisk in the milk to avoid forming any lumps. Once all of the milk has been added, whisk vigorously until the sauce is completely smooth; turn down the heat to medium-low and simmer, whisking periodically to avoid scorching, until the sauce fully thickens, 10 to 12 minutes. Turn off the heat, whisk in the Gruyère, and season with the salt and pepper. The finished sauce should be very thick.

Continued

FENNEL

4 or 5 large fennel bulbs (each 3 to 4 inches), or 6 to 8 small fennel bulbs (each 2 to 3 inches), with some fronds attached

1 tablespoon salt

1 teaspoon freshly ground black pepper

2 tablespoons extra-virgin olive oil

4 tablespoons butter

¾ cup homemade stock (page 346) or other high-quality stock

¼ cup good white wine

CHEESE SAUCE

3 tablespoons butter

3 tablespoons all-purpose flour

2 teaspoons garlic paste (page 344)

2½ cups whole milk

3 ounces cave-aged Gruyère cheese, grated

½ teaspoon salt

¼ teaspoon freshly ground black pepper

BREAD CRUMB TOPPING

2 tablespoons butter

¾ cup coarse bread crumbs (page 363)

1 teaspoon garlic paste (page 344)

½ teaspoon fennel pollen

¼ teaspoon freshly ground black pepper

3 tablespoons roughly chopped fennel fronds (optional)

FOR ASSEMBLY

2 ounces cave-aged Gruyère cheese, grated

2 ounces Parmigiano-Reggiano cheese, ground (see page 376)

Fennel Gratin

CONTINUED

MAKE THE BREAD CRUMB TOPPING In a saucepan over medium-low heat, melt the butter. Add the bread crumbs, garlic paste, fennel pollen, and pepper and cook, stirring often, until the bread crumbs are pale gold. Don't allow them to take on too much color, as they will spend a few minutes in the oven on top of the gratin. Remove the pan from the heat and stir in the chopped fennel fronds.

ASSEMBLE THE DISH Position a rack in the upper third of the oven and preheat the oven to 350°F. Pour the cheese sauce over the fennel (very gently reheat the sauce if it is cold), and then sprinkle with the Gruyère and Parmigiano-Reggiano cheeses. Bake until bubbling and beginning to brown, 15 to 20 minutes.

Remove the baking dish from the oven and scatter the topping in an even layer across the top. Continue to bake the gratin until it takes on a deep golden hue, about 5 minutes. If it needs more color, place the dish under the broiler (make sure it is broiler-proof) for 1 minute, watching it very carefully to ensure nothing burns. Serve immediately.

NOTE The fennel and cheese sauce can both be made up to 1 day in advance and kept in separate containers in the refrigerator until ready to bake and serve.

Blistered Cauliflower with Anchovy, Garlic, and Chile Flakes

SERVES 6 TO 8

It seems like almost overnight people have discovered that cooking cruciferous vegetables with high heat is the way to go. The method in this recipe, like that for crispy Brussels sprouts on page 177, brings out the natural sweetness of the vegetable. If you've never cooked a vegetable this way, this dish is a great introduction.

Cauliflower roasted on its own is very mild and sweet, so I like to balance it out with the deep flavors of anchovy and garlic and with some chile flakes for spice. The bread crumbs are added for texture and for an element of crunch at the end.

Fully preheat the pan to sear the surface of the cauliflower quickly. If you place a cold pan full of vegetables in the broiler, they'll end up steaming rather than crisping up into that beautiful caramelized state you're looking for.

Place an empty baking sheet on the oven rack positioned two rungs from the top and preheat the broiler to scalding hot, at least 10 minutes.

In a small jar or plastic container with a tight-fitting lid, combine 3 tablespoons of the oil, the garlic paste, anchovy paste, chile flakes, and lemon zest. Shake well and set aside.

Cut the cauliflower heads into ½- to ¾-inch slices (don't worry about the little irregular pieces that break off; they will get a nice char). In your largest mixing bowl, toss the cauliflower with the remaining ⅔ cup oil and the salt and pepper. This may look like an excessive amount of cauliflower, but it cooks down significantly.

Carefully remove the hot baking sheet from the broiler (use a double layer of kitchen towels or oven mitts). Place half of the cauliflower across the pan in an even layer. It's important not to crowd the cauliflower on the pan or it will steam instead of sear. If your baking sheet is not large enough, you may have to sear the cauliflower in three batches. Return the pan to the broiler and cook the cauliflower for 15 minutes, stirring every 5 minutes or so, to allow color to develop. The cauliflower is ready when the smaller pieces look caramelized and charred and the larger pieces have dark brown caramelized edges. Place the first batch of cauliflower in a bowl and repeat with the remaining cauliflower.

Once all of the cauliflower has been caramelized, toss it with the garlic-anchovy paste, breaking up any lumps of paste so it is evenly distributed, and return the whole batch to the baking sheet. Return the cauliflower to the broiler for 2 to 3 minutes, until any raw garlic flavor is gone. Toss the cauliflower with the bread crumbs and parsley and serve family-style.

⅔ cup plus 3 tablespoons extra-virgin olive oil

2 teaspoons garlic paste (page 344)

1 tablespoon anchovy paste (from about 8 fillets; see page 370)

¼ teaspoon red chile flakes

1 teaspoon lemon zest (see page 375)

2 heads cauliflower, trimmed of their greens and cored

½ teaspoon salt

¾ teaspoon freshly ground black pepper

1 cup panfried coarse bread crumbs (page 363)

¼ cup chopped flat-leaf parsley

Parsnip Purée

MAKES ABOUT 3 CUPS; SERVES 6 TO 8

I love this and other vegetable purées because they're halfway between a sauce and a side dish. Purées are a nice way of serving a vegetable that has an intense flavor, like parsnips or celery root, which, when long cooked and blended with cream and milk, feel somehow lighter on the palate. Don't let that lightness fool you, however. This purée is quite rich, so a little goes a long way on the plate.

Much like when making a velouté (see page 82), the only way to ensure a silky-smooth purée is to cook the vegetable until it is very soft and squishes easily between your fingers before you blend it. Then, once you're ready to blend, use a slotted spoon to transfer the vegetable to the blender and add just enough of the cooked cream and milk mixture to get the blades moving smoothly. If you have a high-powered blender, this is the time to use the tamper that came with the machine, as it will allow you to get the vegetables moving around quickly without adding a lot of extra liquid. The purée should be as thick as possible, so regardless of the kind of blender you own, add only a little bit of liquid at a time. You can always add more, but you can't take it away.

In a large saucepan or a stockpot over medium heat, combine all of the ingredients. Bring to a simmer and cook until the parsnips have softened completely and the cream is mostly reduced, 35 to 45 minutes. Watch the pot carefully, as it can boil over.

When the parsnips are soft enough to squish easily between your fingers, use a slotted spoon to transfer them to a blender. Purée the parsnips, adding only as much dairy as needed to get the mixture spinning, until very smooth, about 1 minute. Some parsnips have more natural moisture than others. Just remember you want the purée to be as thick as possible yet velvety smooth. (Strain the purée through a fine-mesh strainer if necessary.) Taste and adjust the seasoning with salt and serve warm. Because this purée contains so much fat, it stores well for 2 to 3 days in an airtight container in the refrigerator. Reheat it gently, as it has a tendency to bubble up, and stir frequently with a small whisk to avoid painful spatter burns.

2 large parsnips, peeled and sliced into ¼-inch-thick pieces (about 4 cups)

2½ cups whole milk

1 cup heavy cream

2 teaspoons salt

4 cloves garlic

Variations

Butternut Squash Purée: You will need a 1½- to 2-pound butternut squash. Halve, seed, peel, and cut into ¼-inch-thick pieces, then proceed as directed for parsnips. Because squash does not have a lot of natural moisture, you should have an extra ½ cup milk and ½ cup cream on hand to thin out the purée as needed.

Celery Root Purée: You will need about 2 pounds of celery root. Peel and slice into ¼-inch-thick pieces, then proceed as directed for parsnips. Because celery root has a lot of natural moisture, you may not need to add any, or only very little, of the cooked milk and cream mixture to the blender. To deepen the green color of this purée as shown in the photo at left, add 1 teaspoon spinach purée from the Spinach-Gruyère Soufflé (page 199) to the blender.

From left: Parsnip Purée, Butternut Squash Purée, Celery Root Purée

Potato Dumplings

SERVES 6 TO 8

I wanted to include a dumpling recipe in this book because dumplings are a versatile, easy comfort-food dish to make year-round. I did a lot of research, testing dozens of traditional dumpling recipes, but none of them were quite right. Eventually I settled on this simple potato version, which is a creative and somewhat unexpected way to serve potatoes.

This is similar to what you'd find in a dish like chicken and dumplings (and, in fact, I like to serve these dumplings alongside the Porcini-Braised Chicken Thighs on page 232), but less floury and more potato-forward. These dumplings would also be wonderful with a light tomato sauce and some Parmesan cheese, or with a little brown butter and fried sage alongside roast pork.

This is a sensitive recipe, so it's important to use a kitchen scale (see page 373) to measure out 24 ounces (1½ pounds) of riced potatoes. If you use too much potato, the mixture might not bind properly and the dumplings may fall apart; if you use too little potato, the dumplings will be too heavy with flour and egg. It's wise to buy a few extra potatoes just in case.

You will need a potato ricer, as a potato masher will not yield a fluffy enough result. The dumplings are at their best and lightest when the potatoes are riced a day ahead of time and allowed to dry out on a baking sheet in the refrigerator overnight. But if you're making this recipe the same day you want to serve it, you can freeze the riced potatoes for 25 minutes to achieve a similar effect.

Preheat the oven to 375°F. Pierce the potatoes all over with a fork, set them on a baking sheet, and bake for about 1 hour, until they can be very easily pierced with a skewer or sharp knife. Remove the potatoes from the oven and let them cool briefly until they can be handled but are still quite warm to the touch, then use a kitchen towel to peel the skin from the flesh. Rice the potatoes and weigh out 24 ounces. Save any leftover potato for another use.

Line a baking sheet with parchment paper and spread the riced potatoes across the pan. Place the pan, uncovered, in the refrigerator overnight to dry out the riced potatoes, or in the freezer to cool for 25 minutes if making the dumplings the same day.

In a small cup or mixing bowl, lightly beat together the eggs and egg yolks until blended. In a another mixing bowl, whisk together the flour, potato starch, 2½ teaspoons of the salt, the pepper, and the nutmeg.

Place the chilled potatoes in a mixing bowl 8 to 10 inches in diameter. Lightly dust the flour mixture across the surface of the potatoes all at once and, using a fork, gently mix to combine (do not overmix). When the mixture looks uniform, add the eggs.

Continued

2 pounds russet potatoes

2 eggs

2 egg yolks (see page 377)

¾ cup all-purpose flour (see page 376)

2 tablespoons potato starch

¼ cup plus 2½ teaspoons salt

½ teaspoon freshly ground black pepper

1/16 teaspoon freshly grated nutmeg

4 quarts water

3 tablespoons butter, melted

3 tablespoons chopped flat-leaf parsley

2 tablespoons finely minced chives

Potato Dumplings

CONTINUED

Use the fork to mix until everything once again looks uniform. Then, using both hands, form the mixture into a ball. Very lightly knead it a few times until it forms a homogenous dough.

In a large saucepan, combine the water and the remaining ¼ cup salt and bring to a boil. Taste the seasoning water and remember how salty it is. As you cook the dumplings, some water will evaporate, leaving the cooking water saltier, so it's important to add fresh water as needed to bring it back to this level of seasoning. Break off a small piece of the dough and roll it between your fingers to make a dumpling about the size of a Ping-Pong ball. Don't smash or compact it too much; keep the pressure light and even throughout.

Add the dumpling to the boiling water. When it floats, set your timer for 6 minutes, and allow the dumpling to simmer (not boil) until the timer sounds. Remove it with a slotted spoon or a spider (see page 374) and taste it. The dumpling should be fluffy and well seasoned and not soggy or sticky. It will firm up as it rests. If the dumpling seems too loose and is falling apart, mix another 1 to 2 tablespoons of flour into the potato mixture.

If the tester dumpling turns out well, shape about 12 more dumplings the size of Ping-Pong balls and add them all at once to the water. When the dumplings float, set the timer for 6 minutes, and then leave them to cook, turning them occasionally as they expand. Make sure the water isn't at a hard boil or the dumplings may break apart.

Transfer the dumplings to a Dutch oven. Replenish the boiling water with additional fresh water and adjust the salt as needed. Using the remaining dough, shape and cook a second batch of dumplings. You should have about 25 dumplings total.

Preheat the oven to 400°F. Add the butter, parsley, and chives to the dumplings and mix gently to distribute evenly. Cover and heat in the oven for 7 to 10 minutes, until warmed through. Serve immediately.

Crispy Brussels Sprouts with Pickled Mustard Seeds

SERVES 6 TO 8

I always liked cooking Brussels sprouts at my old communal dining space, Family Supper, because I love to get people excited about things they think they don't like. A certain generation of people (mine included) grew up with a poor impression of sprouts based on the way they were (over)cooked, but something magical happens when you blast brassicas with hot, direct heat. They caramelize, with a blistery, crackly outside, a tender interior, and a deeply satisfying flavor. The addition of pickled mustard seeds brings just the right amount of acid and sweetness to round out the dish.

2½ pounds Brussels sprouts

½ cup extra-virgin olive oil

1¾ teaspoons salt

½ teaspoon freshly ground black pepper

3 tablespoons pickled mustard seeds (page 350)

Place an empty baking sheet on an oven rack as close to the heat source as possible and preheat the broiler.

Cut the base off of each Brussels sprout, and then cut each sprout in half lengthwise, discarding any floppy outer leaves.

In a large mixing bowl, toss the sprouts with the oil. Sprinkle in the salt and pepper and toss well to combine (this is a good place to practice the aerial salting method described on page 375).

Carefully remove the hot baking sheet from the broiler (use a double layer of kitchen towels or oven mitts) and lay the sprouts in a single layer across the pan. Return the pan to the oven and set a timer for 6 minutes. After 6 minutes, stir the sprouts and rotate the pan 180 degrees to ensure the sprouts caramelize evenly. Set the timer for another 6 minutes. The sprouts should have a nice char on some areas and be vibrant green.

At the 12-minute mark, add the mustard seeds to the baking sheet and stir well. Broil for an additional 2 minutes. The sprouts should now be ready. When you taste one, it should be tender but not completely soft. (The sugars in the pickled mustard seeds will have caramelized a bit and can burn your mouth if you're not careful.) I like to test one big sprout and one little sprout to get an average. Remove the finished sprouts from the hot baking sheet and serve immediately.

Orange-Caraway Glazed Carrots

SERVES 8

Some of the cookbooks I learned to cook from recommend sprinkling sugar on top of carrots to glaze them, somehow hoping that the sugar would marry with the natural juices in the carrots just so to create the perfect glaze. Unfortunately, you can't predict how much liquid will come out of a vegetable, so I developed a more controlled technique that also yields a deeper and richer flavor.

MAKE THE CARROTS Place an empty baking sheet in the oven and preheat the oven to 400°F.

Cut off the tip of a carrot at a 45-degree angle and discard the tip. Rotate the carrot a quarter turn and cut 1½-inch pieces at a 45-degree angle. Continue rotating and cutting along the length of the carrot to create an irregular bias shape. (This is called an oblique cut.) Repeat with the remaining carrots.

In a large mixing bowl, toss the carrots with the oil and salt. Carefully remove the hot baking sheet from the oven (use a double layer of kitchen towels or oven mitts). Spread the carrots in an even layer on the hot baking sheet. Return the pan to the oven and roast until the carrots are tender (but not too soft) and have some dark caramelization around the edges, 25 to 35 minutes. The carrots should not be al dente. Instead, they should have no bite left but they should not be squishy either. Remove from the oven.

MAKE THE GLAZE In a small saucepan, combine the vinegar, sugar, and salt over low heat and bring to a very gentle simmer, stirring to dissolve the sugar. Cook until the mixture is the consistency of maple syrup and the color has darkened, about 5 minutes. Keep an eye on the glaze, as it can burn very easily.

Stir in the orange zest and pour the glaze into a small heatproof bowl or ramekin to stop it from cooking further. As the glaze cools, it will thicken slightly to a honey-like consistency, but when you add it to the carrots in a hot pan, it will return to a maple syrup–like texture. Do not refrigerate the glaze, as it will harden.

To serve, in a sauté pan over medium-high heat, melt 1 tablespoon of the butter. Add the carrots and the caraway seeds and cook, stirring occasionally, until the carrots are heated through and the butter is bubbling, about 3 minutes. Add the glaze and toss the carrots a few times to ensure they are evenly coated with the glaze, 1 to 2 minutes. The finished carrots should look smooth and beautifully glossy, not sticky or gooey. If necessary, add the remaining 1 tablespoon of butter to loosen the glaze and coat the carrots with an even sheen. Serve immediately (but don't taste before blowing on them first, because the caramelized sugars are very hot).

CARROTS

2 bunches (about 16 large) carrots, tops discarded and peeled

2 tablespoons extra-virgin olive oil

¾ teaspoon salt

1 to 2 tablespoons butter

1 teaspoon toasted caraway seeds (see page 378)

GLAZE

⅓ cup aged sherry vinegar (see page 370)

¼ cup maple or muscovado sugar

½ teaspoon salt

½ teaspoon orange zest (see page 375)

NOTE If your glaze didn't reduce enough before you added it to the carrots, you can thicken it slightly by cooking it for an additional minute in the pan with the carrots. If your glaze was overcooked and a little too thick before adding it, toss it with the carrots for barely a minute before removing from the heat.

Caramelized Delicata Squash

SERVES 4

Unlike caramelizing onions, which is all about low and slow cooking, this take on caramelization relies on an understanding of heat and movement in the pan. To get that beautiful golden sear on squash, don't crowd the squash pieces in the pan. If they are packed too tightly, they will steam instead of sear. Even if you can fit all of the squash into the pan at once, don't. Cook it in two batches. Thinly cut delicata squash doesn't need to be peeled. The skin offers a nice textural contrast.

The move that will really help you here is the flip. You see chefs using the flip in busy restaurants and on TV. Instead of using a spoon or spatula, which can cause your ingredients to break, they quickly shove the pan forward and up so the ingredients lift up and flip over, falling back into the pan. Try this several times per batch. Flipping turns the squash over quickly and creates a fast, even sear. (And for the sake of your wrist and arm, practice with a lightweight pan! This is one of the main reasons chefs use the black steel pans I recommend on page 373.)

1 (1½- to 2-pound) delicata squash, unpeeled

5 tablespoons extra-virgin olive oil

½ teaspoon salt

⅛ teaspoon freshly ground black pepper

Flaky finishing salt

Carefully cut the stem end off the squash, then cut the squash in half lengthwise. Scoop out and discard the seeds. Cut each half crosswise into half-moons about ⅛ inch thick, or about the thickness of two quarters. This is one of those times when being accurate with your knife cuts is important, as each piece needs to be as close to the same size as possible to cook evenly.

In a large bowl, toss the squash with 3 tablespoons of the oil, the salt, and the pepper. In a lightweight sauté or black steel pan, heat 1 tablespoon of the olive oil over medium-high heat. Add half of the squash and cook, flipping the pieces frequently (every 10 to 15 seconds), until tender and golden brown on both sides (some blistery dark spots are okay), 4 to 5 minutes. During cooking, move the pieces with a spoon or tongs as needed to ensure each one makes contact with the pan.

Transfer the first batch of squash to a plate or baking sheet and gently spread out the slices so they will cool. Avoid piling the squash slices into a bowl, which can cause them to continue cooking and break apart. Cook the second batch of squash in the same way with the remaining 1 tablespoon oil. Taste and adjust the seasoning if necessary.

To serve, briefly warm all of the squash together in a large sauté pan. Sprinkle with flaky salt and serve immediately.

Oven-Glazed Shallots

SERVES 4

Soft, sweet, tangy, and salty—this is probably the best expression of an allium there is. Cooking shallots slowly and then glazing them with aged balsamic vinegar, which is slightly viscous, helps create a glossy lacquer and brings out all of the shallots' natural sweetness.

Although you can prepare this dish year-round, it's particularly lovely when you start to see fresh shallots at the market in early fall. The fresh ones will cook much faster than the storage ones, so keep a close eye on them while they cook. This is a good side dish to make ahead of time. It's more elegant than a knotted nest of caramelized onions, and you can serve it straight out of the pan if you like.

Preheat the oven to 400°F. Trim and peel the shallots but leave a bit of the root end intact so the shallots don't break apart during cooking. In a mixing bowl, toss the shallots with the oil and salt.

Heat a Dutch oven over medium-high heat until very hot. Add the shallots and cook, stirring frequently, until they are a deep chestnut color on all sides, 7 to 8 minutes. Cover the pot, transfer it to the oven, and cook until the shallots are completely soft and offer no resistance, 20 to 30 minutes, depending on their size.

Add the vinegar, return the pot to the oven, and cook, uncovered, for 5 minutes more. Stir the shallots carefully so they don't fall apart too much and cook for another 5 minutes, until the vinegar is just caramelized but not burning. Keep a close eye on the vinegar, as it can burn easily.

Serve immediately for the best presentation. The shallots can be made up to 1 hour in advance, however, and then reheated in a 375°F oven for 5 to 7 minutes, until heated through. (They will keep in an airtight container in the refrigerator for up to 1 week and can be used any time you would use caramelized onions, such as on sandwiches and in salads.)

1½ pounds shallots (see Note, below)

3 tablespoons plus 1 teaspoon extra-virgin olive oil

1½ teaspoons salt

1 tablespoon plus 1½ teaspoons 10-year aged balsamic vinegar (see page 370)

Variation

Use this balsamic glazing method for cipollini onions. The onions may take a few minutes longer to cook.

NOTE Select large shallots if you can, as they shrink considerably after peeling and during cooking. Plan on serving each person 2 or 3 large shallots.

Caramelized Lentils du Puy

SERVES 6 TO 8

Puy lentils (*lentilles du Puy*), which are cultivated in the Auvergne region of France, are special, and you shouldn't substitute another kind if you can help it. Check online or with your local market to find the certified ones, which cook up very tender without falling apart or splitting. This is a time when the slightly higher price is justified.

The finished dish is surprisingly umami-forward due to the glaze, which has tomato paste and anchovies. I like to cook lentils until they are almost done and then let them continue cooking with almost no heat or movement at all for the final 20 minutes so they don't burst open. Once the lentils are cooked through, it's important to caramelize them in two batches so they get nice, crisp edges.

When making the mirepoix, take a little extra time to carefully and finely dice the vegetables. This care and attention will come through in the final presentation.

MAKE THE LENTILS Spread the lentils across the top quarter of a baking sheet. Carefully sort through the lentils to remove any rocks, dirt, or other particulates; move the clean lentils down in rows to the bottom of the baking sheet, moving back and forth like a typewriter. Rinse the sorted lentils in a strainer, then add them to a saucepan with the water and the wine. Bring to a simmer over medium-high heat, and then lower the heat slightly so the lentils are actively simmering but not rapidly boiling. When the liquid reaches a rolling simmer, set a timer for 20 minutes. After 20 minutes, the lentils should be al dente.

Add the salt to the lentils and stir well. Turn off the heat but keep the pot, uncovered, on the burner for 20 minutes. After 20 minutes, taste for doneness; the lentils should be completely tender but not falling apart. (If they need more time, gently bring them back to a simmer and carefully watch and taste.) Drain the lentils in a fine-mesh strainer and spread them across the baking sheet to cool.

MAKE THE MIREPOIX Heat the oil in a 10- to 12-inch nonreactive sauté pan over medium-high heat. Add the onion, celery, carrot, salt, and pepper and cook, stirring occasionally, until the onion is translucent and the carrot and celery are tender but toothsome, 2 to 3 minutes. Transfer to a plate and set aside.

MAKE THE GLAZE In a small saucepan, combine the wine, thyme, and garlic and bring to a boil. Turn down the heat to a gentle simmer and cook until the wine has a thick, syrupy consistency. Be sure to stop cooking before too much wine evaporates. You want to reduce the liquid to about 1 tablespoon, which takes anywhere from 5 to 10 minutes. Pour the reduction through a fine-mesh strainer into a small bowl.

In a small jar with a tight-fitting lid, combine the reduction, vinegar, tomato paste, sugar, garlic paste, anchovy paste, and mustard. Shake thoroughly to combine and set aside.

Continued

LENTILS

1½ cups Puy lentils

6 cups water

2 cups red wine

1 tablespoon plus 1 teaspoon salt

MIREPOIX

2 tablespoons extra-virgin olive oil

1 cup finely diced yellow onion

1 cup finely diced celery

1 cup peeled and finely diced carrot

½ teaspoon salt

¼ teaspoon freshly ground black pepper

GLAZE

1 cup red wine

1 thyme sprig

1 clove garlic

2 tablespoons aged sherry vinegar (see page 370)

2 tablespoons tomato paste

2 tablespoons muscovado or dark brown sugar

1 tablespoon garlic paste (page 344)

1 tablespoon plus 1 teaspoon anchovy paste (from about 10 fillets; see page 370)

1 tablespoon plus 1 teaspoon Dijon mustard

FOR ASSEMBLY

5 tablespoons extra-virgin olive oil

⅓ cup roughly chopped flat-leaf parsley

2 tablespoons high-quality extra-virgin olive oil, for finishing

Caramelized Lentils du Puy

CONTINUED

ASSEMBLE THE DISH Divide the lentils, the mirepoix, and the glaze into two batches each (keep them all separate). Heat 2 tablespoons of the oil in a nonreactive sauté pan over medium heat. Add a batch of the glaze. It will probably sizzle and splatter, but that's okay; just step back a little from the stove. Stir the glaze with a wooden spoon for about 1 minute, until the edges darken, the oil separates from the glaze, and the glaze looks a bit scrambled. Add a batch of the lentils, turn up the heat to medium-high, and stir the lentils frequently for about 2 minutes, until some of the edges of the lentils begin to darken and crisp slightly. Add a batch of the mirepoix and cook for an additional minute. Transfer the mixture to a mixing bowl.

Rinse and dry the pan and repeat with 2 tablespoons of the remaining oil and the remaining glaze, lentils, and mirepoix. Add the second batch of the lentil mixture to the mixing bowl, as well. Rinse and dry the pan once more.

To serve, heat the remaining 1 tablespoon oil in the sauté pan over medium-high heat. Add all of the lentil mixture and mix until hot, 1 to 2 minutes. Return the lentils to the mixing bowl and toss with the parsley and finishing oil. Serve immediately.

Duchess Potatoes with Smoked Onion Soubise

SERVES 8

This is a refined version of twice-baked potatoes. I developed this recipe after playing around with making a smoked onion *soubise* (a rich white sauce made with onion purée) and wanting a way to show off the results. Although these potatoes happen to be vegetarian, they have an incredibly meaty quality from the smoky onions. This dish works any time you'd serve a baked potato—alongside a luxurious rib eye (page 263), a simple chicken breast (page 227), or even next to a salad for a comforting lunch.

I use two kinds of potatoes here because each one has different characteristics, and while the best variety for making fluffy mashed potatoes for the filling is russet, the best potatoes for making the delicate outer shells are Yukon Golds. As with the Potato Dumplings on page 172, you will need to use a potato ricer to get the necessary fluffy result. You will also need a pastry bag with a star tip (or a resealable plastic bag) for piping the filling into the shells.

MAKE THE POTATO SHELLS Preheat the oven to 400°F. Place the Yukon Gold potatoes in a baking dish and toss with 2 tablespoons of the oil and the ¾ teaspoon salt. Pour water to a depth of about ¼ inch into the baking dish, then cover the dish with aluminum foil. Place in the oven and cook the potatoes until they can be easily pierced with a fork, 45 to 60 minutes. The potatoes should be just tender, not overcooked, and still slightly waxy. They need to hold their shape and their skins need to stay intact, so cook them carefully.

Transfer the potatoes to a plate and allow them to cool for 10 to 15 minutes, then refrigerate for at least 1 hour or up to 8 hours. Do not peel.

MAKE THE SMOKED ONION SOUBISE While the potatoes are cooking, in a small saucepan, melt the butter over medium heat. Add the smoked onions and season with the salt and pepper. Turn down the heat to low and sweat (see page 377) the onions for 4 to 5 minutes. Add the cream and water and simmer until the onions are completely soft and the cream has reduced and thickened slightly, 20 to 25 minutes.

Transfer the onion-cream mixture to a blender and purée until very smooth, 1 to 2 minutes. Set up a chinois (see page 373) or fine-mesh strainer over a clean bowl and pass the onion purée through it to remove any particles, pushing down with a small ladle or rubber spatula.

MAKE THE FILLING Place the russet potatoes and water to cover by 1 inch in a large saucepan over high heat. When the water starts to simmer, add 3 tablespoons of the salt, cover, adjust the heat to maintain a simmer, and cook until the potatoes are tender with a tiny bit of resistance at the center when pierced with a fork, 40 to 45 minutes. Turn off the heat but keep the potatoes in the hot water until they can be easily pierced

Continued

POTATO SHELLS

4 large, waxy potatoes, such as Yukon Gold

3 tablespoons extra-virgin olive oil

¾ teaspoon plus ½ teaspoon salt

SMOKED ONION SOUBISE

2 tablespoons butter

2 cups smoked onions, roughly chopped (see page 377)

1 teaspoon salt

½ teaspoon freshly ground black pepper

1¼ cups heavy cream

½ cup water

FILLING

1½ pounds russet potatoes

3 tablespoons plus ¾ teaspoon salt

1 egg yolk (see page 377), beaten

½ teaspoon freshly ground black pepper

1 teaspoon flaky finishing salt (optional)

Duchess Potatoes with Smoked Onion Soubise

with a fork, 5 to 10 minutes longer. Remove the potatoes from the water and let cool just until they can be handled, then use a kitchen towel to peel the skin from the still-warm flesh. Pass the potatoes through a potato ricer into a small bowl.

Add 1 cup of the onion soubise to the riced potatoes and mix together with a fork. Add the egg yolk and mix well. Season with the remaining ¾ teaspoon salt and the pepper and set aside. Do not refrigerate.

Once the waxy potatoes are chilled, slice them in half crosswise. Use a melon baller or small spoon to very gently hollow out as much of the potato as possible, discarding the scooped potato and leaving a layer of flesh about ⅛ inch thick attached to the skin for stability. Set the potato halves, hollow sides up on a baking sheet and set aside. The shells can be stored, lightly covered with plastic wrap, at room temperature for up to 4 hours.

To test how the filling will bake up, preheat the oven to 400°F. Line a small baking sheet or baking dish with parchment paper and spoon a tablespoon or so of the filling onto the parchment. Bake until the edges of the filling begin to brown, 7 to 10 minutes. This will tell you if the filling will lose its shape and get runny when you pipe it into the potatoes. If it seems quite firm, add a few additional tablespoons onion soubise for flavor. If it is wet or runny, whip in another beaten egg yolk. Leave the oven on.

To fill the potato shells, brush the inside of each shell evenly with the remaining 1 tablespoon oil, then dust the insides with the remaining ½ teaspoon salt. Place the filling in a pastry bag fitted with a large star tip (or fill a large resealable plastic bag with the filling and cut off one of the corners). Pipe the filling into the potato shells, filling them to about 1 inch above the rim.

Place the filled potatoes on a baking sheet. Place the baking sheet on the center rack of the oven and bake until the edges of the filling are deep golden brown and the potatoes are piping hot, 15 to 20 minutes. If you have an extra potato, taste one to see if it needs a little finishing salt. Serve immediately.

Eggs

Eggs might be my favorite food. They're incredibly versatile, and chances are you have some in your kitchen right now. Eggs have a neutral flavor that complements almost anything, and a single egg can help turn a side dish into a meal. I love all of the ways you can cook an egg, and I even have nine chickens in my backyard to ensure I always have a fresh supply on hand.

Fortunately, it's becoming increasingly easy to find high-quality eggs— ones with thick shells, deep-orange yolks, and viscous whites—and I advise you to seek them out. The difference in quality between fresh, local eggs from pastured hens and eggs laid by factory-farm chickens is dramatic, and even the highest-quality eggs are still relatively inexpensive.

The egg is a terrific ingredient with which to learn new techniques. After all, if you don't poach one properly, it's not a great loss. The egg is also fragile (the yolk is easily broken, the white can be overwhipped) and deeply nourishing (a dish of soft scrambled eggs was the first meal my mother cooked for me after the birth of my daughter, August). It's important to honor the egg, to be attentive while it cooks, and to master the techniques used in the following recipes. And once you do all that, you are sure to surprise people by showing them just how impressive the humble egg can be.

Soufflés: Spinach-Gruyère Soufflé, Smoked
Salmon Soufflé, Ham Soufflé, Corn Soufflé ‖ 195

**Spring Vegetable Hash with Poached Duck Egg
and Whole-Grain Mustard Hollandaise** ‖ 203

Quiche with Wild Mushrooms, Gruyère, and Chives ‖ 204

**Soft Scrambled Eggs with Caviar and
Herbed Crème Fraîche** ‖ 207

Crispy Fried Egg with Fresh Corn Polenta ‖ 208

Soufflés

SERVES 4 TO 6

I learned to make a soufflé when I was seven years old. Since then, I've picked up a few tricks, but one lesson that hasn't changed over the years is what my mother taught me: even an imperfect soufflé is still delicious. Of course, you shouldn't set out to fail, but if your soufflé doesn't rise proudly (or suffers some other minor imperfection), all hope is not lost. You'll still have a great dinner.

That said, there are a few things that will increase your chances of making a perfect soufflé. First and foremost is properly whisking the egg whites. I am a huge advocate of whisking by hand, at least until you have the technique committed to memory. When you're in touch with the process, you're a better cook because you learn to look for changes that you might completely miss if using a machine.

To create the fluffy, voluminous egg whites that lead to a tall soufflé, it's imperative that no egg yolk or other fat, such as oil, finds its way into the whites. So be very careful when separating eggs and keep all of your equipment clean and dry.

To further help a soufflé stand tall, butter the inside of the soufflé dish and line it with fine bread crumbs, creating a wall for the soufflé to crawl up so it can puff higher. Once the soufflé is in the oven, you must not open the oven door to check on things. To avoid the temptation, invest in an oven thermometer to figure out whether your oven runs hot or cold, and then adjust the temperature according to what you learn.

Soufflés start to deflate as soon as they come out of the oven, but they'll stay hot for about twenty minutes and taste just as good even after they deflate, so don't stress too much about timing everything perfectly. I think of soufflés as rustic, everyday fare, but if you want your presentation to make a big splash, have the table fully set before the soufflé is ready, so you can present it in its full glory the moment it is ready to emerge from the oven.

Use this base recipe as the foundation for any kind of soufflé. You can try one of the variations that follow, or you can get creative with the produce and cheese you have in your refrigerator. All of my soufflés here, with the exception of the corn variation, use the same base; the variations have ingredients added to the base just before the egg yolks are whisked in.

Continued

Soufflés

CONTINUED

Preheat the oven to 375°F and place the rack in the middle position. Brush a 2-quart soufflé mold with the 2 tablespoons room-temperature butter. Add the bread crumbs, shaking and turning the mold so the sides and bottom are evenly coated. Pour out any excess crumbs and set the mold aside.

In a small saucepan, melt the 5 tablespoons butter over medium heat. Add the shallot and cook until translucent, 1 to 2 minutes. Add the flour and whisk vigorously to combine, allowing the mixture (the roux) to take on just the slightest bit of blond color, 2 to 3 minutes. Gradually whisk in the milk and cream to make a béchamel, working slowly to avoid lumps. When they have both been added, whisk vigorously until smooth, then immediately turn down the heat to medium-low and simmer, whisking frequently to prevent scorching. When the mixture is slightly thickened, after 5 to 6 minutes, remove the pan from the heat and scrape the mixture into a shallow metal mixing bowl. Add the salt, pepper, cayenne, and nutmeg and whisk briefly; let the mixture cool for 15 minutes.

When the mixture is just slightly warm to the touch, whisk in the spinach, salmon–cream cheese mixture, ham, or sautéed corn (depending on the variation you are making), then whisk in the egg yolks one at a time, whisking rapidly after each addition. If your variation calls for the addition of cheeses and/or herbs, fold them in now.

See page 378 for instructions on how to whip the egg whites and when to add the cream of tartar.

Scoop approximately one-third of the whipped egg whites into the egg yolk mixture. Using a rubber spatula and a light hand to retain as much air as possible, mix everything together until fully incorporated. This lightens the thick base significantly so that the two mixtures are more evenly matched when you add the remaining whites. Carefully fold in the remaining egg whites (see page 375).

Pour the batter into the prepared soufflé mold. Bake undisturbed (do not open the oven door!) in the middle of the oven until a thermometer inserted into the center of the soufflé reads 180°F (as you gain experience with this recipe, you'll be able to tell when your soufflé is done by how high it rises, and then you can retire the thermometer), about 50 minutes. Serve immediately.

Continued

2 tablespoons butter, at room temperature, plus 5 tablespoons butter

¼ cup fine bread crumbs (page 363)

3 tablespoons very finely minced shallot

5 tablespoons all-purpose flour

1½ cups whole milk (see exception for Corn Soufflé, page 200)

½ cup heavy cream

1 teaspoon salt

½ teaspoon freshly ground black pepper

1/16 teaspoon cayenne pepper

⅛ teaspoon freshly grated nutmeg (omit for Corn Soufflé)

6 egg yolks (see page 377)

7 egg whites

⅛ teaspoon cream of tartar, if not using a copper bowl

Soufflés

Spinach-Gruyère Soufflé

This is the soufflé we ate the most often when I was growing up. It has a golden brown exterior, which opens up to reveal a beautiful bright green interior, like a surprise gift (see the photo, page vi).

Wash the spinach well (see page 378), then blanch and shock as directed on page 375, leaving it in the boiling water for 30 to 60 seconds, until the stems are tender. Let the spinach cool completely in the ice bath before removing it and fully squeezing out the water with your hands. The spinach should weigh about 6 ounces and be roughly the size of a baseball when all of the water is squeezed out. Reserve the shocking water.

In a blender, purée three-fourths of the spinach and 4 to 6 tablespoons of the reserved shocking water (just enough to get the spinach to move freely and fully purée) on high speed until uniformly very smooth, about 1 minute. Roughly chop the remaining spinach and add it and the purée to the soufflé base as instructed, then whisk in the yolks one by one, and fold in the Gruyère and Parmigiano-Reggiano. Bake as directed.

1 bunch spinach

3 ounces Gruyère cheese, finely grated on a Microplane grater (see page 374)

1 ounce Parmigiano-Reggiano cheese, finely grated on a Microplane grater (see page 374)

Smoked Salmon Soufflé

An echo of the classic pairing of bagels and lox, this light, airy soufflé is a good option for brunch. It's one of the more savory soufflés and is delicious served alongside a lightly dressed salad of tomatoes in the summer.

In a food processor, combine the salmon and cream cheese and blend for 30 seconds, until smooth. Add the salmon–cream cheese mixture to the soufflé base as instructed, then whisk in the yolks one by one, and fold in the chives, green onions, and dill. Bake as directed.

4 ounces smoked salmon

1 (8-ounce) package cream cheese, at room temperature

3 tablespoons finely minced chives

2 green onions, thinly sliced on the bias

1 tablespoon roughly chopped dill

Ham Soufflé

When making meat-based soufflés, serve a slightly smaller portion to each person and plan to accompany the soufflé with a large side of seasonal vegetables. Even though this version is heavier and slightly richer than the spinach soufflé, it is still light and pillowy and makes a lovely counterpoint to a large crisp salad or quickly sautéed kale. Leftovers make a delightful breakfast.

Melt the butter in a black steel pan over medium heat. Add the ham and cook (you may want to use a splatter guard as it tends to sizzle) until slightly crisp, 4 to 5 minutes. Add the thyme in the final minute of cooking, then turn off the heat and set aside until cool. Add the ham to the soufflé base as instructed, then whisk in the yolks one by one, and fold in the Cheddar, Parmigiano-Reggiano, and green onions. Bake as directed.

Continued

1 tablespoon butter

4 ounces good-quality ham (such as Niman Ranch brand), very finely minced

½ teaspoon chopped thyme

3 ounces smoked Cheddar cheese, finely grated on a Microplane grater (see page 374)

1 ounce Parmigiano-Reggiano cheese, finely grated on a Microplane grater (see page 374)

3 green onions, thinly sliced on the bias

Soufflés

Corn Soufflé

The natural sweetness of corn makes this soufflé ideal for a light brunch or lunch or an unexpected side to a meaty main course like Lamb Loin Chops (page 286). Make this in the summer when fresh corn is available, since you need the cobs as well as the kernels.

   This variation is slightly different from the others. It calls for a corn purée made from a blend of corn kernels and corn cob–infused milk in place of the plain milk called for in the soufflé base.

Cut the corn kernels off the cobs and set the kernels aside. Break the cobs in half and place in a small saucepan. Add the milk and cream, bring to a simmer over medium-high heat, turn down the heat to a bare simmer, and then cook the cobs for 10 minutes. Remove from the heat and set aside.

In a sauté pan, melt the butter over medium heat. Add the shallot and cook for 1 minute. Add the garlic and cook for 30 seconds or so. Add the reserved corn kernels, salt, and pepper and sauté for 7 to 10 minutes, until corn kernels no longer taste raw. Remove from the heat and set aside ¾ cup of the sautéed corn.

Place the remaining sautéed corn in a blender. Discard the cobs from the milk, add the milk to the blender, and blend until completely smooth, about 1 minute.

Follow the instructions for Soufflés on page 196, substituting the corn purée for the milk, adding it to the butter-flour mixture (the roux) along with the cream. Simmer for an additional 2 minutes, until the mixture is thick and well combined and is the consistency of thick cake batter. Remove from the heat and carefully scoop the base into a metal mixing bowl. Add the salt, pepper, and cayenne (omit the nutmeg for this recipe) and whisk briefly; let the mixture cool for 15 minutes. Add the reserved sautéed corn to the soufflé base as instructed, then whisk in the yolks one by one, and fold in the pecorino romano and chives. Bake as instructed.

2 large ears yellow corn, shucked

1½ cups whole milk

½ cup heavy cream

3 tablespoons butter

3 tablespoons very finely minced shallot

4 cloves garlic, thinly sliced

¾ teaspoon salt

½ teaspoon freshly ground black pepper

1½ ounces pecorino romano cheese, finely grated on a Microplane grater (see page 374)

3 tablespoons finely minced chives

Spring Vegetable Hash with Poached Duck Egg and Whole-Grain Mustard Hollandaise

SERVES 4 TO 6

We make some variation of hash with meat and vegetables every Sunday for brunch at Beast. If you have leftover duck confit (see page 235), this is your recipe, although you could easily substitute slab bacon or cubed ham in its place.

It's easier than you think to poach multiple eggs at once. I always poach one or two eggs more than my number of guests in case one breaks, just to be safe.

In a 4- to 6-quart Dutch oven, warm the duck fat over medium-low heat with the garlic, 1½ teaspoons of the salt, ½ teaspoon of the pepper, and the thyme. As soon as tiny bubbles begin to rise, add the potatoes and stir well. They should be just submerged, so add more fat if necessary. Turn the heat to medium, and as soon as tiny bubbles begin to rise again, cook for 9 to 12 minutes, testing for doneness frequently after 9 minutes. To test, remove a potato and poke it with a fork; it should break apart but still be slightly waxy. Using a spider (see page 374), transfer the potatoes to a baking sheet to cool. Reserve the fat.

Heat a black steel pan over medium-high heat until hot. Add the duck confit, bacon, or ham; turn down the heat to medium, and sauté until beginning to crisp, 2 to 3 minutes (if using bacon, sauté for 7 to 10 minutes). Remove from the heat and set aside.

In a large black steel pan, heat 2 tablespoons of the reserved fat over medium heat. Add the onion and sauté until just starting to become translucent, 6 to 7 minutes. Add the potatoes and let them sit, without stirring, for about 1 minute, until a brown crust begins to form. Gently stir to brown all sides. One at a time, stirring after adding each ingredient, add the carrots, then zucchini, then snap peas and asparagus together, then the reserved duck confit. Sauté until the vegetables are tender, 1 to 3 minutes. Taste for seasoning and adjust if necessary. Set the pan aside off the heat.

Crack 3 or 4 of the eggs into individual ramekins or teacups. In a 2-quart saucepan, combine the water and vinegar and bring to a boil. Turn down the heat to low to slow the boil to a few small bubbles. Gently dip the edge of a ramekin into the water and slip out the egg. Immediately follow with the other 3 eggs. Turn up the heat slightly to create a very gentle simmer. Keep an eye on the water; you don't want a rolling boil. After 2 minutes (or 1½ minutes if using chicken eggs), pull out 1 egg with a slotted spoon to check for doneness. The yolk should feel runny, but the white part immediately next to the yolk should feel set. The eggs can take up to 3 minutes to cook (chicken eggs up to 2 minutes); transfer the finished eggs to a shallow bowl. Dot the eggs with 1 teaspoon of the butter, ⅛ teaspoon of the remaining salt, and half of the remaining pepper. Repeat with remaining eggs and dot them with the remaining butter, salt, and pepper.

To serve, arrange the hash on individual plates, dividing it evenly. Carefully place 1 egg on top of each serving of hash and spoon about 3 tablespoons of the hollandaise over the top. Garnish and serve immediately.

4 cups duck fat (from making Lacquered Duck Confit, page 235) or extra-virgin olive oil

3 cloves garlic

1¾ teaspoons salt

½ teaspoon plus ⅛ teaspoon freshly ground black pepper

2 thyme sprigs

4 cups skin-on cubed Yukon Gold, Yellow Finn, or other waxy potatoes, in ¾-inch cubes

1½ cups roughly shredded duck confit or cubed slab bacon or ham

1 cup diced yellow onion

1 cup peeled sliced small spring carrots, in ¼-inch-thick rounds

1 cup diced zucchini, in ½-inch dice

1 cup sliced sugar snap peas, on bias in ½-inch-wide strips

1 cup sliced asparagus, in ½-inch-thick rounds

6 to 8 duck or chicken eggs

3 cups water

1 tablespoon distilled white vinegar

2 teaspoons butter, at room temperature

¾ cup Pickled Mustard Seed Hollandaise (page 32)

Roughly chopped flat-leaf parsley, finely minced chives, microgreens, or edible flowers, for garnish (optional)

Quiche with Wild Mushrooms, Gruyère, and Chives

SERVES 8

I like quiche because you can serve it any time of day. It's very likely that you have everything on hand to make it, and you can add almost anything you want to it. Just be sure that whatever vegetables you use are squeezed and drained of their liquid before adding them to the filling or the quiche will be soggy.

The buttery *pâte brisée* pastry shell that is used here can be prebaked up to a day ahead. Don't be afraid of baking an already golden brown pie crust for a second time. The difference in flavor from a too-light crust will change your mind on the subject! Once the quiche filling is added, the crust won't burn; it will simply become a deep, beautifully burnished brown with a delicious toasted flavor.

Preheat the oven to 350°F. Clean the mushrooms (see Notes, pages 150 and 160) and slice into ⅛-inch pieces. Cook the mushrooms in two batches to avoid crowding in the pan. Heat a black steel pan over medium heat and add 1 tablespoon of the butter. When the butter melts, add ¼ cup of the shallot and sweat (see page 377) for 1 to 2 minutes, until just translucent. Add half of the mushrooms and season with ¼ teaspoon of the salt and ⅛ teaspoon of the pepper. Increase the heat to medium-high and stir until the mushrooms start to color on their edges and the moisture they release evaporates. Lower the heat to medium and continue to cook and stir until completely soft and beginning to get some golden color, 6 to 7 minutes. In the final 30 to 60 seconds, add the sherry and let it cook out. Set the mushrooms aside on a plate to cool, and repeat with the remaining mushrooms, butter, shallot, ¼ teaspoon salt, and ⅛ teaspoon pepper. When the mushrooms are cool enough to handle, gather them into a kitchen towel or place them in a fine-mesh strainer and squeeze out the liquid. Finely chop the mushrooms and set aside.

Crack the eggs into a mixing bowl and whisk vigorously until slightly foamy, about 30 seconds. Add the remaining 1¼ teaspoons salt and ½ teaspoon pepper, the nutmeg, milk, cream, and chives and whisk for 15 seconds to combine.

Place the prebaked quiche shell, in its pan, on a baking sheet. Sprinkle the cheese in an even layer on the bottom of the shell. Add the mushrooms in an even layer and press them gently into the crust. Carefully pour in the egg mixture to just below the top of the quiche shell. Put the baking sheet on the center rack of the oven and pour the last bit of egg mixture into the shell (so you don't spill while moving the quiche to the oven).

Bake until the quiche has puffed slightly and the top is golden brown and set in the middle, 50 to 60 minutes. Remove the quiche from the oven and let cool for 10 minutes. Use a small, sharp knife to cut any excess crust level with the top of the quiche pan; cut by pushing from the inside out (with the handle of the knife hovering over the filling), so the crumbs fall on the countertop instead of into the quiche.

Let the quiche rest at room temperature for 2 hours before serving. Carefully remove the outer ring of the quiche pan. Slice the quiche into 8 pieces and serve.

8 ounces wild mushrooms (such as morel, porcini, or chanterelle) or button or cremini mushrooms

2 tablespoons butter

½ cup finely minced shallot

1¾ teaspoons salt

¾ teaspoon freshly ground black pepper

1 tablespoon dry sherry

5 eggs

¼ teaspoon freshly grated nutmeg

1¼ cups whole milk

1¼ cups heavy cream

¼ cup finely minced chives

1 pâte brisée shell (page 356), prebaked

2½ ounces cave-aged Gruyère or extra-sharp Cheddar cheese, finely grated on a Microplane grater (see page 374)

Soft Scrambled Eggs with Caviar and Herbed Crème Fraîche

SERVES 2

Unfortunately, most of us have had overcooked scrambled eggs, which are rubbery and unpleasant. But when eggs see gentle heat and are scrambled slowly and patiently, they become rich and soft. Remove them from the heat when they're just a touch undercooked and they'll finish cooking on the plate. Paired with caviar and herbed crème fraîche, this dish is nothing short of luxurious. Serve it with Beet-Cured Salmon with Creamy Herbed Cucumbers (page 56) for a sophisticated brunch, or toast a slice of the quick brioche (page 362) and keep it simple.

Years ago, my sous chef Mika and I were cooking at a big food festival and Daniel Boulud prepared soft scrambled eggs with crème fraîche and caviar for all of the chefs at a late-night party. The dish was the ultimate expression of generosity and fun: he had a great time making it, and we had a great time eating it. This dish is my homage to Daniel Boulud and that memorable night.

A final note: The eggs must come to room temperature before cooking so they cook evenly, and because this dish has so few ingredients, it's imperative to use the best-quality eggs you can find.

In a small bowl, stir the heavy cream into the crème fraîche to thin it. Set aside.

Crack the eggs into a bowl and beat vigorously but carefully with a fork. Try not to make any foam, which creates edges that stick up around the sides of the pan and overcook. Stir in the salt, pepper, and half-and-half.

The key to soft scrambled eggs is low heat, allowing the eggs to settle into themselves, and gentle and patient stirring. In a 10-inch black steel or nonstick sauté pan, warm the butter over low heat until completely melted and just beginning to make a tiny bubbling sound in the center of the pan, about 1 minute. Add the eggs and let them rest undisturbed for about 30 seconds, then give them a brief stir with a flat-edged wooden spatula. Let the eggs settle for about 30 seconds more, then stir again. Continue to stir gently; for smaller curds, stir a little more frequently, for larger curds, stir less often.

They are ready after an additional 3 to 4 minutes, when they're mostly set but still have a very slight moist sheen; the timing depends on how low you've set the heat (this varies greatly from stove to stove). Remove the eggs from the heat when they are just a shade undercooked; they will finish cooking on the plate from the residual heat.

Divide the eggs between two plates and top each portion with one-half of the crème fraîche and one-half of the caviar. Garnish the plates with the chives and serve immediately.

1½ teaspoons heavy cream

2 tablespoons Herbed Crème Fraîche (page 22; substitute dill for the tarragon)

6 eggs, at room temperature

½ teaspoon salt

⅛ teaspoon freshly ground black pepper

1 tablespoon plus 1 teaspoon half-and-half

2 teaspoons butter

½ ounce caviar or trout roe

½ teaspoon very finely minced chives

Crispy Fried Egg with Fresh Corn Polenta

SERVES 4

When I first envisioned this dish, it was a smooth corn purée with a crispy fried egg. But as I started testing, my chef de cuisine Jake Stevens taught me a trick he learned while working at the Tasting Kitchen in Venice, California: grating fresh ears of corn on a box grater. This captures all of the juices and starches, which helps to emulsify the kernels into something that resembles polenta texturally but tastes like fresh corn.

Frying the egg this way—until the egg whites begin to bubble and the bottom gets all golden brown and crispy but the yolk stays perfectly runny—makes for a dramatic presentation.

This is designed to be a small, rich plate that you can serve with toast for breakfast or with a salad for lunch or dinner.

MAKE THE FRESH CORN POLENTA Lay two pieces of parchment paper on a baking sheet. Shuck the corn and remove any silk. Snap each ear in half. On the largest holes of a box grater, grate the corn to the cob over the parchment to capture all of the kernels and corn juices. Carefully lift the paper and pour everything into a bowl.

In a saucepan, heat 2 tablespoons of the butter over medium-low heat. Add the corn and its juices, the salt, and the pepper and cook, stirring constantly. Don't add any liquid unless you really have to, but if the corn sticks and looks very dry, add 1 or 2 tablespoons water. Stir and taste often for about 5 minutes, until no liquid is left and none of the corn tastes raw. Turn off the heat and stir in the remaining 2 tablespoons butter. Divide the corn among four plates.

MAKE THE EGGS Cook the eggs one at a time. Crack the first egg into a ramekin or teacup. Heat a 9-inch (or smaller) black steel or nonstick sauté pan over medium-high heat. Add 3 tablespoons of the oil and heat until the surface is rippling slightly but not smoking. With the pan on the burner, tilt the pan at a 45-degree angle toward you and pour the egg into the hot pool of oil. If the oil is hot enough, the white should spread only a little—as soon as this happens, use a shallow soupspoon to spoon the edges of the egg white back onto the egg so the shape stays compact. Lift the edges of the egg ever so slightly with the spoon to ensure they aren't sticking to the pan. Using the spoon, gently but quickly baste the hot oil onto the egg white, being careful to avoid the yolk. Continue spooning the hot oil onto the white until the white is almost set, about 45 seconds.

Just before the white is fully set, sprinkle the entire egg with one-quarter of the finishing salt and pepper. When the white is opaque, using a fish spatula (see page 373), transfer the egg directly on top of a serving of corn. Repeat with the remaining eggs, adding the remaining 1 tablespoon oil as necessary, then garnish each plate with a celery leaf and serve immediately with hot sauce alongside.

FRESH CORN POLENTA

4 ears yellow corn

4 tablespoons butter, at room temperature

¾ teaspoon salt

¼ teaspoon freshly ground black pepper

EGGS

4 eggs

4 tablespoons extra-virgin olive oil

½ teaspoon flaky finishing salt

¼ teaspoon freshly ground black pepper

Celery leaf, for garnish (optional)

Hot sauce, for serving (optional)

Seafood

Cooking seafood often intimidates home cooks, but it's actually one of the fastest, simplest proteins to prepare at home, and it's perfect if you're cooking only for one or two people. Because seafood cooks so quickly, preparing it offers a good opportunity to master your timing skills.

Although some techniques for cooking fish are similar to those for other meats, fish generally requires a more delicate touch when searing or poaching because it's fragile. The curvature of a metal fish spatula (see page 373) helps maneuver fish in a way that keeps it intact.

Preparing seafood begins with shopping, and there is an element of social responsibility when it comes to this task. Check out the Monterey Bay Seafood Watch list and inform yourself about the most sustainable options available. Fish farming is changing, too. Some progressive initiatives are being implemented across the globe to develop new ways to responsibly increase the supply of this limited resource.

Beyond that, always ask your fishmonger what day the seafood came in and where it came from. Look at it, smell it, ask if it's ever been frozen. These are all fair questions, and your fishmonger would do the same if he or she were shopping for fish. Don't hesitate to get specific about the cut or size you want. Good seafood is expensive, and you should get your money's worth. Fresh seafood has a brief shelf life, so buy it the day you plan to use it.

These recipes are designed to highlight a variety of techniques. Preparing seafood properly is all about focus and timing. Because seafood cooks quickly, it's important to have your *mise en place* ready before you start—compared to other proteins, seafood is less forgiving, and can go from perfect to overdone in a matter of seconds. This shouldn't intimidate you, but rather, encourage you to become more attentive in your kitchen habits.

Butter-Poached Halibut

SERVES 4

I love butter-poaching fish. It's the gentle, luxurious cousin to steaming. Butter enhances the rich flavor that already exists in a meaty white fish like halibut, and because the fish is removed from the clarified butter before serving, it never feels greasy or excessive.

For this recipe, ask for the center cut of the halibut, from the fattest piece in the case (if you don't see one, ask the fishmonger if he or she has more in the back). Your fish must be evenly thick so all of the pieces cook at the same rate. Use the smallest pot that accommodates all four halibut pieces without crowding but that will allow the fish to be fully submerged in the butter.

Preheat the oven to 350°F. In a 4-quart ovenproof saucepan, heat the butter over medium heat until melted and starting to simmer, 5 to 7 minutes. Once white foam begins to form on the surface of the butter, use a small ladle or shallow spoon to gently skim the foam and discard it. Turn down the heat to medium-low and continue the gentle bubbling, removing any foam every 2 to 3 minutes, until no more foam appears. This may take up to 20 minutes.

Once the surface of the butter looks clear and glassy (you may have a few small pieces of milk solids on the bottom; this is okay as they'll be strained out), set a fine-mesh strainer over a bowl and line the strainer with a double layer of cheesecloth. Pour the butter through the strainer and discard the cheesecloth. Wash and dry the saucepan.

Return the clarified butter to the saucepan while the butter is still warm. Add the salt and stir well. Taste the butter; it should be nicely seasoned. Gently add all of the halibut to the saucepan; the fish must be completely covered with butter. If it is not completely submerged, try using a slightly smaller pan, or top off with a tiny bit of extra-virgin olive oil. Place the pan, uncovered, in the oven and set a timer for 8 minutes.

Remove the saucepan from the oven. Using a slotted spoon or fish spatula (see page 373), take the smallest fillet out of the butter. Press on it gently, and at one of the natural breaks of the flesh, pull the flesh back slightly and peek inside to make sure the meat is opaque almost entirely through. There should still be a very slight translucence just at the center. Thicker pieces of halibut may take up to 10 minutes to cook.

To serve with Spring Pea–Mint Relish and Beurre Blanc as shown (see the photo, right), make the relish up to 6 hours and the Beurre Blanc up to 1 hour before serving. Do not attempt to poach the halibut and make the Beurre Blanc at the same time, as they both require your full attention. Keep the Beurre Blanc warm in a thermos until you're ready to serve. Poach the halibut immediately before serving.

Remove the halibut from the butter and plate each piece individually. Spoon about 2 tablespoons of Beurre Blanc on top of each portion of halibut and top with an equal amount of room-temperature relish. Garnish with pea tendrils, torn pieces of mint, or edible flowers.

---

2 pounds butter

2 teaspoons salt

1½ pounds center-cut halibut fillet, skin off, split into 4 uniform pieces (about 5 ounces each)

Seasonal Variations

Spring (pictured): Spring Pea–Mint Relish (page 8) and Beurre Blanc (page 43), with pea tendrils, fresh mint, or edible flowers, for garnish (optional)

Summer: Fresh Corn Polenta (from Crispy Fried Eggs with Fresh Corn Polenta, page 208) and Savory Tomato Confiture (page 11)

Fall: Caramelized Lentils du Puy (page 185)

Winter: Caramelized Delicata Squash (page 181) and Beurre Rouge (page 43)

NOTE The poaching butter can be reused two more times. Strain the butter into an airtight container and freeze it. Place the container in a bowl of hot water to melt the edges of the frozen butter enough to remove it from the container. In a saucepan over low heat, melt the butter, then follow the recipe to poach the fish.

Seared Sea Scallops

SERVES 4

I love preparing scallops in the summer when I don't want to spend a lot of time cooking a large protein. The trick to this dish is searing the scallops properly to develop a sweet, umami-rich crust. If they don't sizzle the second they hit the pan, you're probably crowding them or your pan isn't hot enough. Stop and wait for the pan to reach the ideal temperature before continuing, rather than ruin your chances at achieving golden perfection.

When shopping for scallops, look for large, fresh sea scallops (the bigger, the better) that haven't been soaked in the phosphate solution that's often used to preserve and plump them. If you're not sure, ask your fishmonger if the scallops have been treated. I like to cook scallops about halfway through, so there's a hint of translucence when you cut into the center. The texture can turn rubbery when overcooked, and a medium-rare finish allows the delicate flavor of the scallop to shine through.

Remove the side muscle, or foot, of each scallop (it looks like a baby scallop and easily pulls away) if necessary and carefully examine all of the scallops to ensure no grains of sand are present. Gently rinse the scallops in cold water and pat very dry with a paper towel. Season the scallops evenly on both sides with the salt and pepper.

Heat a black steel pan over high heat until very hot. Add the oil and heat until the surface is rippling but not smoking. Pour off any excess oil; there should be only a thin, even film of oil on the pan. Add half of the scallops at once. The scallops should audibly sizzle as soon as you place them in the pan. If they don't, quickly pull the scallops out and wait for the pan to get hotter. Press down firmly with a fish spatula (see page 373) to ensure even browning. Cook for 1 to 2 minutes, until the scallops have a nice, golden brown surface on the underside. If your scallops are crowded or the pan isn't hot enough, they will not develop this surface.

Flip the scallops and press down again with the spatula to ensure as much surface contact as possible. Cook for 45 seconds to 1½ minutes, depending on the thickness of the scallops. When the second sides are golden brown, remove the pan from the heat. The whole process should take 2 to 3 minutes. When you cut into a scallop, it should not be cooked all the way through; the middle third should still be translucent.

To serve with Basil Pistou and Half-Dried Tomatoes as shown (see the photo, left), dollop 5 or 6 generous tablespoons of the pistou on a platter and arrange 4 to 6 scallops on top. Scatter 15 to 20 tomatoes around the scallops and squeeze the lemon wedges over the top. Garnish with the edible flowers. (I like to serve this dish family-style, assembling at least a couple of platters, but if you're plating individual portions, use about 2 tablespoons pistou, 3 scallops, and a small handful of cherry tomatoes per plate.)

12 large sea scallops

¾ teaspoon salt

¼ teaspoon freshly ground black pepper

2 teaspoons extra-virgin olive oil

4 lemon wedges, seeded (see page 375)

Edible flowers, for garnish (optional)

Seasonal Variations

Summer (pictured): Basil Pistou (page 6) and Half-Dried Tomatoes (page 350)

Fall: Fennel Gratin (page 164)

Winter: Roasted Beets and Pink Grapefruit with Frisée and Mint Crème Fraîche (page 137)

Spring: Spring Pea Risotto (page 147)

Pan-Seared Salmon

SERVES 4

Salmon is the iconic food of the Pacific Northwest, where I've lived my entire life. But even if you don't live around here, you can likely get excellent wild-caught salmon. This is a great opportunity to learn about carry-over cooking, which is when foods continue to cook internally even after being removed from the heat. You want to remove the salmon from the pan when it is one shade lighter than how you'd like to eat it. Because of its vibrant color, it's very easy to see to what extent salmon is cooked through. I like salmon best when it's cooked medium, with a thin swath that's still translucent in the thickest part of the fillet.

Preheat the oven to 350°F. Season both sides of each piece of salmon with ¼ teaspoon of the salt and ⅛ teaspoon of the pepper.

Heat a black steel pan over high heat until very hot. Add the oil and heat until the surface is rippling but not smoking. Add all of the salmon, skin side down, and press lightly with the back of a fish spatula (see page 373) to ensure a good sear on the skin. Cook until the fish looks opaque approximately halfway up the sides, about 3 minutes.

Add the butter to the pan. Allow it to melt, and then baste it over the fish with a spoon for about 30 seconds, until the butter has lightly cooked the surface of the fish.

Place the pan in the oven and cook for 3 minutes. Remove from the oven and again baste the fish with the butter. Return the pan to the oven and cook for another 3 to 5 minutes, depending on the thickness of the pieces. The thicker the pieces, the longer they will take to cook. Very thick pieces, near 2 inches, may take up to 9 minutes total. To check for doneness, remove the pan from the oven, and using a fish spatula or the sharp pointed end of a paring knife, pull back slightly at one of the natural breaks of the flesh of a smaller piece. Peek inside and make sure the meat is almost entirely opaque. A little translucence should remain at the center. Like a steak, the salmon should spring back when gently pressed but not feel overly firm.

To serve with Oven-Glazed Shallots and Horseradish Crème Fraîche as shown (see the photo, right), make the crème fraîche up to 1 day ahead of time. The glazed shallots can be made up to 1 hour in advance, then reheated in the pot in which they were cooked just before serving.

Place each piece of salmon on a plate. Arrange 3 or 4 glazed shallots alongside the salmon and top with a tablespoon of the crème fraîche and a sprig of dill.

1½ pounds center-cut salmon, skin on, cut into 4 uniform pieces

1 teaspoon salt

½ teaspoon freshly ground black pepper

1 tablespoon extra-virgin olive oil

3 tablespoons butter, at room temperature

Seasonal Variations

Fall (pictured): Oven-Glazed Shallots (page 182) and Horseradish Crème Fraîche (page 25)

Winter: Quick-Sautéed Greens with Garlic, Lemon Confit, and Chile Flakes (page 163) and Beurre Rouge (page 43)

Spring: Beurre Blanc (page 43) and Spring Pea–Mint Relish (page 8)

Summer: Tomatoes with fried caper rémoulade (see page 125; omit crab and French dressing)

Sole Piccata

SERVES 4

This dish is a cleaner, brighter version of a traditional chicken or veal piccata. In fact, it bears only a passing resemblance to the piccata preparations of old-school red sauce joints, though the core flavors remain the same. Lemon and capers are essential elements of piccata, and pairing fish with Lemon Confit and Fried Caper Relish (page 20) is my way of paying homage to the classic dish. Think of it as a deconstructed take that allows each individual component on the plate to shine. I like it when there's a little variety in every bite, so instead of covering the whole fillet in a buttery wine sauce, you can mix and match little bites of fish, confit, and fried caper.

Fish fried in a shallow pan is one of the quickest meals a home cook can make. Because cooking sole takes less than two minutes, timing is important. The sauce should be totally finished and the table set before you even think about starting the fish.

It's okay to use any flat white fish like turbot or flounder in lieu of sole, keeping in mind that the cooking time will change according to the thickness of the fillet.

Season the fish on both sides with the salt and pepper. Spread the flour on a plate. One at a time, lay each piece of fish on the flour and press gently, then flip to lightly flour the other side. Place the dredged fish on a plate.

Heat your two largest sauté pans over medium-high heat, add 2 tablespoons of the butter and 1 tablespoon of the oil to each pan, and heat until the butter begins to foam slightly and starts to turn a very light golden color. Add half of the fish fillets in a single layer to each pan and tap each piece lightly with a fish spatula (see page 373) to ensure the fillets make good contact with the pan. Don't worry if your butter is browning; as long as it doesn't turn black, it will add nice depth of flavor. When the first fillets to go into the pan have cooked for 1 minute, begin flipping all of the fillets in the order in which you put them in. When they have cooked for 30 seconds on the other side, check 1 fillet by gently flaking off an end piece. Make sure each piece is nearly cooked then remove the pans from the heat—the fish will continue cooking slightly. Squeeze a lemon wedge over each pan of fish.

Carefully transfer the fish to individual plates, dividing them evenly. Spoon about 3 tablespoons of the relish over each portion.

To serve with Quick-Sautéed Greens with Garlic, Lemon Confit, and Chile Flakes as shown (see the photo, left), arrange a small serving of greens alongside the fish.

1 pound sole or other thin, flaky white fish fillets (about 8 fillets)

1 teaspoon salt

½ teaspoon freshly ground black pepper

½ cup Wondra flour (see page 371)

4 tablespoons butter

2 tablespoons extra-virgin olive oil

2 lemon wedges, seeded (see page 375)

Lemon Confit and Fried Caper Relish (page 20), for serving

Seasonal Variations

Winter (pictured): Quick-Sautéed Greens with Garlic, Lemon Confit, and Chile Flakes (page 163)

Spring: Asparagus (omit Black Garlic Hollandaise; page 144)

Summer: Hollandaise (page 32) and Half-Dried Tomatoes (page 350)

Fall: Butternut Squash Purée (page 171)

Poultry

This is a technically diverse chapter that is arranged from the simplest recipe to the most involved. If you cook your way through the chapter, you'll pick up skills that apply to other proteins, and you'll master some exciting techniques that don't always get the attention they deserve.

Poultry is often seen as a workhorse in the kitchen—it can be an everyday ingredient, but certain techniques, like making confit, can elevate it to something extraordinary. Although braising is often thought of for larger, tougher meats, it's a great way to turn poultry into a rich, hearty main course with minimum fuss.

Chicken is a go-to protein for many home cooks because it's inexpensive, cooks quickly, and has a neutral flavor that makes it endlessly adaptable. And it can be great prepared simply, too. A perfectly seared chicken breast is one of life's greatest pleasures. That said, dried out chicken is one of life's great disappointments, and there are a few easy ways to improve your chicken cookery.

Season and sear your chicken aggressively. Salty, crispy brown chicken skin is the ultimate comfort food, and with good reason. The key to successfully cooking poultry (and most every protein) is to get a good initial sear and later to rest it properly. All meats, including chicken and duck, should be served warm but not too hot. Piping-hot meat is meat that hasn't rested long enough.

Many home cooks aren't very familiar with cooking duck, which can be a bit harder to source. But its depth of flavor, which is reminiscent of red meat, makes it worth the hunt. I prefer to use fresh Muscovy or Moulard ducks for their deep, rich flavor. The duck confit on page 235 is one of my favorite recipes in this book and the cover photograph. I love the way the tender meat inside contrasts with the thin, crisp glazed skin on top. Toss a little shredded confit into the melon and radicchio salad on page 126 in lieu of the crispy prosciutto or add it to a breakfast hash (see page 203). Preparing confit is a preservation technique that has the added bonus of being savory and delicious.

———

Brined Chicken Breasts

SERVES 4 TO 8

This dish is the single most convincing argument for brining I can put forth. The difference between a chicken breast that's been brined and pan-seared and one that's just been pan-seared is like night and day. The brine imparts moisture and flavor into what can be an uninspiring piece of meat. Although a hungry person can easily eat an entire breast, if you're preparing hearty sides, you may want to plan on a half breast per person.

Leaving the skin on the breast is crucial, too. Not only is it delicious, it also provides the meat with some protection from drying out. Skin-on breasts are usually sold on the bone, which needs to be removed in order to sear the breast evenly. It is easy to do: Lay the breast, skin side up, on a cutting board and look for the layer of bone under the meat. Insert a small, sharp knife between the bone and the meat and, running the knife along the edge of the bone, slice off the meat. Flip the now boneless breast over and remove the loose flap of meat, aka the tender, and reserve for another use. (The tender won't cook evenly with the rest of the meat, and because of its small size, it gets overseasoned in the brining process.)

This is a perfect headache-free main when you're cooking for friends; once the meat is brined, it cooks up quickly, leaving you time to relax and receive compliments from your friends about how they've never tasted a chicken breast so juicy.

In a small saucepan over high heat, bring the water to a boil. Remove the pan from the heat and add ½ cup of the salt and the sugar and stir until dissolved. Add the ice to cool the brine to room temperature. Put the chicken breasts in a resealable plastic bag, pour the brine over them, and seal closed. Place the bag in a container that allows the meat to be fully submerged in the liquid, and refrigerate for at least 1 hour and no more than 1½ hours (or the meat will be too salty).

Remove the chicken from the brine, discard the brine, and dry the chicken very well on a kitchen towel. Allow to come to room temperature, about 1 hour. Season each breast on both sides with ½ teaspoon of the remaining salt and ¼ teaspoon of the pepper.

Place a baking sheet in the oven and preheat the oven to 400°F.

Heat a black steel pan over high heat until very hot. Add 1 tablespoon of the oil and heat until the surface is rippling but not smoking. Working in batches to avoid crowding the pan, add 2 chicken breasts, skin side down. Weight them down with a heavy heatproof plate to create an even sear across the surface of the skin and cook for 2 to 2½ minutes, until crisp and golden brown. Transfer the breasts to a plate, then

Continued

4 cups water

½ cup plus 2 teaspoons salt

6 tablespoons sugar

1½ pounds ice, or 3 cups cold water (see page 378)

4 boneless skin-on chicken breasts (see recipe introduction)

1 teaspoon freshly ground black pepper

3 tablespoons extra-virgin olive oil

3 tablespoons butter

Seasonal Variations

Spring (pictured): Asparagus with Black Garlic Hollandaise (page 144) and herb salad (page 353)

Summer: Melon with Radicchio, Crispy Prosciutto, and Caramelized Honey–Black Pepper Vinaigrette (page 126)

Fall: Crispy Brussels Sprouts with Pickled Mustard Seeds (page 177)

Winter: Mom's Simple Salad (page 115)

Brined Chicken Breasts

CONTINUED

rinse the pan and dry it well. Repeat the process with 1 tablespoon of the oil and the remaining 2 breasts. Rinse and dry the pan well. Return the pan to medium-high heat. Add the remaining 1 tablespoon of oil and 2 of the seared breasts, skin side up, to the pan.

Add 1½ tablespoons of the butter to the pan. Once the butter has melted, repeatedly spoon it over the chicken to baste the meat. Place the 2 basted chicken breasts, with all of their juices and butter, aside on a clean plate. Add the other 2 chicken breasts to the hot pan, skin side up, and baste using the remaining 1½ tablespoons butter. Place the breasts, with all of their juices and butter, on the plate.

Carefully remove the hot baking sheet from the oven. Place all of the chicken breasts on the baking sheet and pour the juices and butter over the meat. Return the baking sheet to the oven and roast until the thickest part of the breasts reaches 140°F, 6 to 9 minutes.

Remove the baking sheet from the oven, transfer the breasts to a platter, and pour any juices over the meat. Loosely tent the chicken with aluminum foil, and let rest for 4 to 5 minutes. Slice each breast on the bias (across the grain, with your knife at a 45-degree angle) into 7 or 8 slices.

To serve with Asparagus with Black Garlic Hollandaise as shown (see the photo, page 226), make the hollandaise and cook the asparagus while the chicken is coming to room temperature after brining. Remove the asparagus from the ice water and pat it dry on a kitchen towel; leave the blanching water on the stove.

While the cooked chicken is resting, bring the asparagus blanching water back to a simmer and quickly reheat the stalks in it, about 30 seconds. Check the consistency of the hollandaise; if it has thickened up too much, whisk the hollandaise in a bowl set over the warm blanching water to gently warm and loosen the sauce slightly or whisk in about 1 teaspoon warm water. Lay 5 or 6 stalks of asparagus on each serving plate and spoon about 2 tablespoons of hollandaise over the asparagus. Arrange the chicken slices alongside the asparagus, dividing them evenly, and tuck small tufts of herb salad in the back.

Seared Duck Breasts

SERVES 4 TO 6

Here is a simple, easy-to-assemble meal to make for yourself or for a crowd. Plan on serving a half breast per person if you have a lot of side dishes or a full breast per person for a hungry crowd.

Even chefs have a tendency to undercook duck breasts. I find that duck breast is a little like hanger steak, in that it is not necessarily something you want to eat rare because it gets too chewy. Aim for a nice medium to medium-rare. Nailing this preparation is an easy way to surprise and impress your guests. The technique involves slowly rendering out the fat to get beautifully crispy skin, then finishing the breasts in the oven, though not for too long. It's better to pull out the breasts early and let them rest for a long time, so the meat takes on that gorgeous ruby hue and remains juicy throughout.

While the duck is cold, pull off the tenders (the loose flap of meat on the underside of the breast) and reserve for another use. Score the skin on each breast in a ¼-inch crosshatch pattern, cutting only through the skin and avoiding the flesh (see the photo, page xii). Place the scored breasts on a plate and let them come to room temperature, about 1 hour.

Season each breast with about ½ teaspoon salt and ⅛ teaspoon pepper on the skin side and about half that much salt and pepper on the meat side. The exact amount of seasoning will depend on the size of the breasts, but season aggressively, rubbing in the salt and pepper with your fingers since much of the salt will come off during searing.

Place a baking sheet in the oven and preheat the oven to 400°F.

Heat a black steel pan over medium-high heat until hot but not smoking, about 1 minute. Place 2 breasts, skin side down, in the pan. Turn down the heat to medium-low and, using tongs, move the breasts around and press down frequently (keeping the skin side down) to ensure even coloring across the skin until the fat is rendered, 5 to 6 minutes. The heat must be kept medium-low to ensure that the fat renders slowly and completely and that the skin doesn't burn. If the fat on a duck breast is rendered properly, the skin will be fully crisp. Transfer the breasts to a plate, discard the fat in the pan, and repeat with the remaining 2 breasts. Once all of the breasts are on the plate, wipe out the pan.

To finish cooking the duck, heat 1 tablespoon of the oil in the same pan over high heat until rippling but not smoking. Add 2 breasts, skin side down as before, and sear for 15 seconds, then flip the breasts onto the meat side. Immediately place 3 tablespoons of the butter and about one-third of the thyme sprigs in the pan and, as the butter melts, repeatedly spoon it over the breasts to baste the meat. Transfer the breasts and

Continued

4 large duck breasts (preferably Muscovy), kept cold

3 teaspoons salt

1 teaspoon freshly ground black pepper

2 tablespoons extra-virgin olive oil

6 tablespoons butter, at room temperature

1 bunch thyme

Seasonal Variations

Summer (pictured on page 230): Arugula dressed with Caramelized Honey–Black Pepper Vinaigrette (see page 126) and Peach Confiture (page 12)

Fall: Mixed Chicories with Grapes, Candied Walnuts, and Aged Balsamic Vinaigrette (page 133)

Winter: Fennel Gratin (page 164)

Spring: Spring Pea Risotto (page 147)

Seared Duck Breasts

CONTINUED

thyme to a baking sheet. Pour the butter and juices over the meat. Repeat with the remaining 1 tablespoon oil, 2 breasts, and 3 tablespoons butter and with another one-third of the thyme sprigs.

Carefully remove the hot baking sheet from the oven, place the 4 breasts skin side up on it, and pour over the butter and juices. Return the baking sheet to the oven and roast until the thickest part of the breast reaches an internal temperature of 107°F to 110°F, 3 to 5 minutes. Keep a close eye on each breast and remove each one as soon as it reaches temperature; the timing may vary depending on the size. To test for doneness without a thermometer, flip a breast meat side up. Firmly press the thickest part of the breast with your index and middle fingers; the meat should bounce back ever so slightly. If it's hard, the breast is overcooked; if there's no bounce at all and the meat feels squishy, it's too rare.

Spread the remaining thyme sprigs on a large plate or in a shallow baking dish. Place the breasts skin side up on top of the thyme and pour over any butter and juices. Tent loosely with aluminum foil and let rest for 15 minutes. Discard the thyme. Slice each breast on the bias (across the grain, with your knife at a 45-degree angle) into ¼-inch pieces.

To serve with arugula dressed with Caramelized Honey–Black Pepper Vinaigrette and Peach Confiture as shown (see the photo, left), arrange the duck slices on individual plates, top each portion with a tablespoon of the confiture, and nestle a small tuft of dressed arugula on the side. Duck is rich and needs to be served with something bright and palate cleansing; the sweet fruit of the peaches plays off the slightly gamey meat beautifully.

Porcini Braised Chicken Thighs

SERVES 6 TO 8

This is a rustic one-pot meal that can be served directly out of the Dutch oven in which it is cooked. Porcini mushrooms have an earthy, savory quality that combines with the stock, wine, and concentrated meat flavor from the thighs to create a lovely richness. The contrast of crisp skin against tender braised meat and soft vegetables is fantastic as well.

I recommend using this recipe to learn how to braise (as an added benefit, it's less expensive than Balsamic Braised Short Ribs on page 273). If you don't have a Dutch oven, it's possible to sear the chicken in a large sauté pan, transfer it to a roasting pan to finish cooking in the oven, and serve it in a pretty casserole dish.

This simple meal is all about balance, and people are always impressed by how delicious it is. I don't always save the vegetables from a braise because they often wind up limp and soggy, but these are very much worth eating.

In a large Dutch oven, heat 1 tablespoon of the oil over medium heat. Add the carrot, onion, and celery and sauté for 6 to 7 minutes, until the vegetables get some color. Add the porcini, garlic, thyme, and bay leaves and mix to combine. Turn off the heat but leave the Dutch oven on the burner.

Preheat the oven to 375°F. Season each chicken thigh with ½ to ¾ teaspoon salt (depending on its size; a large thigh will weigh about 10 ounces and a small one about 6 ounces) and ¼ teaspoon pepper.

Heat a black steel pan over high heat until very hot. Add 1 tablespoon of the oil and heat until the surface is rippling but not smoking. Working in batches to avoid crowding the pan, add 4 chicken thighs, skin side down, and lower the heat slightly, to medium-high. Weight down the thighs with a heavy plate to create an even sear across the entire surface and cook for 5 to 6 minutes, until evenly golden but not too dark in any spots. Check after the first 1 to 2 minutes to ensure no black spots are forming and lower the heat as needed. Place the thighs, skin side up, in a single layer on top of the vegetables in the Dutch oven. Repeat the searing two more times with the remaining oil and chicken thighs, rinsing the pan and wiping it completely dry after each batch.

In a saucepan over medium heat, bring the stock and wine to a simmer. Pour the stock mixture into the Dutch oven; the edges of the chicken should be submerged but the skin should be exposed. It's important not to cover the chicken skin completely or it won't get crisp.

Cover with a tight-fitting lid (or with aluminum foil if using a roasting pan), place in the oven, and cook for 1¼ hours, or until the chicken is completely tender. Turn up the oven temperature to 400°F, remove the cover, and continue to cook until the chicken skin is crisp, about 15 minutes.

Continued

4 tablespoons extra-virgin olive oil

1½ cups sliced, peeled carrot, on the bias in 3-inch pieces

3 cups roughly chopped yellow onion, in 1½-inch pieces

1½ cups roughly chopped celery, in 2-inch pieces

1 ounce dried porcini mushrooms

10 cloves garlic

3 thyme sprigs

2 fresh or 4 dried bay leaves

12 bone-in, skin-on chicken thighs, at room temperature

2 to 3 tablespoons salt

3 teaspoons freshly ground black pepper

4 cups homemade stock (page 346) or other high-quality stock

1 cup dry white wine

Seasonal Variations

Fall (pictured): Potato Dumplings (page 172)

Winter: Long-Cooked Broccoli (page 156) and Hazelnut Sauce Verte (page 5)

Spring: Crispy Baby Artichokes (page 152) and Orange-Caraway Glazed Carrots (page 178)

Summer: Arugula with Cherries, Shaved Sheep's Milk Cheese, and Sherry Vinaigrette (page 122)

Porcini Braised Chicken Thighs

CONTINUED

Remove from the oven, discard the thyme sprigs as best you can, and serve directly from the pot.

To serve with Potato Dumplings as shown (see the photo, page 233), cook and rice the potatoes the day before and make the dumpling dough while the chicken is braising. After removing the pot from the oven, set it aside and poach your dumplings. Remove and strain 1 cup of the chicken braising liquid; mix this into the dumplings and reheat them as directed on page 175. Meanwhile, crisp the skin on the braised chicken. Bring the dishes to the table and serve family-style. Encourage people to try the vegetables from the braising liquid. They are delicious!

Lacquered Duck Confit

SERVES 6 TO 12

This is one of the dishes I'm most proud of, and it's an impressive dish to serve when you're entertaining. It was inspired by a recipe in *The Silver Palate Cookbook* by Julee Rosso and Sheila Lukins, which I read avidly when I was first starting to cook. It takes 3 days to complete, so plan ahead.

Even though this recipe takes a few days to make, a lot of that time is passive. Also, because the recipe is a multistep process, you can prep most of the components ahead of time, and then finish the dish quickly so you can relax and enjoy your party. Although this recipe serves 6, I recommend making 12 legs at once because it's a labor-intensive recipe. If you choose to serve six people, you can store the six remaining legs, submerged in their fat, in the refrigerator for up to a month. If you would like to serve all 12 at once, you can do that, too, you'll just need to spend more time searing and glazing all of the legs at the end of the recipe.

Making duck confit at home can seem intimidating, but you'll get so much out of the investment. Duck fat isn't cheap, but once you've made the first batch of confit, you'll reuse the fat to make more, and it only tastes better as you continue to use it (up to a point—after three or so uses, it becomes too salty). Duck fat itself is one of the most flavorful and versatile fats around, and thanks to my love of making confit, I always have some on hand for cooking. As the fat cools, you also end up with a layer of what I call duck jelly, which can be added to the French onion soup on page 102. (Be aware that duck jelly is very salty, so season whatever you use it in accordingly.) Leftover duck confit is wonderful in the melon and radicchio salad on page 126 or the breakfast hash on page 203.

Day 1

MAKE THE SPICE BLEND Toast all of the spices except the nutmeg and black pepper and finely grind everything together (see page 378).

MAKE THE DUCK LEGS Rinse the duck legs and dry well on paper towels. At the base of the long bone opposite the meaty side, use a sharp paring knife or good kitchen shears to score all the way around the circumference of the bone to cut away the tendon, which helps prevent the meat from tearing. Meat shrinks as it cooks, and if you don't sever the tendon, it will pull the meat taut and give you a less attractive presentation.

In a small bowl, combine the salt and the spice mix. Season each leg evenly on both sides with about ¾ teaspoon of the mixture, then place in a tightly packed single layer in a hotel pan (see page 373; or use your largest roasting pan). Cover and refrigerate overnight.

Continued

SPICE BLEND

½ teaspoon black peppercorns

6 allspice berries

1 teaspoon coriander seeds

4 whole cloves

½ cinnamon stick

6 juniper berries

¼ teaspoon freshly grated nutmeg

½ teaspoon freshly ground black pepper

DUCK LEGS

12 duck legs (preferably 6 to 8 ounces each, from Muscovy ducks)

3 tablespoons salt

2 large heads garlic, halved crosswise (no need to peel)

½ bunch thyme

4 fresh or 8 dried bay leaves

4 quarts rendered duck fat (more, if the duck legs are larger than 8 ounces each)

LACQUER

½ cup aged sherry vinegar (see page 370)

½ cup packed muscovado or dark brown sugar

½ teaspoon salt

Seasonal Variations

Fall (pictured on page 238): Parsnip Purée (page 171), Cracked Green Olive and Armagnac Prune Relish (page 19) and Parsley Sauce Verte (page 5)

Winter: Quick-Sautéed Greens with Garlic, Lemon Confit, and Chile Flakes (page 163) and Savory Tomato Confiture (page 11)

Spring: Crispy Baby Artichokes (page 152)

Summer: Melon with Radicchio, Crispy Prosciutto, and Caramelized Honey–Black Pepper Vinaigrette (page 126; omit the prosciutto)

Lacquered Duck Confit

CONTINUED

Day 2

Remove the duck from the refrigerator and preheat the oven to 325°F. Dry each duck leg with paper towels, wash and dry the pan thoroughly, and place the legs, skin side up, back in the pan along with the garlic, thyme, and bay leaves. In a saucepan over low heat, gently warm the duck fat until melted. Pour the fat over the duck legs, covering them completely by at least ¼ inch.

Cut a piece of parchment paper to fit over the top of the pan, cover the pan with the parchment, and then cover the parchment with a piece of aluminum foil. Place the pan in the oven and set a timer for 1 hour so you can check the progress. Depending on the size of the legs, they may take anywhere from 1½ to 3 hours to cook. To check for doneness, carefully remove 1 leg from the fat and place it on a plate. Using tongs, press down with medium pressure at the place where the meat and the bone join in the crook of the thigh (known as the ball joint). The meat should easily release from the bone.

When the duck is cooked, remove the foil and parchment and let the legs cool for 20 minutes in the duck fat. If you are planning to store some or all of the duck legs for more than 1 week, transfer the legs you wish to store to an ovenproof container. Remove and discard the garlic, thyme, and bay leaves from the fat and pour in enough fat to completely cover the legs. Tightly cover the container and refrigerate for up to 1 month (see Note, right, for reheating instructions for the stored legs).

For the legs you plan to serve soon, line a baking sheet with parchment paper and transfer the legs to it. Reserve 2 tablespoons of the cooled duck fat for every 3 legs you plan to serve. Cover the baking sheet and the reserved fat and refrigerate overnight or for up to 1 week. Transfer any remaining duck fat to storage containers and freeze for future use; it will keep for up to 3 months.

Day 3

MAKE THE LACQUER On the day of serving, remove the duck legs from the refrigerator and let them come to room temperature, about 2 hours.

In a small nonreactive saucepan, heat the vinegar over medium-high heat. Add the sugar and salt and stir to dissolve. Boil until slightly thinner than honey, 3 to 4 minutes. Remove from the heat and let cool to room temperature. After cooling, the consistency should be slightly thicker but still brushable; if the mixture thickens too much after cooling, add a splash of sherry vinegar. (If you're serving six, you'll have leftover glaze, which keeps in the refrigerator for up to 2 weeks. To reheat, slowly bring to a gentle simmer before using. Leftover glaze can also be used in a vinaigrette or marinade.)

Continued

NOTE To reheat the stored legs, cover the container with foil and place in a 325°F oven until the fat has melted, 25 to 35 minutes (don't let the legs cook). Then proceed with the instructions in the last paragraph of Day 2.

Lacquered Duck Confit

CONTINUED

Preheat the oven to 400°F. Place a large black steel pan over medium-high heat and add 2 tablespoons of the reserved duck fat. When the fat is rippling but not smoking, add 3 of the duck legs skin side down, and sear, weighting them down with a heavy plate, until golden brown, 1 to 2 minutes. Check frequently for an even, crisp surface. Transfer the legs to a baking sheet, wipe the pan clean, and repeat with the remaining reserved duck fat and duck legs, browning only as many as you plan to serve that day.

Add all six legs back to the pan in a single layer skin side up. If making 12, divide the legs among two pans. Brush the crispy skin of each leg with a thin layer of the lacquer. Add about ¼ cup water to the bottom of each pan to prevent the sugars from sticking. Cook in the oven until the lacquer is bubbling, 5 to 6 minutes. Remove from the oven and, using tongs, pick up each leg by the bone and carefully transfer to a serving plate.

To serve with Parsnip Purée, Cracked Green Olive and Armagnac Prune Relish, and Parsley Sauce Verte as shown (see the photo, left), make the purée 2 to 3 days in advance and reheat over a low flame just before serving. Stir it frequently to ensure it's not sticking. Make the relish up to 3 days in advance, and the sauce verte shortly before serving as it doesn't keep well. Start the sauce verte after removing the duck from the refrigerator on the day you're serving it. Applying the lacquer to the duck should be the last step, done just before serving. Swipe ¼ to ⅓ cup of the parsnip purée on each plate and top with a duck leg. Add about 1 tablespoon of the olive relish and 2 teaspoons of the sauce verte on top.

Pork

I cook a lot of pork. It's one of the things Beast is known for (people always ask about the glazed pork belly), but I also frequently make pork at home because it's versatile and easy to cook perfectly.

Be picky about the pork you buy. Pigs need to be treated well to taste good. This is true for every meat, but it is particularly true of pork, the flavor and texture of which are deeply influenced by how the animal was raised. Factory farming, in which pigs are often kept in confined areas and pumped full of antibiotic-laced feed designed to fatten them up quickly, is an inhumane industry with serious environmental consequences. And on top of that, the meat is flavorless.

If you can, buy pork directly from a farmer who pasture-raises heritage breeds. Try cooking the meat of a few different breeds to discover which you like best. Red Wattle hogs taste different from Berkshires, which are distinct from Durocs. Each breed has its own flavor, and all of these breeds will disappear from the marketplace if they are not supported by shoppers. If you're not able to buy straight from a farm, look for labels indicating the meat is hormone- and antibiotic-free, with an animal welfare certification if possible. The pork you buy should have taut muscle fibers, a slightly shiny appearance, and an appetizing rosy color. It should never be mealy, sticky, or overly pale. High-quality pork is undoubtedly more expensive, but it's worth it.

The recipes in this chapter teach you how to properly season, brine, glaze, braise, sear, rest, and slice various cuts of pork, which are all skills you can apply to other kinds of meat. Pork, like all meats, should be brought to room temperature before searing so it will cook evenly, and it should be allowed to rest before slicing or serving, at which point it will be warm, not piping hot.

Pan-Seared Pork Chops

SERVES 4

My mom cooked pork chops all the time when I was growing up, and now I know why: they're a great, quick weeknight dinner. If you have the time to make a brine and let the pork sit in it for a few hours before cooking, the meat will be more flavorful. But if you don't, you can still make delicious pork chops with just salt and pepper, as long as you don't overcook them.

How do you know when your pork chops are perfectly cooked? When you press on the meat right along the bone, it should feel ever-so-slightly springy and gently bounce back. If the meat feels firm, it's overcooked. When you make an incision in the meat near the bone, the interior should be opaque but rosy, not pale and white.

Resting is the key to moist, flavorful meat, especially a cut with the bone still in, as it allows the muscle fibers to relax and the delicious interior juices to evenly redistribute throughout, instead of spilling out onto your cutting board.

In a small saucepan over high heat, bring the water to a boil. Add ¼ cup of the salt and the sugar and stir until dissolved. Add the ice to cool the brine to room temperature. Put the pork chops in a resealable plastic bag, pour the brine over them, and seal closed. Place the bag in a container that allows the meat to be fully submerged in the liquid, and refrigerate for 2 hours.

Remove the chops from the bag, discard the brine, and dry the chops very well with paper towels. Allow the meat to come to room temperature, 1 to 2 hours. Season each chop on both sides with ½ teaspoon of the remaining salt and ¼ teaspoon of the pepper.

Place a baking sheet on the center rack of the oven and preheat the oven to 400°F.

Heat a black steel pan over high heat until very hot. Add 1 tablespoon of the oil and heat until the surface is rippling but not smoking. Working in batches to avoid crowding the pan, immediately add 2 chops and sear, pressing down hard with tongs, until golden on both sides, about 2 minutes per side. Don't let too many dark spots form; you're aiming for a nice golden brown. Remove the pan from the heat and turn the chops onto the fat-cap side to let some of the fat render. Set the seared chops on a plate. Rinse and dry the pan and repeat with the remaining oil and the remaining pork chops.

Carefully remove the hot baking sheet from the oven and place all 4 chops on it. Roast in the oven for 3 to 5 minutes, until the thickest part near the bone reaches 120°F. Remove the chops from the oven, transfer them to a platter, and allow to rest, loosely tented with aluminum foil (not tightly wrapped or they will continue to cook) for 5 minutes before serving.

To serve with New Potato Salad with Fava Beans and Morels as shown (see the photo, right), make the potato salad up to 1 day in advance or while the pork chops are brining (add the fava beans just before serving). Put a pork chop on each plate and spoon about 1 cup of the potato salad alongside.

1 cup water

¼ cup plus 2 teaspoons salt

3 tablespoons muscovado or maple sugar

1½ pounds ice, or 3 cups ice water (see page 378)

4 bone-in center-cut pork chops (10 to 12 ounces each and 1 to 1½ inches thick)

1 teaspoon freshly ground black pepper

2 tablespoons extra-virgin olive oil

Seasonal Variations

Spring (pictured): New Potato Salad with Fava Beans and Morels (page 149)

Summer: Long-Cooked Zucchini (page 156) and Savory Tomato Confiture (page 11)

Fall: Escarole Caesar Salad (page 129)

Winter: Fennel Gratin (page 164)

Fennel-Brined Pork Loin

SERVES 6 TO 8

A whole center-cut pork loin, which is large, cylindrical, and has a fat cap, is a beautiful cut (see the photo, page 240; not to be confused with a long, skinny tenderloin). It's also quite practical for dinner parties because you can cook the whole thing ahead of time, then present it tableside to stunning effect. You will need to plan ahead, however, as the pork needs to brine for 24 to 30 hours. I use this same fennel brine at Beast for a variety of cuts because it has a complex and lovely flavor.

Pork loin is fairly lean, so it can dry out in the oven. That's why the brine, which contributes both moisture and another layer of flavor, is essential. Using a pork loin to learn how to properly prepare and rest roast is a delicious and less expensive option than beef. Make sure your side dishes are served nice and hot, but remember, the pork should be only warm when you serve it. If it is hot, it has not rested long enough.

MAKE THE BRINE In a small sauté pan over medium heat, toast all of the spices except the bay leaves (see page 378). Cut a 1-foot square of cheesecloth and fold it over once. Place the spices, bay leaves, garlic, and thyme in the middle of the cloth, gently roll it lengthwise into a small sachet, and tie both ends with kitchen twine (like a wrapped candy).

In an 8-quart stockpot, combine the water, salt, sugar, and sachet and bring to a boil. When the salt and sugar have dissolved, turn down the heat slightly and simmer until the water is flavored with the aromatics, about 20 minutes. Do not allow the mixture to boil rapidly or the water will reduce and the mixture will become too salty. Remove the pot from the heat and add the ice to dilute the brine and cool it to room temperature.

MAKE THE PORK LOIN Trim the fat cap of the pork loin between ⅛ and ¼ inch thick if necessary. Score the fat cap in a crosshatch pattern ¼ inch wide (and very shallowly, cutting only through the fat and avoiding the flesh; see the photo, page 240). Place the pork loin in a deep casserole dish or Dutch oven and add the brine to cover completely. (Cut the loin in half crosswise if it doesn't fit in the dish.) Place a piece of parchment paper over the top and weight it down with a plate to keep the loin submerged. Refrigerate for at least 24 hours or up to 30 hours.

Preheat the oven to 400°F. Line a shallow baking dish with the thyme.

Remove the pork from the brine, place it on several layers of paper towels, and dry well; discard the brine. Tie the pork loin with kitchen twine (see the photos, page 271), then season with the salt and pepper.

Continued

BRINE

4 juniper berries

4 allspice berries

1 star anise pod

1 tablespoon coriander seeds

1 tablespoon black peppercorns

1 tablespoon fennel seeds

2 teaspoons yellow mustard seeds

4 fresh or 8 dried bay leaves

1 head garlic, halved crosswise

½ bunch thyme

8 cups water

¾ cup salt

¾ cup sugar

4 pounds ice, or 8 cups cold water (see page 378)

PORK LOIN

1 (4- to 5-pound) boneless pork loin (not tenderloin), trimmed of silver skin

1 bunch thyme

1 tablespoon salt

1 teaspoon freshly ground black pepper

3 tablespoons extra-virgin olive oil

6 tablespoons butter, at room temperature

Seasonal Variations

Summer (pictured): Crispy Baby Artichokes (page 152), Hazelnut Romesco (page 14), and herb salad (page 353)

Fall: Crispy Brussels Sprouts with Pickled Mustard Seeds (page 177)

Winter: Butternut Squash Purée (page 171) and Hazelnut Sauce Verte (page 5)

Spring: Asparagus with Black Garlic Hollandaise (page 144)

Fennel-Brined Pork Loin

CONTINUED

Heat a black steel pan over high heat until very hot. Add the oil and heat until the surface is rippling but not smoking. Place the pork, fat side down, in the pan and sear, pressing down with tongs and rotating every 2 to 3 minutes, until golden brown all around. Add the butter, turn off the heat, and once the butter has melted, spoon it over the pork 4 or 5 times to baste the meat.

Place the pan in the oven. After 10 minutes, flip the pork and use a spoon to baste it with some of the melted butter. Continue to cook until the internal temperature reaches 120°F, 5 to 7 minutes (depending on the thickness of the roast).

Remove the pan from the oven, then remove the pork from the pan, placing it on top of the thyme in the baking dish. Allow the loin to rest, loosely tented with aluminum foil (not tightly wrapped or it will continue to cook), for a minimum of 20 minutes and up to 30 minutes before slicing.

To serve with Crispy Baby Artichokes and Hazelnut Romesco as shown (see the photo, page 246), make the romesco up to 3 days in advance but let it stand at room temperature for at least 2 hours before serving. Pare the artichokes and hold them in water with lemon juice up to 8 hours in advance, then parcook them up to 4 hours in advance. Sear the artichokes while the pork is resting so you can serve them hot.

Snip the twine on the pork and cut the pork loin across the grain at 1½-inch intervals. Spoon about ¼ cup of romesco onto each plate, place the pork on top, and divide the artichokes evenly among the plates. Garnish with the herb salad.

Sherry-Glazed Pork Belly

SERVES 6 TO 8

I was nervous about making pork belly at Beast because a lot of people shy away from how fatty it is. In a restaurant where customers eat a set menu, serving something they might not like is a risky proposition. However, I shouldn't have worried, because this is now one of my most popular dishes, and everybody who tastes it loves it.

This dish is all about balance—the sherry glaze brings an acidic touch that cuts through the richness, and the toasted *levain* bread that it's served on soaks up some of the porky juices.

This recipe takes 3 days to complete, and although most of the time is passive, you do need to plan ahead. Because of the time it requires, I don't recommend halving the recipe, even if you're only serving four. If you don't serve all of the pork belly, you can freeze the remainder for another use, such as slicing into strips and pan frying them for a glamorous BLT or cutting into chunks for tossing into a breakfast hash (page 203).

A note about the brine: Most of my brines are 5 percent salt by weight, but this one is 7 percent salt because the belly really needs it. At 5 percent, it tastes underseasoned, so follow the measurements carefully.

Day 1

PREP THE PORK BELLY While the pork belly is still cold, place it, fatty side up, on a cutting board. With the tip of a knife, create a ⅛-inch-deep crosshatch pattern across the entire surface of the fat. Don't cut through the muscle; the idea is to make shallow cuts in the fat, which will help it render as it cooks, giving you a beautiful crispy surface (see the photo, page 240).

Place the pork in a Dutch oven or stockpot that's only slightly larger than the belly itself. Make sure the vessel fits in your refrigerator and that it's deep enough to fully submerge the pork in the brine.

MAKE THE BRINE In a black steel pan over medium heat, toast all of the spices except the bay leaves (see page 378). Cut a 1-foot square of cheesecloth and fold it over once. Place the spices, bay leaves, and garlic in the middle of the cloth, gently roll it lengthwise into a small sachet, and tie both ends with kitchen twine (like a wrapped candy).

In a large stockpot, combine the water, salt, sugar, and sachet and bring to a boil. When the salt and sugar have dissolved, turn down the heat slightly and simmer for 5 minutes, then remove from the heat and let steep for another 10 minutes to allow the flavors to develop and deepen. Add the ice to cool the brine to room temperature.

Pour the brine over the pork. The pork should be completely submerged. Place a piece of parchment over the belly and weight it down with a heavy plate or other heavy object, cover, and refrigerate for 24 to 28 hours.

Continued

PORK BELLY

1 (3½- to 4-pound) pork belly, kept cold

2 tablespoons extra-virgin olive oil

Flaky finishing salt

BRINE

4 juniper berries

4 allspice berries

1 star anise pod

1 tablespoon coriander seeds

2 teaspoons black peppercorns

2 teaspoons fennel seeds

2 teaspoons yellow mustard seeds

4 fresh or 8 dried bay leaves

½ head garlic, halved crosswise

6 cups water

¾ cup plus 1 tablespoon salt

⅓ cup plus 2 teaspoons sugar

3 pounds ice, or 6 cups water (see page 378)

BRAISING LIQUID

2 (750-ml) bottles white cooking wine (a dry yet inexpensive Riesling)

2 cups homemade stock (page 346) or other high-quality stock

1 yellow onion, chopped

3 carrots, peeled and chopped

1 head garlic, halved crosswise

1 teaspoon black peppercorns

4 fresh or 8 dried bay leaves

GLAZE

½ cup aged sherry vinegar (see page 370)

½ cup packed muscovado or maple sugar

1 teaspoon salt

TOAST

1 small loaf bread, such as whole-wheat levain or artisanal ciabatta

2 teaspoons extra-virgin olive oil

Sherry-Glazed Pork Belly
CONTINUED

Day 2

Remove the pork from the brine, place it on several layers of paper towels, and dry well. Discard the brine. Preheat the oven to 325°F.

Heat a black steel pan over high heat until very hot. Add the oil and heat until rippling but not smoking. Add the pork and weight it down with a plate to achieve an even sear across the surface. Check it frequently—once the first side is evenly golden brown, flip the belly and continue to cook, moving it around in the pan as needed to ensure even coloration. Cook until both sides are a deep chestnut brown, about 6 minutes per side.

MAKE THE BRAISING LIQUID Transfer the seared pork to a nonreactive (enameled cast iron or stainless steel) Dutch oven and add the wine, stock, onion, carrots, garlic, peppercorns, and bay leaves; the liquid should cover the pork by at least ½ inch. Cover with a lid or parchment paper and aluminum foil and cook in the oven for 4 to 5 hours, until the pork is completely fork-tender. Remove from the oven, then uncover and let the pork cool in its braising liquid for at least 30 minutes or for up to 2 hours.

Using two spatulas, carefully remove the pork from the liquid without letting it fall apart and place it in a shallow baking dish. Top it with a smaller baking dish and weight the second dish down with something heavy, like a large can of beans. (The weight helps press the pork into an even shape for later portioning.) If you don't have a baking dish that fits inside the first one, use a small baking tray (from a toaster oven) or other flat object that can be evenly weighted down; a piece of cardboard wrapped in aluminum foil will work in a pinch. Refrigerate the pork with the weight overnight. Strain the leftover braising liquid into a container, cover, and refrigerate for at least 12 hours or for up to 24 hours.

The next day, skim the solid fat from the top of the braising liquid and discard. Set aside ½ cup of the braising liquid for finishing the pork belly and reserve the remainder for braising something else or for mixing with stock to use as the base for a rustic soup.

Day 3

MAKE THE GLAZE In a small nonreactive saucepan, heat the vinegar over medium-high heat. Add the sugar and salt and stir to dissolve. Boil until slightly thinner than honey, 3 to 4 minutes. Remove from the heat and let cool to room temperature. After cooling, the consistency should be slightly thicker but still brushable; if the mixture thickens too much after cooling, rewarm and add a splash of sherry vinegar.

Seasonal Variations

Fall (pictured on page 250): Fresh Corn and Summer Vegetable Succotash (page 159) and herb salad (page 353)

Winter: Kale with Pickled Apples, Gruyère Crisps, and Creamy Dijon Vinaigrette (page 134)

Spring: Bread Salad with Asparagus, Pickled Rhubarb, and Flat-Leaf Parsley (page 116)

Summer: Arugula with Cherries, Shaved Sheep's Milk Cheese, and Sherry Vinaigrette (page 122)

GLAZE THE PORK BELLY Preheat the oven to 400°F. Remove the pork from the refrigerator and make sure no vegetables or peppercorns are stuck to it. While it is still cold, slice it into eight 2-inch squares. Reserve any leftover scraps for another use (see recipe introduction).

Heat a black steel pan over medium-high heat. Add the pork squares, scored side up, and the reserved ½ cup braising liquid and cook until the liquid starts to bubble slightly, about 1 minute. Turn off the heat, then brush glaze over the top of the pork with a pastry brush. Try to paint it on in a single thick layer that doesn't spill down the sides of the squares, as it will burn on the bottom of the pan. Sprinkle the top of the pork with finishing salt, then place the pan in the oven for 5 minutes.

Remove the pan from the oven and check to be sure the braising liquid has not evaporated (add more liquid or a splash of water if necessary). Brush another layer of glaze on the pork, sprinkle with more finishing salt, and return the pan to the oven for 5 minutes more.

MAKE THE TOAST While the belly is glazing for the second time, cut the bread into ¾-inch-thick slices. Cut each slice into a 2½-inch square, leaving crust on one side if possible. Brush one side of each bread square very lightly with some of the oil and arrange the squares in a single layer on a small baking sheet.

Remove the pork from the oven, brush with glaze for a third and final time, and place the pork and bread in the oven for a final 5 minutes. When the bread is light golden brown but not hard and the pork is hot all the way through, place a square of pork belly on each square of toast. (Leftover glaze will keep in the refrigerator for 2 weeks, and can be used in a marinade or vinaigrette.)

To serve with Fresh Corn and Summer Vegetable Succotash and herb salad as shown (see the photo, page 250), cut the vegetables for the succotash and store them in separate containers for up to 8 hours. Prepare the succotash about 20 minutes before serving, just prior to glazing the pork for the first time. Leave the succotash in its sauté pan off the heat while you finish glazing the pork. Just after putting the toast and the pork with its final glazing in the oven, warm the succotash over medium-high heat for about 2 minutes, until just heated through. Spoon about 1 cup of succotash onto each serving plate, set the pork belly–topped toast on top, and place a small tuft of herb salad alongside.

Milk-Braised Pork Shoulder

SERVES 6 TO 8

Many people associate pork shoulder with barbecue. It is, after all, the cut used for making pulled pork. But I think it's really nice to prepare a shoulder as a roast. It has a fair amount of fat, which gives it a certain softness, almost like a pork version of a pot roast. I love the richness of this dish, especially in the winter.

Milk-braised pork has Italian roots, but the flavor profile of this sauce—with the leeks, sage, and black pepper coming through—reminds me a little bit of a southern-style gravy. The sauce looks and tastes very rich, but because it's made with milk (as opposed to cream) and thickened with roux and puréed vegetables, it's not nearly as heavy as you might think.

Take the twine off the roast (if there is one) and unroll the shoulder. You'll see a solid center of meat with two smaller flaps. Cut off each of the flaps. Roll up each flap into a log, and then roll the middle piece into a log. You should have 3 logs of roughly the same size. Tie each log with kitchen twine (see the photo, page 271), then season each log with 2 teaspoons salt and ¼ teaspoon pepper. Set aside on a plate. Preheat the oven to 325°F.

Cut a 1-foot square of cheesecloth and fold it over once. Place the sage, thyme, and bay leaves on the cloth, roll it lengthwise into a small sachet, and tie both ends with kitchen twine (like a wrapped candy). Set the sachet aside. (Making an aromatic sachet makes it easier to remove all of the spices later, so you don't accidentally blend them into the gravy.)

Heat a black steel or cast-iron pan over high heat until very hot. Add 1 tablespoon of the oil and heat until the surface is rippling but not smoking. Add a pork roast and sear, turning every 2 to 3 minutes to achieve an even sear on all sides. Set the roast aside on a platter. Rinse the pan and wipe it completely dry, then add 1 tablespoon of the remaining oil and sear another roast. Repeat this process for the third roast, again using 1 tablespoon of the remaining oil, then clean and dry the pan one last time.

In the same pan, heat the remaining 1 tablespoon oil over medium-high heat. Add the onion, celery, and leek and sauté for 2 to 3 minutes, until the edges are beginning to caramelize lightly. Remove from the heat.

Put the pork roasts in a large Dutch oven and add the milk, stock, garlic, sautéed vegetables, and aromatic sachet. Add the remaining 1 teaspoon salt and bring the mixture to a simmer over medium heat. Cover the pot, transfer to the oven, and cook for 2 hours. Remove the cover, then cook, uncovered, for an additional 1 to 1½ hours, allowing the liquid to reduce and achieve a rich gold color. Stir carefully and baste the pork with the braising liquid. The meat is done when it is completely tender and falls apart slightly when you push it with your finger. The liquid in the Dutch oven will look curdled after cooking. This is okay, as it will all be blended later.

Continued

1 (3½- to 4-pound) boneless
pork shoulder

2 tablespoons plus 1 teaspoon salt

¾ teaspoon freshly ground black pepper

12 sage leaves

3 thyme sprigs

4 fresh or 8 dried bay leaves

4 tablespoons extra-virgin olive oil

½ large yellow onion, roughly diced

1 celery stalk, roughly diced

1 leek, white and pale green parts only

6 cups whole milk

2 cups homemade stock (page 346)
or other high-quality stock

6 cloves garlic

2 tablespoons dry sherry

1½ tablespoons butter

1 tablespoon all-purpose flour

Fried sage leaves (see page 376),
for garnish

Seasonal Variations

Winter (pictured): Quick Sautéed Greens with Garlic, Lemon Confit, and Chile Flakes (page 163) and Caramelized Delicata Squash (page 181)

Spring: Orange-Caraway Glazed Carrots (page 178)

Summer: Mom's Simple Salad (page 115) and biscuits (page 360)

Fall: Pan-Seared Wild Mushrooms with Parsley and Parmesan (page 160)

Milk-Braised Pork Shoulder

CONTINUED

Remove and discard the sachet. Carefully remove the roasts from the pan and let them cool slightly. Cut the twine off the roasts and let the meat rest while you make the sauce. Strain the braising liquid through a fine-mesh strainer into a bowl, reserving the milky liquid and the vegetables separately.

Combine 2 cups of the vegetables with about 2 cups of the braising liquid in a blender and purée on high speed until totally smooth, about 3 minutes. If you have leftover braising liquid, reserve it for another use, like adding it to stock for a rustic soup or for cooking baked beans. Add the sherry to the braising-liquid blend and set aside.

In a saucepan over medium heat, make a roux by melting the butter, whisking in the flour, and then continuing to whisk until light golden, about 1 minute. Whisk in the braising-liquid blend slowly to avoid lumps, then continue to whisk until smooth. Turn the heat down to a very gentle simmer, whisking frequently, for 5 to 7 minutes, until the sauce thickens slightly. Taste and adjust the seasoning.

Preheat the oven to 325°F. Cut each roast into slices 1½ to 2 inches thick. The pork should be falling-apart tender, so don't expect perfectly clean slices. Pour the sauce into a shallow baking or casserole dish and nestle the pork slices in the sauce. Place in the oven until the slices and the sauce are warmed through, 10 to 12 minutes.

To serve with Quick-Sautéed Greens with Garlic, Lemon Confit, and Chili Flakes and Caramelized Delicata Squash as shown (see the photo, page 255), start cooking the squash during the last 20 minutes of braising time and let both batches sit in the pan (it's okay to crowd both batches into one pan once all of the slices are caramelized). Sauté the greens while the pork is reheating in the sauce. When you're ready to serve, reheat the squash over medium-high heat until warmed through, about 1 minute.

Spoon about ¼ cup of the sauce onto each plate and top with a slice of pork. Tuck some greens and squash alongside the pork and scatter fried sage leaves around the plate.

Beef

Beef can feel like a special-occasion meat, and when prepared right, it is an absolute umami bomb of rich, satisfying flavor. There's a learning curve when it comes to cooking beef, and in part because of that, I find it to be the most gratifying protein to cook. We need to have respect for an animal as large as a cow and learn how to treat its meat properly.

To ensure beef cooks evenly, it must, like all meats, be at room temperature before it comes into contact with any sort of heat. A large cut like rib eye or strip loin can take 2 to 3 hours to come to room temperature, so plan accordingly. The key to delicious beef is a proper sear, followed by a generous resting period. The internal temperature of meat often rises during resting, so you'll want to pull the beef off the heat just before it feels done. As with all meats, I make sure that my side dishes are served piping hot but that the beef is served warm.

The recipes in this chapter illustrate how to marinate, sear, roast, braise, rest, and slice a variety of cuts; of course, most of these skills apply to other meats as well. But I chose these recipes because they cover not only these indispensable techniques but also several cuts. The strip loin roast is a large, showcase dish that feeds eight and is best suited to special occasions, while the flat iron is the opposite: a less showy and less expensive cut that marinates beautifully and cooks quickly.

A final note on beef: I use grass-fed beef because it aligns with my politics, but it's ultimately a personal decision. It's important to consider your source, because the way your beef was raised will impact the way you cook it. Corn-fed or corn-finished beef tends to have more fat and marbling than grass-fed beef, so it can take a hard sear over high heat. Grass-fed beef is usually leaner, so I cook it on slightly lower heat and baste it with plenty of butter after searing to keep it moist. These recipes were all tested with corn-fed beef, because that is still more widely available. If you can access grass-fed beef, please by all means do! Just be sure to lower the flame when you sear, use a little more fat for basting, and cook the beef to about 5 degrees lower than instructed in the recipe.

Bone-In Rib Eyes

SERVES 4

Rib eye is my favorite beef cut and probably the favorite of many others, too. It's a big, sexy, luxurious steak and it's not cheap, so save this recipe for a special occasion. Don't be freaked out by the prospect of serving each person a 1½-pound steak. In this case, nearly half of that weight is bone and fat, so it's not as outrageous as it seems.

Overall this recipe is simple, but you do have to pay attention to the details, like bringing the steaks all the way to room temperature before cooking, seasoning the meat 1 hour ahead of time, searing it in a blazing-hot pan, and pulling the compound butter out of the fridge about a half hour before serving. These little things affect the quality of the finished dish.

Let the steaks come to room temperature, about 2 hours. One hour before cooking, season each rib eye on both sides with 2 teaspoons of the salt and ½ teaspoon of the pepper. Just before cooking, blot steaks dry with a paper towel (but don't rub seasoning off). Place a baking sheet in the oven and preheat the oven to 400°F.

Heat a black steel pan over high heat until very hot. Add 1 tablespoon of the oil and heat until the surface is rippling but not smoking. Place 1 rib eye in the hot pan and press a heavy plate or bowl onto the steak to ensure an even sear. Cook each side until a heavy, crackly crust forms (avoid creating many black spots), 1½ to 2 minutes per side. Set the seared steak on a clean plate. Rinse the pan and wipe it completely dry, and then repeat the process to sear the remaining steaks, using 1 tablespoon oil each time.

Once all of the steaks have been seared, remove the baking sheet from the oven, place the seared steaks on it, and return the baking sheet to the oven. Cook the steaks, flipping after 2 minutes, for 4 to 6 minutes total, until each steak reaches an internal temperature of 114°F to 117°F for medium-rare. Transfer the steaks to a plate and loosely tent with aluminum foil. Allow the steaks to rest for 8 to 10 minutes.

To serve with Blue Cheese Butter, Fried Shallots, and Duchess Potatoes with Smoked Onion Soubise as shown (see the photo, left), make the fried shallots up to 3 days in advance; they don't need to be reheated before serving. Make the potatoes up to 1 day ahead and reheat just before serving. The compound butter needs 2 hours to chill, so make it at least 1 day in advance. On the day of serving, cut four slices, each ½ inch thick, from the log of compound butter and set them aside to soften slightly. After the steaks have rested for 6 to 8 minutes, top each one with a slice of butter and let them rest, uncovered, for about 2 minutes more.

Plate each butter-topped steak with a small duchess potato or two and a scattering of fried shallots. I also like to add a few sprigs of very lightly dressed herb salad to help brighten the plate and refresh the palate.

4 bone-in rib eyes, 1¼ to 1½ pounds each and 1½ inches thick, at room temperature

8 teaspoons salt

2 teaspoons freshly ground black pepper

4 tablespoons extra-virgin olive oil

Seasonal Variations

Spring (pictured): Blue Cheese Butter (page 342), Fried Shallots (page 352), Duchess Potatoes with Smoked Onion Soubise (page 187), and herb salad (page 353)

Summer: Mom's Simple Salad (page 115)

Fall: Fresh Corn and Summer Vegetable Succotash (page 159)

Winter: Kale with Quick-Pickled Apple, Gruyère Crisps, and Creamy Dijon Vinaigrette (page 134)

Seared Marinated Flat Iron Steak

SERVES 6 TO 8

Some steaks just aren't meant to be cooked rare or medium-rare, and the flat iron is one of them. If it's not cooked closer to medium, you end up chewing endlessly because the meat isn't tender enough. Fortunately, flat iron cooks quickly, though this recipe does call for an overnight marinade.

This recipe also illustrates how important resting is. If you slice the steak immediately, it will still have a translucent red band around its interior and it will bleed everywhere. By letting it rest, it will continue to cook until it is medium and that red band turns into a beautiful even pink throughout.

The marinade is a close cousin of a recipe I made for the chicken I served at my wedding, which came from a ginger-lemon chicken dish my mom used to make. I wanted to create something similar for beef, updated with fresh herbs and fish sauce.

Be sure to dry the steak really well before searing, as the sugars in the marinade can create a lot of smoke if it is still wet when it hits the heat. Fan the steak into slices on each plate for a beautiful presentation.

Squeeze the juice out of the lemon slices into a mixing bowl. Add the spent lemon slices to the bowl along with the ¼ cup of oil, the garlic, fish sauce, soy sauce, sugar, ½ teaspoon of the pepper, the chile flakes, thyme, and ginger. Stir well to combine.

Put the steaks in a resealable plastic bag, pour the marinade over them, and seal closed. Massage the bag to distribute the marinade evenly, then place the plastic bag in a container and refrigerate for 24 hours.

Remove the steaks from the bag at least 2 hours before cooking and pick off the ginger and thyme. Discard the marinade. Blot off all of the marinade from the steaks with paper towels, making sure the steaks are very dry. Season each steak on both sides with ½ teaspoon salt and ¼ teaspoon of the remaining pepper. Preheat the oven to 400°F.

Heat a black steel pan over high heat until very hot. Add 1 tablespoon of the oil and heat until the surface is rippling but not smoking. Working in batches to avoid crowding the pan, add 2 steaks to the pan. Press a heavy plate or bowl onto the steaks to ensure an even dark brown sear across the entire surface of the steaks (avoid creating black spots). Cook on each side for 1 minute, transfer to a baking sheet, and then rinse and dry the pan. Repeat with the remaining oil and steaks in two batches.

Once all of the steaks have been seared, place the baking sheet in the oven and cook, flipping the steaks after 3½ minutes, for 7 to 10 minutes total, until each steak reaches an internal temperature of 116°F to 120°F in the thickest part. Remove the baking sheet from the oven and transfer the steaks to a plate to rest for 5 to 7 minutes. Cut on a sharp bias across the grain into ¼- to ½-inch-thick slices.

Continued

1 lemon, sliced

¼ cup plus 3 tablespoons extra-virgin olive oil

6 cloves garlic

2 tablespoons fish sauce (see page 370)

1 tablespoon soy sauce

1 tablespoon sugar

2 teaspoons freshly ground black pepper

¼ teaspoon red chile flakes

6 thyme sprigs

1 (2-inch) piece peeled fresh ginger, thinly sliced

3½ pounds flat iron steak, cut into 6 evenly sized steaks

3 teaspoons salt

Seasonal Variations

Summer (pictured): Long-Cooked Green Beans (page 156), Savory Tomato Confiture (page 11), and herb salad (page 353)

Fall: Pan-Seared Wild Mushrooms with Parsley and Parmesan (page 160)

Winter: Blistered Cauliflower with Anchovy, Garlic, and Chile Flakes (page 168)

Spring: Spring Pea Risotto (page 147)

Seared Marinated Flat Iron Steak

CONTINUED

To serve with tender Long-Cooked Green Beans and Savory Tomato Confiture as shown (see the photo, page 265), make the tomato confiture up to 1 week in advance and bring it to room temperature before serving. On the day of serving, start cooking the green beans after the marinated steaks have rested at room temperature for about 1 hour. When the beans have about 20 minutes of cook time left, start cooking the steaks (they work fantastically on the grill, too).

Arrange four or five slices of steak on each plate in a fan pattern, top with 2 tablespoons of confiture, stack a small serving of green beans alongside, and place a small tuft of herb salad on the side.

Strip Loin Roast

SERVES 8

This strip loin cooks relatively quickly, but the demi-glace cream (see Seasonal Variations, below) accompaniment takes a couple of days to make, so plan ahead if you'd like to serve them together. Call your butcher in advance to get a strip loin, also known as a New York strip. Butchers often cut it into steaks, so if you want an entire roast, it's best to ask ahead.

This cut is a practical way to serve steak to a crowd without having to worry about perfectly cooking individual steaks. After a nice, long rest, the slices of rosy meat make for an impressive and beautiful presentation. Serve this at a special dinner party, or for a holiday meal in place of a more traditional crown roast or leg of lamb. It's rich, deeply meaty, and a great place to show off beef sourced from a high-quality farm.

Preheat the oven to 400°F. Tie each roast (see the photos, page 271) with kitchen twine. Season each roast with 2½ teaspoons of the salt and ¾ teaspoon of the pepper.

Heat a black steel pan over high heat until very hot. Add 1 tablespoon of the oil and heat until the surface is rippling but not smoking. Add 1 roast and press down with tongs to achieve an even sear across the entire surface of the meat. Cook, turning the roast every 2 to 3 minutes, until all sides are deep chestnut brown. Set the meat on a plate and rinse and dry the pan. Repeat with the remaining oil and the remaining roast, then rinse and wipe the pan again.

Return the pan to medium heat, return both roasts to the pan, and add the butter. As the butter melts, spoon it over the beef four or five times to baste it.

Place the pan in the oven and set a timer for 15 minutes. Check the internal temperature: at this point, it should be very low, 80°F to 85°F. Continue to cook the beef until the internal temperature reaches 110°F to 112°F for medium-rare or 116°F to 118°F for medium, 10 to 20 minutes.

Spread the thyme bunch in a shallow baking dish and place the roasts on the thyme. Loosely tent the roasts with aluminum foil and let rest for at least 25 minutes or up to 40 minutes before slicing.

To serve with Demi-Glace Cream, Pan-Seared Wild Mushrooms with Parsley and Parmesan, and herb salad as shown (see the photo, left), make the demi-glace 2 days in advance. On the day of serving, reduce the cream and add it to the demi-glace, then set aside. Sear and roast the beef.

Continued

1 (3-pound) New York strip loin roast, cut lengthwise into two pieces, each about 3 by 4 inches, at room temperature

1 tablespoon plus 2 teaspoons salt

1½ teaspoons freshly ground black pepper

2 tablespoons extra-virgin olive oil

4 tablespoons butter, at room temperature

1 bunch thyme

Seasonal Variations

Fall (pictured): Demi-Glace Cream (page 39), Pan-Seared Wild Mushrooms with Parsley and Parmesan (page 160; you will need to make a double batch), and herb salad (page 353)

Winter: Fennel Gratin (page 164)

Spring: New Potato Salad with Fava Beans and Morels (page 149)

Summer: Tomatoes with Crab, Sungold Tomato French Dressing, and Fried Caper Rémoulade (page 125)

Strip Loin Roast

CONTINUED

While the beef rests, cook the mushrooms. (Feel free to substitute different kinds of wild mushrooms if necessary, but do not use a cultivated variety like oyster mushrooms in place of wild ones.)

Gently reheat the demi-glace cream over low heat until warm.

Snip and untie the roasts, and then cut the meat into ¾-inch-thick slices. Ladle 3 tablespoons of demi-glace cream onto each plate and place a slice of meat, cut side up so the pink interior is exposed, on top. Arrange about ½ cup of mushrooms alongside the meat and garnish with the herb salad.

Balsamic Braised Short Ribs

SERVES 4

Short ribs are full of fat and marbling, which makes them perfect for braising, and the addition of acidic balsamic vinegar helps balance some of the meat's richness. Properly cooked, short ribs make a very sultry meal.

Braising is a good technique for entertaining, because you can essentially set it and forget it, and the leftovers are easily repurposed. Use the meat scraps in a hash (see page 203) or use the braising liquid as a base for Classic French Onion Soup (page 102). It can also be used in a new braise.

You need to keep a few things in mind when you're braising. This cooking method requires a lot of liquid to keep the meat from drying out and you must have a tight-fitting lid or other cover so the liquid does not evaporate. The braising liquid should be highly seasoned, as well. This recipe calls for a tablespoon of salt in the liquid itself, which may seem like a lot, but the meat needs all of it to become properly seasoned in the liquid.

Short ribs take a long time to cook because of the delicious fat and gelatinous tissue that hold them together. The best way to test for doneness is to slice a small piece off the corner and taste it. When it tastes rich and tender, the ribs are done. Overcooked short ribs lose their lusciousness and end up tasting like pot roast, so be attentive and check often.

Season each rib with 1½ teaspoons of the salt and ½ teaspoon of the pepper. (This may seem like an excessive amount of salt and pepper, but much of it will fall off when you sear the meat.)

Heat a black steel pan over high heat until very hot. Add 1 tablespoon of the oil and heat until the surface is rippling but not smoking. Add half of the ribs and sear, pressing down with tongs and turning them as needed, until deep brown on all sides (avoid creating many black spots), 2 to 3 minutes per side. Transfer the seared ribs to an enameled cast-iron or stainless-steel Dutch oven or a half hotel pan (see page 373); don't use an unlined cast-iron pan for braising. Because there's so much acid in this recipe, an unlined cast-iron pan will leave a metallic flavor in your meat. Rinse and dry the pan and repeat with 1 tablespoon of the remaining oil and the remaining ribs. Add the second batch of seared ribs to the Dutch oven and set aside.

Preheat the oven to 350°F. Rinse and dry the pan you used for searing the ribs once again. Heat the remaining 2 tablespoons oil in the pan over medium-high heat. Add half of the celery, carrots, and onion and cook, stirring occasionally, until golden and caramelized, 7 to 10 minutes. Add 1 tablespoon of the tomato paste and cook, stirring frequently, until the vegetables are deep golden brown. Add this mixture to the Dutch oven and repeat with the remaining vegetables, 1 tablespoon tomato paste, and 1 tablespoon oil. Add the prunes, lemon peel, thyme, and garlic to the Dutch oven and set aside.

Continued

4 (1-pound) bone-in short ribs, cut between the bones into 2-rib sections (8 ribs total)

5 tablespoons salt

4 teaspoons freshly ground black pepper

5 tablespoons extra-virgin olive oil

3 celery stalks, cut into 2-inch pieces

4 large carrots, peeled and cut into 2-inch pieces

2 large yellow onions, roughly diced

2 tablespoons tomato paste (preferably Italian)

5 pitted prunes

3 lemon peel strips (from about ½ lemon; see page 375)

4 thyme sprigs

1 head garlic, halved crosswise

3 cups homemade stock (page 346) or other high-quality stock

2 cups red wine

½ cup 10-year aged balsamic vinegar (see page 370)

Seasonal Variations

Winter (pictured): Horseradish Gremolata (page 40) and Orange-Caraway Glazed Carrots (page 178)

Spring: Potato Dumplings (page 172)

Summer: Biscuits (page 360) and Savory Tomato Confiture (page 11)

Fall: Crispy Brussels Sprouts with Pickled Mustard Seeds (page 177)

Balsamic Braised Short Ribs

CONTINUED

In a large nonreactive saucepan over medium heat, bring the stock, wine, and balsamic vinegar to a simmer. Add the remaining 1 tablespoon salt, then pour the stock mixture into the Dutch oven. Cover the pot, place in the oven, and cook until the meat is very tender and nearly falling off the bone but not completely falling apart when teased with a fork or pressed between your fingers, about 2½ hours. Uncover the pot and let the beef cool in the braising liquid until it is cool enough to handle, 30 to 45 minutes.

Transfer the ribs to a cutting board and carefully trim (or just pull off gently with your fingers) the flap of connective tissue where it meets the bone (it should be easy to peel back and cut off near the hole where the bone is; if the bone fell out during cooking, just fish it out of the liquid and discard it).

Strain the braising liquid and discard all of the solids. (I like to save the carrots, which I usually throw into a hash the next day.) Pour the braising liquid into a container and ladle off and discard as much fat from the surface as possible. You'll use some of the braising liquid when serving the beef; freeze the rest for another use. Keep in mind that this braising liquid has incredible flavor but is aggressively seasoned, so use it sparingly.

Preheat the oven to 400°F. Place the trimmed short ribs in a casserole dish and pour a few large ladles of the braising liquid over the top. Reheat the ribs in the oven, uncovered, until fully heated through, 5 to 7 minutes, basting as needed to keep them from drying out.

To serve with Horseradish Gremolata and Orange-Caraway Glazed Carrots (see the photo, page 272), roast the carrots up to 4 hours in advance. Reheat and glaze them immediately before serving. Make the gremolata while the ribs are reheating.

Place 1 short rib on each plate and spoon 2 to 3 tablespoons of the braising liquid around the side. Arrange about ½ cup of glazed carrots to the side of the meat and sprinkle with 1 to 2 tablespoons of gremolata.

Lamb

Lamb shouldn't be served only during the holiday season. Lamb is all about *terroir*, and if you find a good purveyor, you'll be rewarded with grassy, almost floral-tasting meat. The best lamb has a mellow, sweet flavor. It's important to buy young, grass-fed lamb from a local source. I strongly prefer to purchase domestically raised meat rather than lamb flown in from Australia or New Zealand. When you shop, ask your butcher where the animal came from and what it ate.

Many people have negative associations with lamb because they had an off-putting experience with it at some point in their life. It's true that when lamb isn't cooked correctly (or when the animal is past its prime), it can have a gamey flavor. But lamb is incredibly enjoyable as long as it's sourced and cooked with care, and these four recipes all display different and essential techniques that showcase lamb's flavor.

The lamb chop dish is a great entry-level lamb recipe. The cut itself is relatively small, and cooking chops is a good way to learn about preparing meat on the bone. The leg of lamb recipe is for more advanced cooks serving a crowd. It provides a golden opportunity to learn about proper seasoning. It also feeds eight to ten people, so gather your friends and family around the table to feast.

When cooking lamb (and all meats), remember to bring the meat to room temperature before searing so it will cook evenly and to give it a proper rest before serving it warm but not too hot. It's important to rest meat for longer than you might think necessary, especially when it's cooked on the bone. It's much more satisfying to have a juicy, perfectly cooked, well rested piece of meat than something piping-hot that you cut into too quickly. When you taste properly rested meat, you'll be able to tell the difference immediately.

Herbed Leg of Lamb

SERVES 8, GENEROUSLY

Roasted to a perfect pink, with the fat rendered out from slow cooking and a crackly crust from a final blast of heat, this leg of lamb is a gorgeous thing to behold. Treated to an herbal rub, this dish is so celebratory that it can easily replace ham or turkey on a holiday table. In terms of presentation and flavor, this definitely beats out a Sunday roast for me.

Tommy Habetz taught me to make this intensely flavorful rub for pork shoulder at my old communal dining space, Family Supper, but I love the way it translates to other large cuts of full-flavored meat like this one. The outside is quite herby and salty, while the interior is rich and juicy.

Because the lamb marinates for a full day, you will need to plan ahead. You may also have to special order the bone-in leg, so call your butcher well ahead of when you want to serve this dish. You can use a boneless leg of lamb for a less dramatic presentation, but you must cut the amount of salt and pepper in half when seasoning the meat and also lightly season the interior where the bone was removed. You may end up with excess herb rub, but it's better to make the full recipe than to run out. You will need a large roasting pan with a rack for this recipe.

MAKE THE HERB RUB Combine the garlic, rosemary, thyme, bay leaves, lemon peel, fennel pollen, chile flakes, and nutmeg in a food processor. Blend until the rub is evenly combined and has a texture similar to bread crumbs, about 1 minute. With the machine running, stream in the olive oil to make a paste. Scrape the paste into a small bowl and set aside.

MAKE THE LAMB Using a very sharp knife, make small cuts across the surface of both sides of the lamb every ½ to ¾ inch. The cuts should be about 1 inch long by ½ inch deep. These slits will help the marinade soak in and allow the fat to crisp up during cooking. Place the lamb on a rack in a large roasting pan. Pour the wine over the lamb and massage it in to infuse the meat with a bit of additional flavor. Next, rub the lamb all over with the salt and pepper. Work the seasoning in with your fingers, rubbing it thoroughly into the meat. Finally, apply the reserved herb rub all over the lamb, evenly coating it with a thin layer. Refrigerate, uncovered, for 24 hours.

The following day, remove the lamb from the refrigerator and let it come to room temperature, about 4 hours.

Preheat the oven to 275°F. Roast the lamb, uncovered, for 1 hour, until the internal temperature is about 90°F when a thermometer is inserted at several points in the thickest area of the leg; be sure to test all the way into the deepest and largest part of the muscle. Because the leg is such a large cut and of varying shape, it is a good idea to check its internal temperature in several of the thickest places; avoid touching the bone with the thermometer.

Continued

HERB RUB

3 tablespoons minced garlic

¼ cup loosely packed rosemary leaves

¼ cup loosely packed thyme leaves

6 fresh or 12 dried bay leaves, crushed

Peel of 1 lemon, removed in strips and finely minced (see page 375)

2 teaspoons fennel pollen

½ teaspoon red chile flakes

1 whole nutmeg, finely grated on a Microplane grater (see page 374)

½ cup extra-virgin olive oil

LAMB

1 (6- to 7-pound) bone-in lamb leg, with the aitch bone removed (ask your butcher to remove it)

⅓ cup red wine

¼ cup salt

1 tablespoon freshly ground black pepper

Rosemary sprigs, for garnish (optional)

Seasonal Variations

Spring (pictured): Spring Pea Risotto (page 147)

Summer: Little Gem Lettuces with Creamy Pistachio Vinaigrette (page 121)

Fall: Caramelized Lentils du Puy (page 185)

Winter: Blistered Cauliflower with Anchovy, Garlic, and Chile Flakes (page 168)

Herbed Leg of Lamb

CONTINUED

Remove the lamb from the oven and turn the oven temperature to 325°F. When the oven has reached that temperature, continue to cook the lamb for another 20 to 40 minutes, until the internal temperature is at least 112°F at the narrowest part of the leg and no more than 130°F at the thickest part of the leg for medium-rare. As before, check the temperature in several places. Loosely tent the roasting pan with aluminum foil and let the leg rest for a minimum of 45 minutes or for up to 2 hours. (The meat can rest in the roasting pan because it's sitting on a rack.)

About 20 minutes before serving, preheat the oven to 400°F. Put the lamb, uncovered, back in the oven and heat, until a gorgeous deep brown color, about 15 minutes. To carve the leg, slide your knife as close to the bone as possible and cut a large piece of meat off the bone. Slice the meat across the grain into individual pieces.

To serve with Spring Pea Risotto as shown (see the photo, page 280), parcook the risotto (as instructed in the Note for that recipe) several hours in advance and finish cooking it after carving the lamb. Risotto demands a lot of attention while cooking and needs to be served the second it's ready. The carved lamb can be loosely tented with aluminum foil to keep it warm while the risotto finishes, which takes only 15 to 20 minutes.

Plate the risotto in individual portions (about 1½ cups per person) so it stays warm. Serve the lamb with fresh rosemary sprigs on a platter family-style so guests can choose the slices they like best.

Lamb Scallopini

SERVES 4

This is light, crispy, and perfect for a quick meal—no wonder my mom made cutlets once a week. Scallopini are typically veal or pork (this recipe could be easily adapted to one of those meats), but lamb is special because it has a meaty flavor that shines through even when it's thinly pounded.

You will need a meat mallet for this recipe. The lemon is essential here, too. This dish needs a punch of acid because it's quite rich. I make this all the time because it comes together so quickly, but it is perfect for a special lunch. The crispy, crunchy element is what makes this dish so satisfying. Pair it with a delicious sauce, a palate-cleansing side, and a nice glass of rosé.

Insert your knife blade between the bone and the meat of each lamb chop, run the blade along the bone, and remove the meat. This should leave you with 4 little lamb medallions, each about 3 ounces. Cut each medallion across the grain into 3 even slices, each about ½ inch thick. You should now have 12 thin medallions of lamb.

Cut two 6-inch squares of parchment paper. Place a piece of lamb on a piece of the parchment and cover it with the other piece of parchment. Pound the meat with a meat mallet until about ³⁄₁₆ inch thick, or the thickness of three quarters. Repeat with the remaining pieces of lamb, then lay the pounded lamb pieces side by side (use a baking sheet if you'd like), and season both sides evenly with the salt and pepper.

In a shallow mixing bowl, lightly beat the eggs. Put the flour and the bread crumbs on two small plates. To bread the lamb, dip each piece into the egg, then into the flour, and then into the egg a second time, and then into the bread crumbs. Lay the breaded cutlets on a baking sheet.

Set your two largest sauté pans over medium-high heat. Add 2 tablespoons of the butter and 1 tablespoon of the oil to each pan, and heat until the butter begins to foam slightly and starts to turn very light golden on the edges, about 1 minute. Add 6 lamb medallions in a single layer to each pan and press gently with a fish spatula (see page 373) to ensure good contact with the pan. Don't worry if your butter is browning; as long as it doesn't turn black, it will add nice depth of flavor. When the first medallions to go into the pan have cooked for 1 minute, begin flipping all of the pieces in the order that you put them in the pan. The lamb is done when both sides are evenly golden brown, about 2 minutes total, or less. This lamb is thin and cooks very quickly, so don't overcook it. Turn off the heat and squeeze 2 lemon wedges over each pan of lamb.

To serve with a simple radicchio and herb salad and Smoked Paprika and Espelette Crème Fraîche as shown (see the photo, left), make the crème fraîche up to 1 day ahead. Set up the radicchio and herb salad before cooking the lamb, but wait to dress it until you are ready to plate the lamb.

Spoon about 3 tablespoons of crème fraîche on each of four plates, lay 3 scallopini on top, and place a small tuft of radicchio, herb salad, and a lemon wedge on the side.

4 (5- to 6-ounce) lamb rib chops, each 1 to 1½ inches thick
¾ teaspoon salt
½ teaspoon freshly ground black pepper
3 eggs
½ cup Wondra flour (see page 371)
⅔ cup fine bread crumbs (see page 363)
4 tablespoons butter
2 tablespoons extra-virgin olive oil
8 lemon wedges, seeded (see page 375)

Seasonal Variations

Summer (pictured): Radicchio and herb salad (page 353) and Smoked Paprika and Espelette Crème Fraîche (page 22)

Fall: Caramelized Delicata Squash (page 181)

Winter: Hazelnut Romesco (page 14)

Spring: Spring Pea–Mint Relish (page 8)

Lamb Loin Chops

SERVES 2 TO 4

We often cook lamb loin chops at Beast because they're petite, which makes them ideal for a dinner where I'm serving a lot of other dishes. This recipe would work well for a small gathering. And if you're only making one side dish, plan on each person eating two chops.

This is one of the fastest and most instantly gratifying recipes in the book. There's no brine or marinade to contend with, so don't skimp on the salt and pepper. And provided you buy high-quality meat from a reputable source, loin chops are a beautiful, straightforward way to show off perfectly caramelized medium-rare meat. I highly recommend that you eat these chops with your fingers. If you're overly polite and limit yourself to cutlery, you'll end up missing the best parts.

If you can't find lamb loin chops, use different chops of similar thickness, like blade chops, but be sure to keep an eye on them to avoid overcooking.

Let the lamb chops come to room temperature, about 1 hour, and dry well with paper towels. Season both sides as well as the fat cap of each chop with ½ teaspoon salt and ¼ teaspoon pepper. Preheat the oven to 400°F.

Heat a black steel pan over high heat until very hot. Add the oil and heat until the surface is rippling but not smoking. Immediately add the chops and cook, pressing down hard with tongs and flipping them once, until golden on both sides, about 1½ minutes per side. Don't create too many dark spots; you're aiming for a nice golden brown. Remove the hot pan from the heat and immediately turn the chops onto to the fat cap side and let the fat render for 15 to 20 seconds.

Add the butter and 2 sprigs of the rosemary to the pan, and as soon as the butter melts (even with the heat off, this should only take a few seconds), use a large spoon to baste the chops with the butter.

Put the pan in the oven, cook for 2 minutes, then check the chops' internal temperature. The thickest part of the chop, closest to the bone, should be 113°F to 116°F for medium-rare. When you press on the meat right along the bone, it should feel ever-so-slightly springy and gently bounce back. Cook for an additional 2 to 4 minutes as necessary. Meanwhile, place the remaining 2 rosemary sprigs in a shallow baking dish.

Remove the chops from the oven and place them on top of the rosemary sprigs in the baking dish. Loosely tent with aluminum foil and let the chops rest for 7 to 10 minutes.

Continued

4 center-cut lamb loin chops, each 2 inches thick

2 teaspoons salt

1 teaspoon freshly ground black pepper

1 tablespoon extra-virgin olive oil

3 tablespoons butter, at room temperature

4 rosemary sprigs

Seasonal Variations

Fall (pictured): Blistered Cauliflower with Anchovy, Garlic, and Chile Flakes (page 168), Lemon Confit Sauce Verte (page 5), and herb salad (page 353)

Winter: Demi-Glace Cream (page 39) and Potato Dumplings (page 172)

Spring: Duchess Potatoes with Smoked Onion Soubise (page 187) and Smoked Paprika and Espelette Crème Fraîche (page 22)

Summer: Little Gem Lettuces with Creamy Pistachio Vinaigrette (page 121)

Lamb Loin Chops

CONTINUED

To serve with Blistered Cauliflower with Anchovy, Garlic, and Chile Flakes; Lemon Confit Sauce Verte; and herb salad as shown (see the photo, page 287), make the sauce several hours in advance and hold it at room temperature until the lamb is ready to serve. Prepare the cauliflower up until the point where it's tossed with the garlic-anchovy paste and set aside, then cook the lamb. Finish the cauliflower while the lamb is resting.

Plate 1 or 2 lamb chops per person. Add ½ cup of the cauliflower to each plate and top the chop with about 2 teaspoons of sauce verte. Place a small tuft of herb salad on the side.

Fig and Red Wine–Braised Lamb Shanks

SERVES 6

This is a real showstopper of a main course. A lamb shank is a big piece of meat, and it makes for a beautiful braise. I love pairing gamey meats with fruit, and the tannins and acids in the wine help infuse the lamb with a rich, balanced flavor.

When done right, braised lamb shanks have a silky, almost sticky, quality. This is mostly a result of cooking down all of the connective tissue, which can be a little tricky. This lamb needs to be fully cooked to achieve that succulent texture. The meat should not actually fall off the bone, however, which ruins the dramatic presentation. Ask your butcher to weigh each shank so they're as close as possible to the same size, which helps ensure even cooking.

This braise, like many braises, is better if made a day ahead, cooled overnight, and reheated the following day, but you can cook and serve it on the same day as described here. If you do cook it a day ahead, gently reheat the lamb in its braising liquid before straining and plating.

Dry each lamb shank well, then season each shank with 2 teaspoons of the salt and ½ teaspoon of the pepper. (Although this may seem like a lot of salt, much of it will fall off during searing.) Preheat the oven to 350°F.

Heat a black steel pan over medium heat until hot. Add 1 tablespoon of the oil and heat until the surface is rippling but not smoking. Add the carrot, onion, celery, and fennel and sauté for 6 to 7 minutes, until the vegetables take on some color. Transfer the sautéed vegetables to a large Dutch oven or deep roasting pan that will accommodate all of the shanks, and rinse and wipe dry the black steel pan.

Heat the black steel pan over high heat until very hot. Add 1 tablespoon of the oil and heat until the surface is rippling but not smoking. Working in three batches to avoid crowding the pan, immediately add 2 shanks to the pan and cook, pressing down with tongs until a deep brown sear forms on as many sides as possible, 5 to 6 minutes total. Since the shanks have an odd shape, you may have to turn them frequently. It's normal for lamb fat to smoke more than the fat of other meat; open a window and turn on your exhaust fan. Place the seared lamb shanks on top of the vegetables in the Dutch oven. Rinse the pan and wipe it completely dry before repeating with each of the next two batches, adding 1 tablespoon of the oil for each batch. Add these shanks to the Dutch oven along with the figs, thyme, and garlic.

In a saucepan over medium-high heat, bring the wine and stock to a simmer. Pour the stock mixture over the lamb and vegetables and season with the remaining 2 tablespoons salt. Cover and cook in the oven for about 3 hours. Testing for doneness here is a delicate art. You want the meat to start to fall off the bone when pushed without it falling off when you pick up the shank by the bone. The meat shouldn't feel like it's about to slip away from the bone, but you shouldn't have to work at getting the meat off, either. Still, it's better to overbraise than underbraise to ensure tender meat.

Continued

6 (1-pound) lamb shanks, at room temperature

6 tablespoons plus ¼ teaspoon salt

3 teaspoons freshly ground black pepper

6 tablespoons extra-virgin olive oil

2 cups diced, peeled carrot, in large dice

4 cups diced yellow onion, in large dice

1 cup diced celery, in large dice

1 cup diced fennel, in large dice

3 cups dried figs

½ bunch thyme

1 head garlic, halved crosswise

1 (750-ml) bottle good-quality red wine

4 cups homemade stock (page 346) or other high-quality stock

2 bunches green onions, root ends trimmed, for garnish (optional)

1 cup Demi-Glace (page 36), warmed for garnish (optional)

Seasonal Variations

Winter (pictured on page 290): Fennel Gratin (page 164)

Spring: Parsley Sauce Verte (page 5) and Celery Root Purée (page 171)

Summer: Tomatoes with Crab, Sungold Tomato French Dressing, and Fried Caper Rémoulade (page 125)

Fall: Crispy Brussels Sprouts with Pickled Mustard Seeds (page 177)

Fig and Red Wine–Braised Lamb Shanks

CONTINUED

Using a slotted spoon, carefully lift the shanks out of the liquid and place them in a baking dish. Strain the braising liquid, reserving the solids and the liquid. Remove and discard the thyme and garlic from the vegetables. Arrange the figs and vegetables around the shanks and pour about ¼ cup of the braising liquid into the baking dish. Reserve the rest of the braising liquid for another use, such as for the base of a rustic soup. Tent the shanks loosely with aluminum foil and return to the oven to reheat for about 10 minutes.

In a large sauté pan, heat the remaining 2 tablespoons oil over medium-high heat until rippling but not smoking. Add the whole green onions and cook for 4 to 5 minutes, until blistered slightly in spots. Season with the remaining ¼ teaspoon salt.

To serve with Fennel Gratin as shown (see the photo, left), partially assemble and cook the gratin up to 1 day ahead (per the instructions in that recipe). If you're cooking and serving the lamb and fennel on the same day, assemble and bake the gratin while the lamb is braising. Reheat the lamb when the gratin has 10 minutes of baking time left.

Plate individual shanks with the seared green onions alongside. If you want the shanks to look really fancy, with a beautiful sheen, spoon about 3 tablespoons of warm Demi-Glace around each one. Serve the gratin family-style.

Desserts & Pastry

As a savory chef, I rarely follow recipes to a tee. But making pastry is one place I do pay close attention to recipes, because it requires a great deal of precision. I have to give a nod here to the dessert gurus who've helped teach me: Claudia Fleming, Nancy Silverton, and Chad Robertson, as well as my incredible pastry chef, Ellen Laing. Ellen has an unbelievable work ethic and palate, is detail-oriented, and her vision matches mine. She's one of my favorite people among all those with whom I've worked, and she has taught me a great deal over the years—in fact, Ellen and I worked side by side on all of the recipes in this chapter.

Dessert is the last thing your guests remember of a meal, so it's important to make sure the dessert is a good one. This is where you can really take care of your friends and loved ones and create special traditions around food. Some of my strongest and most nostalgic memories are centered around dessert—my grandparents making pie together, for example, or the triple-layer chocolate cake my mother made for my birthday every year.

When you're planning dessert, think about what else you're serving and how the dessert weaves into the rest of the meal. If your main course was very rich and creamy, you might opt for a bright and tart bite at the end. In certain seasons, you may choose something big and comforting, while in others you may crave something small and refined.

Baking and making desserts can be a meditative act. When I'm stressed out, baking helps calm my mind by forcing me to focus on the task at hand. It requires you to be zoned in, and that's one of the most joyful aspects of cooking.

Buttermilk–Black Pepper Ice Cream

MAKES 1½ QUARTS

Years ago, I took some of my staff on a trip to Napa Valley. We had lunch in the garden of a restaurant called Martini House. For dessert, we were served a simple dish of different types of melon cut into a tiny, even dice and salted buttermilk and black pepper ice cream. I had never tasted pepper in a sweet preparation like that, and when developing this recipe, I wanted to pay homage to the dish and that trip.

I often use buttermilk and crème fraîche in desserts because they are more tangy than sweet. Use the highest-quality buttermilk you can find, preferably cultured full-fat buttermilk, often labeled Bulgarian style. The black pepper adds a kick of warm spice and a surprising floral note to the ice cream. Leave it out if you're looking for something a bit simpler; the buttermilk ice cream alone is delicious.

Place a fine-mesh strainer over a bowl. In a small, heavy saucepan, heat the cream and 1 cup of the sugar over medium heat, stirring frequently to dissolve the sugar, until the mixture is steaming and small bubbles are forming around the edges (about 190°F), 4 to 5 minutes.

While the cream is heating, in a mixing bowl, whisk together the egg yolks, the remaining ¼ cup sugar, and the salt until the yolks turn a shade paler, about 2 minutes.

When the cream mixture is ready, remove the pan from the heat. Gradually add the hot cream to the egg yolks, one ladle at a time, whisking well after each addition to ensure the eggs don't curdle or cook, until you've added all of the cream. Pour the egg and cream mixture back into the pan, place over low heat, and use a rubber spatula to move the liquid slowly. It will start to thicken and leave a film on the spatula. You're looking for a film that coats the spatula thickly enough that you can draw a line through it with your finger and it leaves a trail. This will be at about 170°F. (See Note, right, for troubleshooting the custard.) Take the egg-cream mixture off the heat and immediately pour it through the strainer to remove any bits of slightly curdled egg.

Whisk in ¾ teaspoon of the pepper. The flavor will bloom as the custard sits, so don't add all of the pepper just yet. Cover the custard and refrigerate for at least 4 hours or for up to 24 hours until completely cold, or chill it in an ice bath (place 2 quarts water and 2 quarts ice in a large bowl, nest the bowl of custard in the ice water, and stir every 5 minutes). Add the vanilla and buttermilk to the cold custard and whisk well. Taste the custard and add the final ¼ teaspoon pepper to taste—flavors become more subtle when ice cold, so it's okay if the flavor now is a little stronger than what you want at the end.

Freeze the ice cream base in an ice cream maker according to the manufacturer's instructions. Transfer the finished ice cream to a plastic container and place in the freezer to harden, about 2 hours. Depending on the temperature of your freezer, you may want to let the ice cream sit at room temperature for 10 to 15 minutes before scooping so it's not too hard. For easier scooping, bring about 2 cups of water to a boil and pour it into a heatproof vessel. Before each scoop, dip the ice cream scoop into the hot water for a few seconds, dry it, and then scoop the ice cream.

1½ cups heavy cream

1¼ cups sugar

12 egg yolks (see page 377)

½ teaspoon salt

1 teaspoon toasted and very coarsely ground black peppercorns (see page 378)

½ teaspoon vanilla extract

2½ cups cultured full-fat buttermilk

NOTE If during cooking the custard suddenly seems thinner and little lumps of cooked egg cling to the spatula when you lift it, take the custard off the heat and carefully add it to a blender. Remove the plastic insert from the lid of the blender and replace it with a cloth towel to allow some steam to escape, and then blend the custard on high for a few seconds. This will stop the custard from cooking further and will hopefully save it. Overcooked custard results in ice cream with a thin, icy texture because the egg yolks have "broken." Instead of holding the fat and sugar together in a silky way, the broken yolks have separated, giving ample opportunity for ice crystals to form. Undercooked custard has almost the same effect because the egg yolks have not cooked long enough to bind the other ingredients together. It's important to watch the temperature closely as you learn to make an ice cream base.

Malt Ice Cream

MAKES 1½ QUARTS

I adore the unique flavor of malt, with its lovely, deep sweetness. It's a nostalgic flavor, which is nice for a dessert because many people associate sweets with childhood. The first time I had malt was while visiting my great-grandmother in Minnesota, where a lot of old-timey desserts still prevail. I'll never forget my surprise at how different a chocolate malt tasted compared with a regular chocolate shake back home.

Malt powder is essentially sugar that adds a toasty flavor, and it has the added benefit of preventing iciness in ice cream and creating a smooth, creamy texture. At Beast, we pair this ice cream with buckwheat crêpes and sautéed apples (see page 318). Buckwheat and malt both have an earthy sweetness and a hint of nuttiness, making them natural companions.

Malt powder is easiest to find in home-brewing stores or online. Look for DME, or dry malt extract. It's made of soaked barley that's been allowed to germinate, and then is soaked again. The sugary water that results is dehydrated into a powder. DME tastes sweet and earthy and is commonly used by brewers as well as commercial bakers to help yeast perform properly. There are different grades for home brewers, according to the style of beer desired; for this ice cream, light and amber work well. Note that this recipe is *not* designed to use malted milk powder, which is a mixture of malt powder, wheat flour, sugar, and powdered milk.

1½ cups whole milk

¾ cup sugar

9 egg yolks (see page 377)

¾ teaspoon salt

3 cups heavy cream

½ teaspoon vanilla extract

¾ cup malt powder

Place a fine-mesh strainer over a bowl. In a small, heavy saucepan, heat the milk and ½ cup of the sugar over medium heat, stirring frequently to dissolve the sugar, until the mixture is steaming and small bubbles are forming around the edges (about 190°F), 4 to 5 minutes.

While the milk is heating, in a mixing bowl, whisk together the egg yolks, the remaining ¼ cup sugar, and the salt until the yolks turn a shade paler, about 2 minutes; set aside.

In a separate large bowl, whisk together the cream, vanilla, and malt powder. It's okay if there are a few tiny lumps because the mixture will be strained; set aside.

When the milk mixture is ready, remove the pan from the heat. Very gradually add the hot milk to the egg yolks, one ladle at a time, whisking well after each addition to ensure the eggs don't curdle or cook, until you've added all of the milk. Have the cream and malt mixture close by so you can immediately add the custard to it when ready.

Pour the egg and milk mixture back into the pan, place over low heat, and use a rubber spatula to move the liquid slowly. It will start to thicken and leave a film on the spatula. You're looking for a film that coats the spatula thickly enough that you can draw a line through it with your finger and it leaves a trail. This will be at about 170°F. (See Note, page 296, for troubleshooting the custard.)

Continued

Malt Ice Cream

CONTINUED

As soon as the custard is ready, whisk it into the cream and malt mixture so it doesn't continue cooking in the hot pot. Pour the custard mixture through the strainer to remove any bits of slightly curdled egg or undissolved malt powder. Cover the custard and refrigerate for at least 4 hours or for up to 24 hours until completely cold, or chill it in an ice bath (place 2 quarts water and 2 quarts ice in a large bowl, nest the bowl of custard in the ice water, and stir every 5 minutes).

Freeze the ice cream base in an ice cream maker according to the manufacturer's instructions. Transfer the finished ice cream to a plastic container and place in the freezer to harden, about 2 hours. Depending on the temperature of your freezer, you may want to let the ice cream sit at room temperature for 10 to 15 minutes before scooping so it's not too hard. For easier scooping, bring about 2 cups of water to a boil and pour it into a heatproof vessel. Before each scoop, dip the ice cream scoop into the hot water for a few seconds, dry it, and then scoop the ice cream.

Cocoa Nib Meringues with Macerated Summer Berries

SERVES 8

Back when I was catering, and during the early days of Gotham Tavern, our pastry chef Mandy Groom taught me a lot about seasonal desserts and pastries. This meringue was one of them. Meringues are actually quite easy to make, and they are a perfect foil for midsummer berries. Because they're so sweet, you can let the natural tart flavor of the berries shine through. This meringue recipe is also a great way to use up all of the leftover egg whites you end up with after making Buttermilk–Black Pepper Ice Cream (page 296) and Malt Ice Cream (page 299).

Superfine sugar (sometimes called caster sugar) is granulated white sugar that has been ground a little finer than standard granulated sugar. You can buy it at any well-stocked grocery store or you can make your own in a food processor or blender. Simply throw in 1 to 2 cups granulated sugar and blend it for 2 minutes. It will be almost powdery and ready to use in recipes like this one, where you want the sugar to dissolve fast.

This recipe for macerated summer berries is very loose because the final taste depends on the quality and flavor of the berries you have on hand. You can easily substitute blackberries, red currants, or black currants. Raspberries and blackberries will break down after just a few stirs into a lovely sauce, but they need a little bit more sugar to tame their acidity. Blueberries love an extra squeeze of lemon to tone down their natural sweetness a touch.

MAKE THE MERINGUES Preheat the oven to 225°F. Line a baking sheet with parchment paper. In a stand mixer fitted with the whisk attachment, whisk the egg whites on medium speed for about 1½ minutes until slightly foamy. Add the sugar and salt and whip on medium speed for 1 minute. Use a rubber spatula to scrape the sugar from the sides of the bowl, then continue whipping on medium speed for 8 more minutes, until all of the granules of sugar and salt have dissolved and the egg whites are stiff and glossy. Add the vanilla and 2 tablespoons of the cocoa nibs and whip until just combined, about 10 seconds.

Fit a pastry bag with a ½-inch plain tip (or cut ½ inch off the corner of a resealable plastic bag). Bend the tapered end of the pastry bag up so the tip is pointing up and your filling doesn't come pouring out, then stand the bag up in a tall bowl (or measuring cup) and fold the wide end of the bag down around the rim of the bowl like you would a garbage bag over a garbage can. Use a rubber spatula to scrape the meringue from the whisk attachment and the bowl into the pastry bag. Lift the pastry bag out of the bowl and gather the open end.

Holding the tip of the pastry bag about ½ inch above the prepared baking sheet, twist the top of the pastry bag to squeeze the meringue out and pipe a 2½-inch wide by 1-inch high round of meringue. You don't need to move the tip around or away until

Continued

MERINGUES

2 egg whites (see page 377)

⅔ cup superfine sugar

¼ teaspoon salt

½ teaspoon vanilla extract

3 tablespoons cocoa nibs

BERRIES

1 cup strawberries, hulled and quartered

1 cup raspberries

1 cup blueberries

2 teaspoons sugar

1 tablespoon cassis (black currant liqueur)

1/16 teaspoon salt

¼ teaspoon lemon juice

FOR ASSEMBLY

Buttermilk–Black Pepper Ice Cream (page 296), for serving

Whipped crème fraîche (page 354), for serving

Cocoa nibs, for finishing

NOTE Be sure to check your oven temperature with an oven thermometer because if it's even a few degrees hotter than you think, it can cause unwanted browning of the meringues.

Cocoa Nib Meringues with Macerated Summer Berries

CONTINUED

the round is the correct size. Continue until you have 8 rounds, spacing them about 2 inches apart (they will expand a bit in the oven).

Dip a spoon with a 2-inch-round bowl (like a soupspoon) in warm water and push down on the center of a meringue to create a nest. Repeat with the remaining meringues, wiping off the spoon and dipping it in warm water after forming each nest. Sprinkle the remaining 1 tablespoon cocoa nibs evenly across the top of the meringues. Bake the meringues for 1½ hours. To check for doneness, put a warm meringue on a plate that has been frozen for at least 30 minutes. The meringue should crisp up after a few minutes. If it doesn't, return the meringues to the oven for up to 30 minutes more, until the meringues are crisp and dry. They should be pale in color, not brown or toasted looking.

MAKE THE BERRIES While the meringues are baking, in a large bowl, stir together the berries, sugar, cassis, salt, and lemon juice and let sit for 1 hour. The juices will be pulled out of the fruit to create a liqueur perfect for soaking into the meringues.

ASSEMBLE THE DISH To serve, place each meringue on a plate and add a heaping spoonful (about ⅓ cup) of macerated berries and juice. Top with a scoop of ice cream, a dollop of whipped crème fraîche, and a sprinkle of cocoa nibs.

Orange Palmiers

MAKES ABOUT 14 PASTRIES

Rolling out puff pastry with sugar instead of flour adds a layer of sweetness and makes these little pastry cookies crispy with caramelized edges. They're a necessary component in Fresh Strawberry Soup with Roasted Rhubarb and White Chocolate Mousse (page 309), as the cookie creates a delicious barrier between the soup and the mousse so the colors don't run together. They are also a favorite of mine, wholly unadorned, alongside a hot cup of tea or coffee.

¼ cup sugar

¼ teaspoon orange zest (see page 375)

¼ teaspoon salt

1 (8 by 6-inch) piece Puff Pastry (page 331)

Pour the sugar into a small bowl, add the zest and salt, and rub the ingredients together with your fingers.

Sprinkle a clean work surface with 2 tablespoons of the orange sugar and lay the puff pastry on the sugar. Sprinkle the remaining sugar on top of the pastry and roll it out into a rectangle ⅛ inch thick, or the thickness of two quarters. The dimensions of the rectangle are not critical, but it should be rolled quite thin. Starting from a long edge of the rectangle, roll up the pastry into a log. Refrigerate the log, unwrapped, for 30 minutes to make it easier to slice.

Line a baking sheet with a Silpat baking mat (see page 374) or parchment paper. Have another baking sheet of the same size ready to place on top, as well as another sheet of parchment to protect the palmiers. Also have ready a heavy ovenproof pot or pan to rest on top of the palmiers to ensure they bake evenly and become very crisp.

Cut the chilled log into ½-inch-thick slices, discarding both end pieces. Place the slices on the prepared baking sheet with at least 2 inches around each slice to allow for spreading. You may have to bake in batches, depending on the size of your baking sheet.

Refrigerate the pastry slices, uncovered, for 30 minutes. Put any of the palmiers that you can't bake right away in the fridge. Preheat the oven to 350°F.

Place the second sheet of parchment on top of the palmiers on the baking sheet and place the second baking sheet on top of the parchment. Weight the top baking sheet down with the ovenproof pot or pan. Bake for 10 minutes, then remove the weight, the top baking sheet, and the second sheet of parchment. Continue to bake for another 2 to 4 minutes, until the palmiers are golden brown on the bottom. Use a spatula to carefully lift up the palmiers to check the bottom color.

Let the palmiers cool on the baking sheet for about 10 minutes, then transfer them to a rack. Let cool completely. Bake and cool the remaining palmiers the same way. Store the palmiers in an airtight container for up to 2 days.

White Chocolate Mousse

MAKES ABOUT 3 CUPS; SERVES 6

White chocolate is mostly sweet, but it has a nutty character, too. Make sure to use the highest-quality white chocolate you can find. This is a delicious showcase for smooth, rich cocoa butter and goes perfectly with bright summer berries.

Using a paring knife, cut the vanilla bean in half along its length. Use the knife to flatten the pod gently against the countertop, and then scrape out the seeds with the blade. In a small bowl, sprinkle the gelatin over the water and let bloom for about 10 minutes.

To prepare the custard base, in a small, heavy saucepan, combine the cream, vanilla seeds, scraped pod, and salt over medium heat. When the mixture comes to a boil, turn off the heat but leave the pan on the burner.

Place a fine-mesh strainer over a bowl. In a small bowl, whisk together the egg yolks and sugar until the yolks turn a shade paler, about 2 minutes. Ladle a large spoonful of the hot cream into the egg yolks and whisk thoroughly to temper the yolks before slowly adding the rest of the cream, whisking the whole time. Pour the egg and cream mixture back into the pan and set over low heat. As the mixture heats, stir with a rubber spatula, slowly running it over the bottom of the pan. When the mixture has thickened slightly and reached a temperature of 160°F (this happens quickly, as it's a small volume of custard), take the pan off the heat and pour the custard through the strainer into the bowl. Stir for a few minutes to cool. Add the bloomed gelatin to the hot custard and whisk until completely combined. Set aside to cool.

Melt the white chocolate in a double boiler. (A double boiler ensures that the chocolate will melt gently and evenly; if you heat the chocolate in a pan set directly on the stove top, it can burn and ruin the flavor of your mousse.) To make a double boiler, fill a saucepan with water to a depth of about 2 inches. Fit a metal or heatproof glass mixing bowl onto the rim of the pan, making sure it doesn't touch the water below. Bring the water to a simmer over medium heat. Add the chocolate to the bowl and stir as it melts, watching carefully and taking it off the heat as soon as it's almost completely melted, 5 or 6 minutes; the residual heat will do the rest. Pour the white chocolate into the custard base and whisk until smooth. Let the mixture cool, stirring it every 5 minutes or so, until it reaches a temperature of about 85°F, 15 to 20 minutes.

While the custard is cooling, whip the cream to a stage between soft peaks and stiff peaks. Add one-third of the whipped cream to the custard–white chocolate mixture and use a large rubber spatula or spoon to gently fold until uniform. Add the rest of the whipped cream and fold it in very carefully until just combined.

Transfer the mousse to six individual serving vessels such as little glasses or bowls. Cover and refrigerate until cold, at least 4 hours, or for up to 2 days before serving. Garnish with fresh berries and serve immediately.

1 vanilla bean

1 teaspoon powdered gelatin

2 tablespoons water

¾ cup heavy cream

½ teaspoon salt

4 egg yolks (see page 377)

3 tablespoons sugar

10 ounces white chocolate, chopped

2 cups heavy cream

Fresh berries, for garnish (optional)

Fresh Strawberry Soup with Roasted Rhubarb and White Chocolate Mousse

SERVES 8 TO 10

This is one of the more complex recipes in the book, as it involves a number of components, has several steps, and calls for advance planning. But it's a great way to see how recipes build off of one another: for example, the *palmiers* are necessary to keep the white chocolate mousse and strawberry soup from bleeding into each other. The finished dessert is one of the most beautiful and satisfying dishes in the book.

Use the juiciest, ripest locally grown strawberries you can find for this soup because it's really all about intense berry flavor. I like ending a meal with a dessert soup, as it is both simple and refined and a great, unexpected way to showcase seasonal fruit. This soup is perfect on one of the first warm days of early summer.

The sweetness of the strawberry soup is nicely balanced by the tartness of the rhubarb. Rhubarb can be stringy and cook down into mush, but cutting it into small pieces mitigates its fibrousness and roasting, rather than simmering, helps it keep its shape. The rhubarb's electric pink color is preserved by this cooking method, and if you have any leftover roasted rhubarb, it pairs well with the buckwheat crêpes on page 321.

MAKE THE STRAWBERRY SOUP In a small saucepan, combine the water, sugar, salt, orange zest strip, and lemon juice and bring to a boil, stirring to dissolve the sugar. Transfer the syrup to a heatproof bowl and let cool to room temperature. Meanwhile, remove the green tops from the strawberries with a knife.

Discard the orange zest from the syrup. Place the strawberries and the syrup in a food processor. Process for 10 seconds to chop the berries and mix them with the syrup, but not for so long that the strawberries start to create foam. You want a clear soup, not a frothy one.

Pour the mixture into a bowl, cover, and refrigerate for at least 1 hour or for up to 8 hours to allow the flavors to meld. Strain the soup through a cheesecloth-lined fine-mesh strainer into a bowl, pressing with the back of a ladle or spoon to extract some of the pulp from the strawberries. Cover and refrigerate until ready to serve.

MAKE THE ROASTED RHUBARB Preheat the oven to 325°F. Line a baking sheet with parchment paper.

Using a paring knife, cut the vanilla bean in half along its length. Use the knife to flatten the pod gently against the countertop, and then scrape out the seeds with the blade; discard the pod. Place the sugar in a large bowl and add the vanilla seeds. Using your fingers, rub the seeds into the sugar until evenly dispersed. Add the orange zest strips and salt and stir well. Add the rhubarb and toss until evenly coated.

Continued

STRAWBERRY SOUP

1 cup water

¾ cup sugar

⅛ teaspoon salt

1 orange zest strip (see page 375)

1 tablespoon lemon juice

4 pints strawberries

ROASTED RHUBARB

1 vanilla bean

1 cup sugar

3 orange zest strips (see page 375)

⅛ teaspoon salt

3½ cups diced rhubarb, in ½- to ¾-inch dice (from about 1 pound)

FOR ASSEMBLY

8 to 10 Orange Palmiers (page 305)

White Chocolate Mousse (page 306)

8 to 10 strawberries

Fresh Strawberry Soup with Roasted Rhubarb and White Chocolate Mousse

CONTINUED

Spread the rhubarb in an even layer on the prepared baking sheet and roast for 8 minutes. Stir the rhubarb and try a piece. It should still have a little bit of tooth to it but mainly be soft. It's better for the rhubarb to be a little underdone than a little overdone, as you want it to maintain its integrity and not fall apart. If necessary, bake for another 2 to 3 minutes. The sugar may not be fully dissolved yet, but the rhubarb will continue to soften a little and release some liquid that will dissolve the sugar, so don't worry. Remove from the oven and let the rhubarb cool on the baking sheet.

ASSEMBLE THE DISH Ladle about ½ cup of the chilled strawberry soup into each of six shallow bowls. Spoon about ¼ cup of roasted rhubarb in a small pile in the center of each bowl. Place a palmier on top of each pile of rhubarb, nestling it so that it sits flat above the surface of the soup. Spoon a dollop (or quenelle, see page 377) of the mousse on top of each palmier. Garnish with a fresh strawberry.

Apricot–Brown Butter Tart

SERVES 8

This tart is a Nancy Silverton creation that I first learned when I worked at a catering company in college. Nancy's food has so much integrity, and I've always respected the way she works. Even though baking requires more precision than a lot of savory cooking, her brain is just as capable of spontaneity as it is calculation, and her desserts really show that. She has an excellent understanding of flavor and of how things work together in the context of a dish.

This tart involves brown butter, which has an incredibly nutty quality I find hard to resist. The buttery, caramelly filling holds whatever fruit you like, and the tart is a good make-ahead option when you're asked to bring something for dessert. If you do make it ahead of time, store it at room temperature (when refrigerated, the fats get too cool and all of the beautiful flavors are muted).

You can use nearly any fruit in this dish: stone fruits or berries in the summer and frozen fruit in the winter. Or you could even eschew fruit entirely and just make a buttery tart with slivered almonds on top and serve it with whipped crème fraîche (page 354).

12 tablespoons butter, cut into 1-inch slices

1 vanilla bean

1¼ cups sugar

3 eggs, at room temperature

½ cup all-purpose flour (see page 376)

¼ teaspoon salt

2 cups sliced pitted apricots, in ¼-inch-thick slices

1 pâte sucrée pastry shell (page 358), prebaked

Vanilla bean whipped cream (page 355), for serving

Melt the butter in a 2-quart saucepan over medium heat. Meanwhile, place a small metal mixing bowl and whisk to the side. Using a paring knife, cut the vanilla bean in half along its length. Use the knife to flatten the pod gently against the countertop, and then scrape out the seeds with the blade. When the butter has melted and is actively beginning to bubble, add the vanilla seeds and the empty pod halves to the pan, and reduce the heat to medium-low. Whisk continuously until the milk solids at the bottom of the pan begin to brown, 8 to 10 minutes. You are making brown butter, not black butter, so be sure to watch very carefully once the butter turns a pale shade of brown, as it can turn black very quickly. Continue to whisk to ensure the solids don't burn on the bottom of the pan. As soon as the butter is a medium walnut shade, pour it into the mixing bowl. This is very important, because it stops the cooking process at exactly the right moment. Pull out the vanilla pod halves and set the brown butter aside.

In a separate mixing bowl, vigorously whisk together the sugar and eggs until the eggs turn a paler shade, about 3 minutes. Slowly whisk the warm (but not hot) brown butter into the sugar and egg mixture. If the butter is too hot and added too quickly, it can curdle the eggs, so make sure to pour it in slowly and whisk continuously. In a separate small mixing bowl, whisk together the flour and salt, then gently fold this mixture into the wet ingredients, being careful not to overmix.

Preheat the oven to 350°F. Arrange the apricot slices in a pattern on the bottom of the tart shell, spacing them about ½ inch apart. Pour just enough batter over the apricots to cover the fruit. Do not overfill the tart shell, as the filling rises during baking. If the filling rises above the edge of the tart shell, it can seep around the edges of the pan and cause sticking when you try to unmold the tart.

Continued

Apricot–Brown Butter Tart

CONTINUED

Place the tart shell on a baking sheet and bake for 30 to 35 minutes. Check for doneness by first gently pressing in the center of the tart. It's okay if it's quite soft, but it shouldn't be liquidy. Test next by slightly tipping the tart toward you. There should be no significant movement in the filling. If it is still sliding around a little, return the tart to the oven, bake for another 5 to 10 minutes, and check again. The tart is done when the sugary surface on top cracks slightly in a few places and the filling puffs up just a little in the center. The edges may be quite dark. (I've found that I prefer the taste of a slightly darker pastry, rather than one that hasn't baked quite long enough.) Allow the tart to cool for at least 1 hour before removing it from the tart mold.

To serve, slice the tart and top each piece with a dollop or quenelle (see page 377) of the vanilla bean whipped cream.

Bête Noire with Raspberry Sauce

SERVES 16

This cake is so rich that it's like taking a bath in a luxurious pool of chocolate. We serve it at brunch at Beast in tiny little squares, which is more than enough for most people. Since this dessert is so decadent, it's totally acceptable to skip the ganache and serve it with just a bit of whipped cream and raspberry sauce to achieve a sweet-tart balance.

The deliciousness of the cake is dictated by the quality of the chocolate, so buy the best possible, with a cacao content of around 65 percent.

I prefer to use a square pan for baking this dessert because it's easier to cut small squares out of it later. An 8-inch round cake pan will work as well, though the presentation will not be as elegant (cut the cake into wedges instead of squares).

MAKE THE CAKE Preheat the oven to 325°F. Brush an 8-inch square baking pan with 1 tablespoon of the butter and line the bottom with a piece of parchment paper cut to fit (do not skip this step, or removing the cake from the pan later will be difficult). Make a simple syrup by heating the water and sugar together in a small saucepan over medium heat, stirring occasionally, until the sugar dissolves, about 5 minutes. Set aside.

Fill a saucepan with water to a depth of about 2 inches. Fit a metal or heatproof glass mixing bowl onto the rim of the pan, making sure it doesn't touch the water below. Bring the water to a simmer over medium heat. Place the chocolate and the remaining 4 tablespoons of butter in the bowl and stir until melted and smooth, about 10 minutes. Remove the bowl from the heat and slowly add the warm simple syrup to the chocolate mixture, whisking constantly until combined.

In a separate bowl, whisk together the eggs and salt until evenly mixed, about 30 seconds. Add the eggs to the melted chocolate mixture and whisk until combined.

Pour the batter into the prepared pan and place the pan in a roasting pan. Add boiling water to the roasting pan to come halfway up the sides of the baking pan. This water bath ensures the cake will bake evenly, preventing the edges from overbaking before the center is done. Bake for 22 to 26 minutes, until a thermometer (see page 374) inserted into the center of the cake reads 160°F; the edges should be no hotter than 180°F. If you don't own a thermometer, keep in mind the cake will seem barely set and that it's better to remove it from the oven slightly underdone than risk overbaking, which will make the texture chalky. Because there's so much chocolate in the cake, it will firm up with cooling and cut like a dream.

MAKE THE RASPBERRY SAUCE While the cake is baking, in a small nonreactive saucepan, combine the raspberries, sugar, water, corn syrup, lemon juice, and salt. Bring to a simmer and cook, stirring occasionally, until the raspberries have broken down, about 2 minutes. Taste for sweetness and add up to 2 tablespoons sugar if necessary.

Continued

CAKE

5 tablespoons butter, softened

1 cup water

¾ cup sugar

18 ounces bittersweet chocolate, chopped

6 eggs

½ teaspoon salt

RASPBERRY SAUCE

4 cups fresh raspberries (about 15 ounces)

½ cup sugar

½ cup water

1 tablespoon light corn syrup

1 teaspoon lemon juice

¼ teaspoon salt

2 tablespoons cornstarch

2 tablespoons water

GANACHE

1 pound bittersweet chocolate, chopped

½ teaspoon salt

2 cups heavy cream

FOR ASSEMBLY

Vanilla bean whipped cream (page 355)

Fresh raspberries, for garnish

NOTE You can substitute frozen berries for the fresh raspberries in the sauce, but because of their higher water and lower pectin content, increase the amount of cornstarch by 1 tablespoon.

Bête Noire with Raspberry Sauce

CONTINUED

Mix together the cornstarch and water in a small bowl. Stir this slurry into the simmering raspberry mixture and cook for 1 minute. Pour the sauce through a fine-mesh strainer set over a bowl, pressing against the raspberries until all that's left in the strainer is their seeds; discard the seeds. Let the sauce cool, cover, and refrigerate until you're ready to serve.

When the cake has finished baking, allow it to cool for about 30 minutes in the water bath, and then carefully remove it and let it cool completely to room temperature. To make unmolding easier, refrigerate the cake, uncovered, for a few hours.

To unmold the cake, line a baking sheet with parchment paper, place a wire rack on top of the parchment, and quickly flip the cake pan over onto the rack. Most of the time it simply takes a firm tap to release the cake, but if it's being stubborn, slightly warming the bottom of the pan will help release it: on the stove top for a minute, briefly in a bath of hot water, or even with a handheld torch (see page 373) grazed across the bottom of the pan.

Bring about 4 cups of water to a boil and pour it into a heatproof pitcher or jar. Dip the blade of a sharp chef's knife into the hot water, wipe off the water, and cut the cake in half. Dip and wipe the blade again and cut the cake in half again, perpendicular to the first cut, to make quarters. Continue to dip and wipe the knife and cut the cake until you have 16 squares, each measuring about 2 inches. Carefully space the pieces about ½ inch apart on the rack.

MAKE THE GANACHE Place the chocolate in a mixing bowl and sprinkle over the salt. In a small saucepan over medium heat, warm the cream until small bubbles form at the edges, about 5 minutes. Do not let it come to a boil. Pour the cream over the chocolate and let sit undisturbed for 5 minutes to melt the chocolate. Stir the chocolate mixture with a spatula until completely shiny and smooth, about 2 minutes. Let cool slightly (ideally to around 85°F).

Put the ganache into a small pitcher or measuring cup and slowly pour it around the edges of each cake square. The top is usually easy to fill in, so concentrate on getting it evenly on the sides of the cake. Let the squares cool to room temperature before serving, about 2 hours. The ganache-coated cake squares can be refrigerated for up to 3 days but should be allowed to stand at room temperature for at least 1 hour before serving. The excess ganache that pours off the cake can be used to make truffles (chill the ganache for about 1 hour, roll it into balls, and then toss with cocoa powder), or added to hot milk for a killer hot chocolate. Because it is half cream, it should be stored in the fridge, where it will keep for about 1 week.

ASSEMBLE THE DISH For each serving, ladle 2 to 3 tablespoons of the raspberry sauce on a small plate. Place a piece of cake in the pool of raspberry sauce, top with a quenelle (see page 377) of the vanilla bean whipped cream, and garnish with a few raspberries. Serve immediately.

Buckwheat Crêpes with Sautéed Apples and Toffee Sauce

SERVES 8

In France, buckwheat crêpes are traditionally thought of as savory, but in this recipe, they skew slightly sweet. Buckwheat crêpes are one of those warm, comforting desserts that just feel right in the fall and winter, especially when paired with brown sugar and cinnamon-laced apples and ice cream.

The trick to making great crêpes is learning to pour and swirl the batter simultaneously. As soon as you pour the batter with one hand, start tilting the pan with the other so the batter coats the entire surface. Your first few crêpes may turn out thicker or more wrinkled than is ideal, but with practice, the motion will become natural. Use a lightweight pan, which will be easier to pick up and swirl the batter one-handed. There are also special crêpe pans that make the motion easier.

These crêpes are versatile. If you don't have time to make the apples, toffee sauce, and ice cream, you can still enjoy the crêpes with maple syrup, jam, or the sauce from Bête Noire with Raspberry Sauce (page 315).

The apples alone are a quick and fancy, no-baking-required dessert, perfect for when you're looking for something very satisfying but not too complicated. You can use any kind of apple, but I particularly like crisp varieties that hold their shape when cooked, like Jonathan, Jonagold, Braeburn, Winesap, Melrose, or Granny Smith.

MAKE THE CRÊPES Put the flours, salt, sugar, eggs, and milk into a blender and blend on high speed until combined, about 1 minute. With the machine running, slowly pour in the melted butter. For the best results, transfer the batter to an airtight container and allow it to rest in the refrigerator for 1½ to 2 hours before making the crêpes. This allows the flour to become fully hydrated and helps develop the flavor of the crêpes. Stir the batter well before cooking the crêpes.

Heat an 8-inch black steel or small crêpe pan over medium heat. Using a paper towel, wipe the pan with a tiny bit of the room-temperature butter, coating it evenly with a thin layer. Using a measuring cup or a small ladle, quickly pour a 2½-inch pool of batter in the pan with one hand and simultaneously swirl the pan with the other hand to cover the bottom with a very thin layer of batter. If the pan is hot enough, the batter will immediately bubble and turn brown and lacy at the edges. It's important for the pan to be hot, because if the batter cooks on the bottom right away, it will cling to the pan and allow you to swirl the rest around and completely coat the pan. If the pan isn't hot enough (or if it is coated with too much butter), the batter will melt and swirl around but won't cook quickly enough to form a thin crêpe. Having a thick crêpe is okay, but your technique should improve as you work through the batter.

Continued

CRÊPES

¾ cup all-purpose flour (see page 376)

½ cup buckwheat flour (see page 376)

1¼ teaspoons salt

3 tablespoons granulated sugar

5 eggs

2 cups whole milk

8 tablespoons butter, melted, plus 2 tablespoons butter, at room temperature

SPICE BLEND

1 tablespoon toasted and ground cinnamon (see page 378)

¼ teaspoon toasted and ground cloves (see page 378)

¼ teaspoon toasted and ground allspice (see page 378)

SPICED SUGAR

2 tablespoons dark brown sugar

2 tablespoons granulated sugar

¼ teaspoon salt

½ teaspoon lemon zest (see page 375)

1 teaspoon spice blend (recipe above)

SAUTÉED APPLES

3 apples (see recipe introduction)

4 tablespoons butter

3 tablespoons spiced sugar (recipe above)

TOFFEE SAUCE

5 tablespoons butter

½ vanilla bean, split lengthwise and seeds scraped, or ½ teaspoon vanilla extract

1 cup heavy cream

1 cup packed dark brown sugar

½ teaspoon flaky finishing salt

Continued

Buckwheat Crêpes with Sautéed Apples and Toffee Sauce

CONTINUED

When the surface of the crêpe starts to lose its shine and the edges turn brown and dry, use a fish spatula (see page 373) to flip the crêpe. Cook very briefly on the second side, about 10 seconds. Transfer the crêpe to a plate and repeat with the remaining batter, stacking the crêpes on top of each other; you should end up with 16 to 20 crêpes. Very lightly wipe the pan with more room-temperature butter between crêpes if they start sticking. The first crêpe usually looks less than presentable, but they will get better as you continue pouring, swirling, and flipping. The crêpes can be made up to 6 hours ahead of time and kept at room temperature, uncovered, on the plate.

MAKE THE SPICE BLEND Mix together all of the ingredients and set aside.

MAKE THE SPICED SUGAR Mix together all of the ingredients and set aside.

MAKE THE SAUTÉED APPLES Cut the apples into quarters, then notch out the core of each quarter. Cut each quarter into 4 or 5 wedges about ¼ inch thick.

Heat a large sauté pan over medium-high heat. (You may need to cook the apples in two batches to avoid crowding the apples or they won't caramelize correctly.) Add the butter, and when it melts, add the apples. Allow the slices to sear for a few seconds, and then stir so they're evenly coated with butter and starting to sizzle. Let cook, undisturbed, for about 3 minutes, until they begin to color slightly.

Sprinkle the spiced sugar over the apples and stir. Let the sugar bubble and caramelize. When the sugar looks melted and the apples appear slightly softened, after about 5 minutes, remove from the heat and spread out the apples on a plate. It's important to spread them in an even layer across a flat surface because they can overcook and lose their lovely caramelized edges if they are piled on top of one another.

MAKE THE TOFFEE SAUCE Melt the butter in a small saucepan over medium heat. Add the vanilla bean seeds and pod half (if using vanilla extract, you'll add it later), cream, brown sugar, and salt and bring to a boil, stirring to dissolve the sugar. Turn down the heat to a medium simmer and cook for 10 minutes, whisking occasionally. Remove the vanilla pod half and discard; remove the saucepan from the heat. If using vanilla extract, stir it in now.

ASSEMBLE THE DISH To serve, preheat the oven to 400°F. Line a baking sheet with parchment paper. Fold 16 crêpes into quarters, place them on the prepared baking sheet in a single layer, and brush generously and evenly with the melted butter. Bake for 2 or 3 minutes, until warmed through. Using a fine-mesh strainer, dust the confectioners' sugar onto the warm buttered crêpes. Squeeze the lemon wedges evenly across all of them. Spoon 2 to 3 tablespoons of toffee sauce on the bottom of each of 8 plates. Place 2 crêpes on top of the sauce on each plate, lay a few apple slices alongside, and add a scoop of malt ice cream.

FOR ASSEMBLY

4 tablespoons butter, melted

¼ cup confectioners' sugar

2 lemon wedges, seeded (see page 375)

Malt Ice Cream (page 299)

NOTE You will have some leftover spice blend, which can be used in a hot toddy or sprinkled over pies and other pastries.

Pistachio Meringue Cake with Fresh Citrus, Candied Kumquats, and Cardamom Caramel Sauce

MAKES 1 (1-POUND) LOAF; SERVES 8

This is an easy and versatile nutty cake that makes use of the egg whites you might have left over after making ice cream (see pages 296 and 299) or Hollandaise (page 32). Pistachios are delicious in this cake, but you could easily substitute hazelnuts or walnuts if that's what you have on hand. It's great with a variety of winter citrus, too. The combination of these flavors reminds me of something I'd eat in Sicily or North Africa.

The cake is topped with a basic salted caramel sauce flavored with cardamom that is designed to be pourable straight from the fridge. This makes it easy to stir it into coffee, pour over ice cream, or eat from a spoon. Simply omit the cardamom if you're looking for a basic salted-caramel sauce.

To get the most volume from your egg whites, be sure that the mixing bowl has no film of fat in it and that there are no bits of egg yolk in the whites (see page 378).

MAKE THE CANDIED KUMQUATS In a small saucepan, stir together the hot water, sugar, and salt. Place over medium-low heat and cook the syrup while you slice the kumquats about ⅛ inch thick. Discard the ends and the seeds, then add the kumquats to the syrup and bring to a bare simmer. Cook until the fruit is soft and translucent, 7 to 10 minutes. Remove from the heat and let the kumquats cool in their syrup. The kumquats can be stored in an airtight container in the refrigerator for up to 2 weeks.

MAKE THE CAKE Preheat the oven to 350°F. Brush an 8½ by 4½-inch loaf pan with the 1 tablespoon softened butter.

In a small saucepan over medium-low heat, melt the 10 tablespoons of butter. Stir in the rum and vanilla and set aside to cool.

Place 1 cup of the pistachios and ¾ cup of the sugar in a food processor and grind together until the pistachios are sandy, about 10 seconds. If there are too many big pieces of pistachio, they will deflate your cake, so grind for a few more seconds if necessary, but keep an eye on the nuts to ensure you don't overprocess them. They should look powdery, not like they are about to form a paste. Add the flour and process for about 2 seconds to combine. Set aside.

Spread the remaining ¼ cup pistachios on a small baking sheet and bake until lightly toasted, 3 to 4 minutes. Since pistachios already have a brown skin and crisp texture, it can be hard to tell when they're toasted. If you are not sure, allow them to cool and then taste one. You're looking for an only slightly toasted flavor and a remaining green interior. Roughly chop the pistachios and set aside.

In a stand mixer fitted with the whisk attachment, whisk the egg whites on medium speed for about 1½ minutes. They will be slightly foamy. Add the remaining ½ cup sugar and the salt and whip on medium speed for 1 minute. Use a rubber spatula to

Continued

CANDIED KUMQUATS

½ cup hot water

1 cup sugar

¼ teaspoon salt

10 medium or 15 small kumquats

CAKE

10 tablespoons butter, plus 1 tablespoon softened butter

1 tablespoon dark rum

1 teaspoon vanilla extract

1¼ cups raw, unsalted shelled pistachios

1¼ cups sugar

⅔ cup all-purpose flour (see page 376)

6 egg whites (see page 377)

½ teaspoon salt

CARDAMOM CARAMEL SAUCE

1 cup heavy cream

¼ teaspoon decorticated (outer green husk removed) cardamom seeds, toasted and ground (see page 378)

1 cup sugar

¼ cup hot water

¾ teaspoon flaky finishing salt

FOR ASSEMBLY

1 blood orange

1 navel orange

1 red grapefruit

Whipped crème fraîche (page 354)

Pistachio Meringue Cake with Fresh Citrus, Candied Kumquats, and Cardamom Caramel Sauce

CONTINUED

scrape the sugar from the sides of the bowl, then whip the egg whites on medium speed for 8 more minutes, until all of the granules of sugar and salt have dissolved and the egg whites are stiff and glossy.

Using a rubber spatula, fold one-third of the pistachio mixture into the egg whites. Repeat with the remaining pistachio mixture in two batches, folding just until combined. Add the melted butter–rum mixture and again fold just until combined.

Pour the batter into the prepared loaf pan. Bake for 30 to 40 minutes, until the cake pulls away slightly from the sides of the pan, feels springy to the touch, and a skewer inserted in the center comes out clean. Let the cake cool in the pan on a wire rack for 20 minutes. Turn it out onto the rack and let cool completely.

MAKE THE CARDAMOM CARAMEL SAUCE In a small saucepan, combine the cream and cardamom and bring to a simmer over medium heat. Turn off the heat and let steep on the burner while you cook the sugar.

Put the sugar, hot water, and salt in a heavy saucepan with a tight-fitting lid. Pour in both the water and the sugar carefully, keeping the sugar crystals from splashing around the sides of the pan. It may seem like you have very little in the bottom of the pan, but you want to have lots of room when you add the cream because the mixture will spit and bubble. Place the pan over low heat and stir the contents with a wooden spoon until the sugar is dissolved; try to dissolve the sugar before the mixture boils. Rinse your spoon well to remove any sugar crystals and don't stir the mixture again until you add the cream. If there are any unmelted crystals, they can cause the caramel sauce to crystallize instead of remaining smooth. Cover the pan, turn the heat to medium, and cook for 5 minutes to help create condensation to wash down sugar crystals from the sides of the pot. Uncover and continue to cook the sugar until it starts to take on some color. At first it will be just a little blond or caramel colored in certain spots. Keep cooking until the sugar starts to smoke a little and turns deep mahogany brown. Don't worry about the smoke and dark color; undercaramelization results in a flat, undeveloped taste. Remove the pan from the heat and pour in about ¼ cup of the hot cream, stirring with a long-handled wooden spoon. The caramel will bubble like crazy—don't get burned! Keep stirring and slowly add the remaining cream. Continue stirring after all of the cream has been added, until the bubbling has calmed down. Strain the caramel sauce through a fine-mesh strainer into a metal bowl, stirring occasionally as it cools. Taste for salt and adjust as necessary. The sauce will keep in an airtight container in the refrigerator for up to 1 week.

ASSEMBLE THE DISH Supreme the citrus fruits (see page 375). Place the citrus segments in a strainer set over a small bowl. Cut the cake into 1-inch slices. Pour a small pool of caramel sauce on each plate, place a slice of cake overlapping the sauce, and arrange a mixture of the citrus segments alongside. Top with a dollop of whipped cream, a few wheels of candied kumquats, and a sprinkling of toasted pistachios.

Almond and Armagnac Prune Puff Pastries

MAKES 3 (5-INCH) ROUND PASTRIES

This is a classic French pastry called a *pithivier*, which is named for its town of origin in France. It consists of two layers of puff pastry surrounding a sweet (but not *too* sweet) filling of almonds, eggs, and sugar. This particular version includes Armagnac-poached prunes in addition to the almond cream, which adds a little complexity and juiciness to the mix. It's a stunning but simple dessert that you can have waiting in the freezer for surprise guests, or make a week ahead for a complicated dinner party. And it's the perfect way to use puff pastry. It's like an elevated almond croissant and well worth the work.

Unwrap the puff pastry and allow it to warm on the countertop for 15 minutes before rolling. Very lightly dust your work surface with flour (but only if the dough seems a little damp from the fridge or from thawing). With a rolling pin, roll the puff pastry into a rectangle measuring 6 by 22 inches and ⅛ inch thick (the thickness of about two quarters). Cut out four or five 5-inch circles using a plate or plastic container as a guide: rest the plate on the dough and trace the shape with the tip of a sharp knife. Working quickly, while the pastry is still cool, press together the scraps and reroll them ⅛ inch thick. Cut another one or two 5-inch circles. If you have a circle without a matching top, just fill half of the circle and fold the other half over the filling to make a half-moon; this will be your tester.

Line 2 baking sheets with parchment paper. Divide the pastry circles between the prepared baking sheets, turning them upside down as you transfer them so the side that was facing up is now facing down. The dough has a tendency to shrink as it bakes; this helps even it out. Refrigerate the baking sheets while you make the fillings.

MAKE THE ALMOND CREAM In a small bowl, using a rubber spatula, mix together the butter, sugar, almond extract, and salt until smooth. Add the flours and cornstarch and mix well. Finally, add the egg white and mix until uniform. Set aside.

MAKE THE PRUNES Chop the prunes and place the pieces in a small bowl. Mix in the egg yolk and pepper and set aside.

MAKE THE EGG WASH In a small bowl, whisk together the egg and cream until well blended.

MAKE THE GLAZE In a small bowl, mix together the corn syrup and hot water until well combined. Set aside.

To assemble the pastries, remove the baking sheet with the greater number of pastry circles from the refrigerator. Mound the almond cream and the prune filling onto the center of the pastry circles, dividing the cream and filling evenly among the circles and leaving a 1-inch border around the edge of each circle. Using a pastry brush, paint the border with a little egg wash. Remove the second baking sheet from the

Continued

6 by 15-inch piece Puff Pastry (page 331)

ALMOND CREAM

3 tablespoons butter, at room temperature

⅓ cup sugar

⅛ teaspoon almond extract

⅛ teaspoon salt

6 tablespoons almond flour

1 teaspoon all-purpose flour

1 teaspoon cornstarch

1 egg white (see page 377)

PRUNES

10 Armagnac-poached prunes (page 369)

1 egg yolk

⅛ teaspoon freshly ground black pepper

EGG WASH

1 egg

1 tablespoon heavy cream

GLAZE

2 tablespoons light corn syrup

2 tablespoons hot water

Almond and Armagnac Prune Puff Pastries

CONTINUED

refrigerator and top the filled pastry circles with a second pastry circle. Center the second circle over each mound of filling and press gently from the center out to the edges, then press firmly at the edge to seal together the 2 circles of dough, leaving one area unsealed. Before sealing the last bit, remove all of the air from the pocket of filling: start at the 6 o'clock position on the circle, and using a thumb and forefinger on both sides of the pastry, press to close and seal repeatedly until you have nearly reached the noon position on the circle. Before you close the pastry entirely, press out any remaining air, then seal it shut. If you don't carefully remove all of the air, your pastries may burst during baking. They will still be delicious, just not as presentable. Refrigerate the filled pastries for 20 minutes.

Preheat the oven to 375°F. Remove the pastries from the refrigerator and, using a pastry brush, brush the tops with the egg wash. Using a sharp knife, gently score a design that looks like rays of sun radiating from a point at the perimeter of the circle. Don't worry too much about how deep the line is; as long as you can see a line where you cut, it will be visible in the baked pastry. (If you're not planning to bake these right away, wrap them well in plastic wrap and refrigerate for up to 1 day or freeze for up to 1 month; no need to thaw before baking.)

Bake for 15 minutes., until the pastries are puffed and beginning to brown. Remove the baking sheet from the oven and brush the top of the pastries with the glaze. This adds a little sweetness to the puff pastry and gives the pastries a beautiful burnished finish. Return the pastries to the oven, lower the temperature to 325°F, and bake for another 15 minutes. (If baking frozen pastries, bake for 20 minutes at 375°F, then lower the oven temperature to 325°F and bake for 20 minutes more.)

Remove the pastries from the oven and let cool slightly. Serve warm. (Rewarm room-temperature pastries in a 325°F oven for about 15 minutes before serving.)

How to Make a Cheese Plate

A lot of people, myself included, don't always want a sugary dessert at the end of a meal. This is when the cheese plate comes into play, and knowing how to compose one is a great skill to master. As a chef, I love a cheese plate because it gives me the opportunity to showcase real artisans—cheese makers who dedicate their life to their craft and deserve to be celebrated. All I have to do is make the accompaniments (crackers, poached fruits, and so on), and suddenly I have a beautifully composed dish.

The first step in building a cheese plate is to find a cheesemonger whom you respect and trust. These people are professionals who do the curating for you, offering only correctly ripened cheese. They can talk you through the various types of cheese and will often let you taste as you go. It's worth it to spend money on good-quality cheese: buy the best in class of each type, as it almost always pays off in terms of taste. And don't limit yourself to just one region. A lot of domestic cheese makers are turning out products that rival the old European standbys, so ask your cheesemonger what he or she likes from your area as well.

Buy your cheeses no more than a few days in advance of serving so they don't overripen, and store them in cheese paper, not plastic. Plan on serving 3 to 4 ounces of cheese per person. Most cheeses should be served at room temperature, which means pulling them out of the fridge several hours before serving. Cold fat doesn't taste like much; the flavor comes when the cheese warms up a bit. An exception to the rule is if the cheese is very ripe and already soft in its cold state (as sometimes happens with rich washed-rind cheeses). In that case, pull it out of the refrigerator about a half hour before serving.

There are lots of options when it comes to plating. I like to limit my compositions to three or four cheeses that span a variety of types (cow's, sheep's, and goat's milk), flavors, and textures. Variety beyond that can get confusing for the palate. To please as many people as possible, I like to have at least one cheese that's relatively mellow, like a clothbound Cheddar. From there, I mix it up a bit. It's helpful to arrange the cheeses in order of flavor intensity, and then tell your guests which one to start with so they don't blow out their palates with a strong cheese with the first bite.

Beyond the cheese itself, there are a few elements to consider: you'll want vehicles for the cheese, like a few kinds of crackers (pages 365–367), which can be made several days ahead of time. Candied nuts (page 351) provide textural contrast, and poached fruits, like the Champagne-poached apricots on page 368 and the Armagnac-poached prunes on page 369, are nice, especially when contrasted against heady blue cheeses. The sweetness from fruit and honey (buy local honey; it's a great expression of *terroir* that changes throughout the season) can also help a cheese plate feel more like a traditional dessert course if you or your guests might crave something sweet.

Puff Pastry

MAKES 1 (12 BY 15-INCH) PIECE

Puff pastry is easy to come by in the freezer section of the grocery store, but making your own is infinitely better. The process is admittedly a bit time-consuming, but it's a great skill to learn, and having homemade puff pastry in the freezer makes it easy to create a beautiful dessert or appetizer in a pinch.

This recipe is a slightly modified version of the puff pastry in Madeleine Kamman's *The New Making of a Cook*, which was hugely influential when I started cooking professionally. Her book is ideal for home cooks looking to cross over into restaurant-style cooking, as she goes into detail on complicated French techniques like this one and helps demystify the whole process.

Puff pastry has two main parts: a dough layer (*détrempe*) and a butter layer. Laminating the dough means wrapping the *détrempe* around the butter, folding, and rolling it several times. As the dough bakes, the water in the dough evaporates, creating steam, which puffs into dozens of flaky pastry layers. It's not worth your time to make only a small amount of puff pastry, and because it freezes so well, there's no reason not to make a full sheet (or even two) to have on hand all the time.

MAKE THE DOUGH Remove the butter from the refrigerator and slice each stick in half lengthwise; let the pieces sit on the countertop while you prep the other ingredients. Mixing the détrempe should take only about 10 minutes, and your butter shouldn't need to warm any longer than that.

In a mixing bowl, combine the flours and place in the freezer. Combine the water, vinegar, and salt in a small bowl or measuring cup and stir until the salt is dissolved.

Remove the flour from the freezer and make a well in the center. Pour the water mixture into the well and use your fingers like a fork, stationary and slightly separated, to stir the liquid in the center. This motion will gradually pull in some of the flour from the edges as you stir. When some of the flour has fallen into the liquid and the water has taken on the texture of a beaten egg, start to actively mix in the rest of the flour by gradually pulling in a little bit of flour at a time. A dough will begin to form. Don't mash the dough against the side of the bowl or knead it in any way. Just stir it gently and fluff it around until the liquid is *almost* fully, but not completely, incorporated. If the dough is really smooth at this point, you've probably overmixed. The idea is to mix the dough without developing any gluten, the protein that forms when the water and flour mix. This will make the dough easier to roll out and will ensure that the layers in the pastry are distinct and delicate. (While gluten gives structure to baked goods like bread, excess gluten makes tender, flaky pastries like this one leaden and tough.)

Continued

DOUGH

16 tablespoons cold butter

⅔ cup pastry flour (see page 376)

1⅓ cups all-purpose flour (see page 376)

½ cup cold water

½ teaspoon white vinegar

1 teaspoon salt

EGG WASH

1 egg

1 tablespoon heavy cream

Puff Pastry

CONTINUED

The dough will not look too appealing at this point. It should be craggy and dry, with some stringy bits. That's a good thing. Just press it into a disk and don't worry. During resting, the dough will hydrate and become more manageable. If you're left with a lot of flour that's still dry after gathering it into a disk, sprinkle in a teaspoon of water, and press it all together.

Using a sharp knife, cut an X about 1 inch deep into the surface of the détrempe (figure 1). This will help prevent shrinkage, and it will make it easier to roll the dough into a square later. Put the disk back in the bowl and refrigerate it, uncovered, for 30 minutes.

Place a 12 by 18-inch piece of parchment paper or plastic wrap on the countertop and arrange three butter rectangles side by side, touching one another, on top of the parchment. Place the fourth rectangle across the top, perpendicular to the other rectangles. The butter arrangement will be about 4½ inches long and 3 inches wide. Lay a piece of parchment on top of the butter, then bang it with a rolling pin (this allows you to soften the butter without warming it too much), with the rolling pin mirroring the direction of the fourth rectangle of butter so the butter spreads into a 5-inch square. If the shape starts looking crazy, cut off an edge, put the cut piece in the center, and pound it out again. The butter doesn't need perfectly straight edges and corners, but it should still resemble a square. Wrap the parchment around the butter and refrigerate for 30 minutes.

Remove the détrempe and the butter from the refrigerator. You should be able to bend the butter without breaking it (figure 2), and it should be cold but still pliable; bendable but not greasy is the ideal. This is important to remember, as the butter should always have this texture when you're rolling it so it spreads easily and evenly between the layers of dough.

Lightly flour the countertop and set the détrempe on top. Using the rolling pin, roll the détrempe into a 7-inch square. The easiest way to do this without overworking the dough is to roll with one motion from the center of the X. Using the X as a guide, roll the dough out from the center to all four corners, creating a square. Ideally, that's all the rolling you'll need to do, but you can even out the square if need be, rolling from the center out. Don't worry if the shape isn't perfectly even and if the détrempe still looks dry and craggy in areas.

Unwrap the butter and place it in the center of the détrempe square, angled so the corners of the butter square are offset with the corners of the dough—like a square in a diamond (figure 3). Encase the butter in the dough by pulling the corners of the dough up and meeting them in the middle of the butter square (figure 4). Pinch the edges of the dough together to form a square envelope around the butter, carefully creating a seal without trapping in any air (figure 5).

Continued

Puff Pastry

CONTINUED

The next step is the lamination: rolling and folding to create layers of dough and layers of butter. This is what creates the flakiness of puff pastry. Each time the dough is rolled out into a long rectangle and folded like a business letter is called a turn. Generally you will give the dough two turns before wrapping and resting it in the refrigerator. For classic puff pastry, in total, the dough is rolled out and folded six times. The goal is to stretch the dough at the same rate as the butter extends. Temperature is a critical element here. The butter has to be cold enough so that it won't just smoosh yet warm enough so that it doesn't crack. If at any point you start to roll out the dough and it seems as though the butter is cracking and resisting too much, leave it to warm at room temperature for 5 minutes and try again.

Roll in one direction from the center out and try to extend the dough in only one direction. Your goal is a rectangle about 6 inches wide and no less than ½ inch thick (figure 6).

Fold the rectangle in thirds, like a letter (figure 7). This is your first turn. The dough will look like a book (figure 8)—with a spine (the folded edge) on one side and the open edge on the other. Now rotate the "book" so the spine is facing your body, parallel to the countertop's edge (figure 9). Tap gently with the rolling pin to seal the dough as needed. Roll the dough out again to a rectangle about 6 inches long and ½ inch thick. Fold the rectangle in thirds again. Make indentations in the dough with two fingers (figure 10) to indicate that you've given the dough two turns. If any butter is peeking out, sprinkle it with flour.

Wrap the folded dough in plastic wrap and refrigerate for 1 hour. It's okay to refrigerate it for up to 2 hours, just let it soften slightly on the countertop before rolling it out again.

Give the dough two more turns, as above: Start with the spine of the "book" facing your body (figure 9). Roll it out to a rectangle, then fold it in thirds. Turn the "book," roll it out, and fold it in thirds. Now mark the dough with four indentions to indicate you've given it four turns. Wrap it in plastic wrap and refrigerate for 30 minutes.

Give the dough two more turns, as above. You're creating beautiful layers of flaky pastry each time you roll and fold (figure 11).

The dough will need a long rest before you roll it out for use to ensure that it is as relaxed as possible, as it must be rolled out to a thin layer. If possible, refrigerate it for up to 24 hours. If you want to get it done on the same day, chill for a minimum of 2 hours.

When you're ready to roll out the dough for use, remove it from the refrigerator, unwrap it, and let it warm on the countertop for about 15 minutes. Lightly flour the countertop and roll out the dough into a rectangle measuring about 12 by 15 inches (figure 12). If you start to roll and the dough seems too cold or the butter is cracking, stop and let it warm at room temperature for another 5 minutes, then try again. The thicker the dough, the more dramatic the puff, and the longer it will take to bake to the middle. Generally, you want your dough to be ¼ to ⅓ inch thick, or the thickness of four or five stacked quarters. Place the rolled dough on a parchment paper–lined baking sheet and wrap it tightly with plastic wrap. Refrigerate the dough for at least 20 minutes so it is cold when you cut it.

The dough can be used immediately; if you're making a recipe in this book that calls for puff pastry, refer to the recipe for the dimension of the piece you'll need.

If you're going to freeze the dough for future use, do so now, either slicing the dough into smaller pieces or freezing it in a single big sheet. Place the dough on a parchment paper–lined baking sheet, cover the baking sheet with plastic wrap, and chill until the dough is frozen through. Unwrap the baking sheet, then wrap the dough well in plastic wrap, put it in a resealable plastic freezer bag, and return the frozen dough to the freezer. If you're freezing multiple pieces, place parchment paper between them so they are easy to pull out one at a time.

To bake plain puff squares, as pictured on page 330, cut the dough into 2½-inch squares and place them on a parchment paper–lined baking sheet. Turn the dough over so the top is on the bottom. Sometimes the top layer of puff pastry will shrink more than the bottom layers and this flip helps even that out. Chill the dough in the freezer until firm before baking, about 15 minutes. Preheat the oven to 400°F.

MAKE THE EGG WASH In a small bowl, whisk together the egg and cream until well blended. Using a pastry brush, brush the tops of the puff pastry.

Remove the dough from the freezer and bake for 7 minutes, then lower the temperature to 350°F and bake for another 10 to 20 minutes, depending on the size and shape of the pastry. It will look done in the first 10 minutes, but it's important to keep baking so the interior layers are cooked, too. Poke it at the seams, where the layers of pastry are puffing, to see if it's still a little soft. If it is, bake for another 5 minutes or more. It's much better for it to be a little overbaked than underbaked. (If baking frozen puff pastry, brush the frozen sheet with egg wash and add 4 to 5 minutes to each stage of baking.)

Serve immediately with fresh jam or whipped crème fraîche.

Parmesan Straws

MAKES ABOUT 24 STRAWS

My southern grandmother always had a pantry full of cheese-flavored crackers and biscuits and a freezer stocked with rich, doughy little appetizers that she could reheat at a moment's notice. This recipe is my homage to her and is one of the few instances when I feel like my southern roots cross with my French-influenced cooking. These straws have the same flavors as my grandmother's: they are crunchy, crispy, buttery snacks. But the puff pastry makes them more refined. They're tasty on their own, as an accompaniment to soup (like the Smoky Tomato Velouté on page 97), or as a garnish on a salad. Use the puff pastry recipe on page 331 (make the whole recipe, and save half of it in the freezer for another use).

1 (6 by 5-inch) piece Puff Pastry (page 331), chilled

¼ cup ground Parmigiano-Reggiano cheese, grated on a large-holed Microplane grater (see page 374)

1 teaspoon thyme leaves

¼ teaspoon flaky finishing salt

¼ teaspoon freshly ground black pepper

¼ teaspoon Espelette pepper (optional, but delicious)

1 egg

1 tablespoon heavy cream

Preheat the oven to 350°F. Line a baking sheet with parchment paper.

Cut the cold puff pastry into strips ½ inch wide and 4 to 5 inches long. (Work with the shape of the dough you have so there's not much waste.) Twist the puff pastry strips three or four times to create a swizzle. This will also help prevent the pastry from overpuffing. Arrange the pastry twists on the prepared baking sheet and let them rest in the freezer while you prepare the topping.

Put the Parmigiano-Reggiano, thyme, salt, black pepper, and Espelette pepper in a wide, shallow bowl. In a small bowl, whisk together the egg and cream until well blended to create an egg wash. Use a pastry brush to brush a light layer of egg wash on the pastry twists. Turn the pastry twists over and brush the second sides. One at a time, dip the twists in the cheese mixture and roll them around to coat evenly. Place the twists back on the baking sheet. Freeze the pastry twists until firm, about 15 minutes.

Bake for 10 minutes, until the twists are rich golden brown; bake for another 3 to 4 minutes, if necessary. Let the straws cool on the baking sheet on a wire rack until the cheese is set, 5 to 10 minutes. The straws can be eaten warm or at room temperature. Store leftovers in an airtight container at room temperature for up to 1 day.

Pantry

Consider these recipes your secret weapons in the kitchen. Not all of them are necessary to complete the dishes that call for them, but they add a serious punch of flavor and texture. The recipes here are all easy to make, and even though many yield more than what you'll actually end up using, once you have these items available, you'll find yourself constantly reaching for them. Many keep well and can be used across a variety of recipes. For example, throw some pickled mustard seeds into the pan the next time you're making chutney, or add poached fruit to a cheese plate. I like to have at least half of the items here on hand at all times.

Three recipes in this chapter—herb salad, fried shallots, and fried garlic chips—are garnishes. These are my personal T.O.E.s, or "touches of elegance," as my former cook Mira used to say. When you have a finished dish that looks like a 10, but you want to turn it up to 11, add a T.O.E.—that final touch that shows you really took the time to make the plate perfect. I use the herb salad for color and acid almost every time I finish a plate, and the fried shallots and garlic are great for anything that needs a layer of umami, salt, and crunch.

Blue Cheese Butter

MAKES ABOUT ½ CUP

This basic technique for whipping butter with salt and pepper works well with a variety of additions, from the blue cheese used here to chopped herbs (use ¼ cup) or sautéed mushrooms that have been squeezed of their liquid (use ¼ cup). Be sure to use the highest-quality butter you can find and a very dry and crumbly blue cheese. A wet, creamy cheese will emulsify into the butter and turn it an unappealing gray color. Use this compound butter on everything from steak to toast.

> 4 tablespoons butter, at room temperature
> ⅛ teaspoon salt
> ⅛ teaspoon freshly ground black pepper
> 1¾ ounces dry blue cheese, crumbled

Make sure the butter is very soft yet not at all melted. In a small bowl with a wooden spoon, beat the butter, salt, and pepper until fluffy, about 1 minute. Add the blue cheese and stir briefly to combine. The butter should have a slightly irregular consistency, with crumbles of blue cheese scattered throughout.

Lay an 18-inch piece of plastic wrap on the countertop. Spoon the soft butter onto the center of the plastic wrap in a cylindrical log shape about 6 inches long by 2 inches wide. Fold the edge of the plastic wrap that's closest to you over the top of the butter and smooth the log into an even shape with your hands. Make sure the plastic wrap isn't tucked into the log itself or it will create a crease in the butter when chilled. Wrap the log fully in the plastic wrap and twist the ends to form a tight log. Refrigerate until solidified, about 2 hours.

Let the butter stand at room temperature for about 30 minutes, then unwrap and cut into slices. Let the slices soften at room temperature for 20 to 30 minutes before serving. Store any leftover butter tightly wrapped in plastic and sealed in a resealable plastic bag. It will keep for up to 1 week in the refrigerator and up to 1 month in the freezer.

Lemon Confit

MAKES ABOUT ½ CUP

This is an ingredient I like to have around for adding an unexpected pop of flavor to many dishes. I use it anywhere you might use preserved lemon, such as in Parsley Sauce Verte (page 5) or mixed into the crème fraîche that complements the cabbage velouté on page 101. I also add the oil to salad dressings and long-cooked vegetables (like the green beans on page 156). This is probably my number one go-to condiment in the Pantry section. You will need to plan ahead, however, as the recipe takes 24 hours to complete.

> Rinds of 3 lemons (see page 375)
> ¼ teaspoons fennel pollen
> 2 teaspoons sugar
> 1½ teaspoons salt
> 2 cups extra-virgin olive oil
> 2 or 3 cloves garlic

Cut away most of the spongy white pith of the rinds, leaving only the yellow peel and about ¹⁄₁₆ inch (about the thickness of a quarter) of the pith. Cut the trimmed rinds into strips about ⅛ inch wide and 1 inch long (see the photo, right).

Place the lemon strips in a 2-quart saucepan and add the fennel pollen, sugar, salt, oil, and garlic. Place over low heat and slowly bring to a very gentle simmer, with tiny bubbles no bigger than those in Champagne, stirring frequently to ensure the sugar and salt dissolve. Once the mixture begins to gently bubble, keep a close eye on the saucepan, ensuring the heat is as low as possible. I use a diffuser (see page 373) to keep the heat low enough; if the heat gets too high, the lemon rind will fry and become tough rather than soft. Simmer for about 20 minutes, until a piece of lemon removed from the oil is tender all the way through.

Remove the pan from the heat and set aside, covered, at room temperature to allow the flavors marry overnight. Store in an airtight container in the refrigerator for up to 3 months.

Garlic Paste

MAKES 1 TEASPOON

I make this paste when I want to impart a strong, even garlic flavor to a dish but don't want it to taste too hot. Working salt into the garlic with a knife helps mellow its bite and distributes its flavor evenly.

Never buy peeled garlic unless you are slicing the cloves for fried garlic chips (page 353). Prepared garlic has a rancid, extremely off-putting flavor, and once you get used to the real thing, you won't mind the labor of peeling a few glorious cloves. The quantities here can be easily doubled.

1 large clove garlic

¼ teaspoon salt

On a cutting board reserved for savory foods (see page 373), crush the garlic by carefully holding the blade of a chef's knife flat against the garlic and smashing down on the blade with the soft side of a closed fist. Roughly chop the garlic and sprinkle the salt on top. Run the flat side of the knife blade back and forth over the garlic, applying pressure with your other hand and flipping the knife over with each pass, to massage the salt into the garlic and make a fine paste.

The paste will keep, covered in olive oil, in an airtight container for up to 3 days in the refrigerator.

Herb Oil

MAKES ABOUT 1 CUP

This is a flavorful, brightly colored oil that can be used
to make beautiful designs on top of soups or sauces. It's
elegant and gives a much-needed pop of color when you
don't want to use a textural element like the herb salad on
page 353. For example, you can float a few drops of it on top
of a rich sauce, like the Demi-Glace Cream (page 39), for a
stunning presentation. Herb oil is easiest to dispense from
a fine-tipped plastic squeeze bottle. You can substitute other
herbs, too.

> 4 cups water
>
> 8 cups ice
>
> 1 cup roughly chopped chives
>
> 1 cup loosely packed flat-leaf parsley leaves
>
> 1 cup neutral oil (such as grapeseed or canola)

To prepare an ice bath, in a mixing bowl, combine the water
and ice. Set a small mixing bowl on top of the ice and water.

Put the chives and parsley into a blender, pour in the oil, and
blend on the highest speed for 2 minutes.

While the herbs and oil are blending, place a large nonreactive
sauté pan over medium-high heat and heat for 1 to 2 minutes.
The pan is ready when a drop of water flicked onto the surface
evaporates immediately on contact. Turn the heat to medium
and carefully pour in the herb oil. Whisk vigorously for
about 15 seconds, and then immediately pour the oil into the
small bowl on top of the ice bath. Stir with a spatula until the
mixture is cool to the touch, about 20 seconds.

Line a fine-mesh strainer with a doubled piece of cheesecloth.
Pour the herb oil through the strainer, and then transfer to
a squeeze bottle. The oil will keep in the refrigerator for up
to 1 week or in the freezer for up to 3 months. Defrost for
2 to 3 hours at room temperature before using.

Homemade Stock

MAKES 5 TO 6 QUARTS

Learning to make stock is a fundamental kitchen skill that will enhance your cooking. It is time-consuming, but much of that time is passive, and this recipe will make enough stock for you to use some now and freeze some for later. I highly recommend making a batch of stock once a month.

To make stock, you slowly cook bones in the oven overnight, which extracts the most flavor and saves room on the stove top for other recipes. Feel free to use a different mixture of bones than what's listed below. I tend to avoid pork bones for stock because they're so gelatinous they can lead to a sticky final result if the plan is to reduce it later. I also avoid using many green vegetables and herbs because I find they impart an off-putting, overly herbaceous note. The final liquid should taste very savory, clean, and balanced; once strained, you may end up sprinkling in some quality salt and sipping it straight.

    8 pounds duck or chicken bones

    5 pounds veal or young beef shank bones
    (a combination of knuckle bones and marrowbones)

    2 pounds oxtails or cross-cut beef shanks
    (with lots of meat)

    4 yellow onions, halved but not peeled

    4 carrots, peeled and cut into 4-inch pieces

    3 celery stalks, cut into 4-inch pieces

    4 fresh or 8 dried bay leaves

    1 head garlic, halved crosswise

    1 tablespoon black peppercorns, toasted (see page 378)

    2 thyme sprigs

Preheat the oven to 450°F. Using your largest roasting pans, arrange the bones in the pans in a single, closely packed layer. Chicken and duck bones roast much faster than veal and beef bones, so keep them in separate pans, making it easy to remove them from the oven first. Roast the bones until deep, mahogany brown—past the point of golden—and the pan itself has accumulated dark brown, almost burnt-looking, bits of caramelized fat and proteins. Underroasting the bones will result in an unpleasant boney flavor, rather than a rich, deeply delicious flavor. You may have to roast the bones in batches, depending on the size of your oven. The roasting time is largely dependent on your oven. The quality of your stock depends on the quality of the bones and the degree to which you roast them. It may take as long as 2 hours, depending on how many bones you can fit without overcrowding them. Check them every 20 to 30 minutes and turn them occasionally to ensure they roast evenly. (This is a mostly passive activity.) Be careful to not over-roast the bones. If you have hot spots in your oven, be sure to move the bones around occasionally.

About 30 minutes after the chicken bones begin roasting, carefully pour off the liquid from the pan to keep the bones from steaming. I keep a ceramic bowl to the side of my oven for this purpose.

Once all of the bones are roasted, transfer them to a 6-inch-deep, restaurant-quality hotel pan (see page 373) and turn the oven temperature to 250°F. Pour off any liquid remaining in the roasting pans, place the pans on the stove top over medium-low heat, and add about 2 cups water to each pan. Using a wooden spatula, carefully scrape up the dark brown bits from the bottom of the pans, creating a murky, watery gravy. Add this liquid to the hotel pan with the roasted bones. (If the bits on the pan are black and charred, skip this step, as they will give your stock a bitter finish.)

Add the onions, carrots, celery, bay leaves, garlic, peppercorns, and thyme to the pan with the bones, and then pour in water to come within about 1½ inches of the rim. Cover the pan with parchment paper, and then with aluminum foil and place the pan in the oven. Cook for at least 12 hours or for up to overnight if you choose. I always leave the bones in the oven overnight.

Remove the pan from the oven, and then remove the bones and vegetables from the pan with tongs. Discard the bones and vegetables. Strain the liquid through a fine-mesh strainer into two large pots. Place the pots over high heat and bring the stock to a gentle bubbling simmer. Adjust the heat to maintain a gentle simmer and let the stock in each pot reduce by half, about 1½ hours. Skim off any impurities (protein "foam" and fat) as needed every 20 to 30 minutes, and be sure the liquid is gently moving at all times. You should end up with a total of 5 to 6 quarts of highly concentrated stock.

At this point, the stock will be rich and flavorful and cloudy with proteins. Do not season it with salt or other flavoring agents (unless you want to drink it as is); the seasoning will happen in whatever recipe calls for the stock. Pour the stock into airtight containers and refrigerate or freeze until ready to use. It will keep for up to 1 week in the refrigerator or for up to 3 months in the freezer.

NOTE After refrigerating, it's easier to skim off foam and fat. Simply lift off any fat that has come to the surface and discard.

NOTE If you have saved bones in the freezer to make stock, be sure to use them quickly once defrosted. Bones have a short shelf life as compared to meat, and any degradation of quality will come through in the flavor of the stock. If the defrosted bones have a strong smell, discard them.

Quick Pickles

MAKES ABOUT 2½ CUPS

This is Beast chef de cuisine Jake Stevens's pickle recipe. He likes to pickle zucchini, though I am personally partial to chard stems because they're so brightly colored (especially if you pickle each color individually). I like to serve these sweet pickles with Fried Pork Rillettes (page 70), any charcuterie, or a cheese plate. You can also chop them up and use them as a topping for sandwiches, similar to a sweeter version of *giardiniera*, a pickled vegetable relish. For an equally delicious, more savory pickle, also try the variation below.

VEGETABLES

4 cups sliced vegetables (such as zucchini, carrots, asparagus, chard stems, or pickling cucumbers), in slices about ¼ inch thick (about 1 pound)

½ yellow onion, sliced ¼ inch thick

2 tablespoons salt

BRINE

1 teaspoon brown mustard seeds

½ teaspoon celery seeds

½ teaspoon red chile flakes

½ cinnamon stick

6 allspice berries

6 cloves

1 cup distilled white wine vinegar

1 cup cider vinegar

1½ cups water

1 cup sugar

2 cloves garlic, smashed with the flat side of a knife

½ teaspoon ground turmeric

½ teaspoon Colman's dry mustard

MAKE THE VEGETABLES Combine the vegetables, onion, and salt in a bowl and mix well. Cover and refrigerate for 4 hours.

MAKE THE BRINE In a small nonreactive sauté pan over medium heat, lightly toast (see page 378) the mustard seeds, celery seeds, chile flakes, cinnamon, allspice, and cloves until fragrant, 30 to 60 seconds. Remove from the heat. In a small saucepan, combine the vinegars, water, sugar, garlic, turmeric, dry mustard, and toasted spices and bring to a boil, stirring to dissolve the sugar, then turn off the heat.

Remove the vegetables from the refrigerator. Fill a bowl with cold water. Add the salted vegetables to the bowl and swish them around to wash well, then drain and wash a second time.

Reheat the brine to a boil. Add a couple of vegetable slices and simmer for 20 to 30 seconds. Taste for salt. If needed, add up to 2 teaspoons more salt. (Different vegetables require different amounts of salt, so sometimes you may not need to add any salt to the brine.) After you have determined the correct saltiness for the brine and you are happy with your test pickles, add one-fourth of the rinsed vegetables to the brine. Bring the liquid back to a boil and then, using a slotted spoon, transfer the vegetables to a container with a tight-fitting lid. Repeat with the remaining vegetables in three batches, bringing the brine to a boil after each addition. When the last batch is added to the container, pour the brine over the vegetables in the container. Let cool for 2 hours, then cover and refrigerate. The pickles will keep in the fridge for up to 1 month.

VARIATION For quick pickles that are more savory than sweet, combine 3 tablespoons toasted coriander seeds (see page 378), 2 tablespoons toasted yellow mustard seeds, 1 cup distilled white vinegar, 1 cup cider vinegar, 1 cup water, and 8 smashed cloves of garlic in a small saucepan. Bring to a boil, and then turn off the heat. Add 1 cup roughly chopped dill to the brine. Proceed as directed to pickle the vegetables.

Half-Dried Tomatoes

MAKES ABOUT 1 CUP

These bright, acidic cherry tomatoes add a burst of color and flavor to everything from scrambled eggs to Crème Fraîche Tarts (page 48) or Seared Sea Scallops (page 217).

- 2 pints cherry tomatoes
- 2 tablespoons extra-virgin olive oil
- ½ teaspoon salt
- ½ teaspoon freshly ground black pepper
- 1½ teaspoons finely minced summer savory or thyme

Preheat the oven to 300°F. Cut the tomatoes in half crosswise. Place the tomatoes, cut side up, on a parchment paper–lined baking sheet. Drizzle with the oil and sprinkle with the salt, pepper, and savory. Roast for 45 minutes to 1 hour, until the tomatoes are beginning to color on their edges and have lost about half of their moisture. The tomatoes will keep, covered with plastic wrap at room temperature, for up to 1 day.

Pickled Mustard Seeds

MAKES ABOUT 1 CUP

This recipe makes a fairly large batch, but the seeds will last a long time in the refrigerator. Use them for any kind of relish (feel free to substitute them for dried mustard seeds in Savory Tomato Confiture on page 11), throw a few spoonfuls into roasted vegetables, or add them to Hollandaise (page 32).

- ¾ cup sugar
- 2½ teaspoons salt
- ½ cup water
- ¾ cup white wine vinegar
- ¼ cup yellow mustard seeds
- ¼ cup brown mustard seeds
- 1 clove garlic

In a small saucepan over high heat, combine all of the ingredients and bring to a boil over high heat, stirring to dissolve the sugar. Lower the heat and simmer, stirring occasionally, for 25 to 35 minutes, until the mixture has thickened to the consistency of syrup (but is not as thick as honey). Let cool, transfer to a nonreactive airtight container, and refrigerate for up to 1 month.

Candied Nuts

MAKES 3 CUPS

This recipe might make more nuts than you need for use in a recipe, but they are wholly addictive as a snack, so I doubt you'll have trouble finding a use for them. Boiling the nuts in simple syrup creates a texturally rewarding nut, one that's glassy and very crunchy but not cloying because some of the sugar gets absorbed into the nut, rather than just sitting on top of it.

This technique works for just about any type of nut, but keep a close eye on the nuts as they cook, stirring frequently and checking often for doneness, as different nuts cook at different rates. For this reason I recommend cooking different types of nuts separately.

3 cups water

3 cups sugar

3 tablespoons salt

2 cups (about 8 ounces) walnuts, hazelnuts, or pecans

3 tablespoons extra-virgin olive oil

½ teaspoon flaky finishing salt

In a 4-quart saucepan, combine the water, sugar, and salt and bring to a boil over medium-high heat, stirring to dissolve the sugar. Add the nuts and return the mixture to a boil, stirring constantly. When the nuts are boiling, turn down the heat to very low and cover the pan. Allow the nuts to simmer gently on the lowest heat possible for 45 minutes. (The heat must be quite low to avoid reducing the sugar and prematurely candying the nuts.)

Preheat the oven to 300°F. Grease a baking sheet with 2 tablespoons of the oil. With a spider (see page 374), remove the nuts from the syrup and spread them out on the prepared baking sheet. Sprinkle with flaky finishing salt. Discard the syrup.

Roast the nuts for 5 minutes and remove from the oven. Stir the nuts, then return them to the oven for another 4 to 5 minutes. Remove, stir, and return to the oven for another 4 to 5 minutes. Remove, stir, and return to the oven for a final 2 to 5 minutes of roasting. The total cook time should be 15 to 20 minutes, until the nuts are evenly golden brown and glossy. Cut a nut in half to make sure it is light golden throughout and carefully taste it to make sure it's cooked evenly.

The nuts may not be crunchy while hot; allow them to cool, harden, and become glassy, 20 to 25 minutes. Toss with the remaining 1 tablespoon oil before serving. Store the nuts in an airtight container at room temperature for up to 1 week.

Fried Shallots

MAKES ABOUT 1½ CUPS

Fried shallots are a staple in Southeast Asian restaurants, and I've been using them at Beast for years. They're totally addictive. Glassy, crunchy, crisp, salty, and savory, they're dangerous to leave unattended.

> 8 large shallots
> 8 cups canola oil
> ½ teaspoon salt

Peel the shallots and leave the root end intact. Slice the shallots crosswise on a mandoline (see page 373) so the shallot rings are as thick as a nickel. Divide the shallot slices into two batches.

In a 6- to 8-quart Dutch oven or heavy pot, heat the oil to 275°F over medium heat. Line a baking sheet with paper towels and set it near the stove. When the oil is ready, add the first batch of shallots and stir with a slotted spoon every few minutes to ensure even browning. Cook for 3 to 4 minutes, until the slices are an even golden brown with a very tiny amount of white still showing. The shallots will continue to cook very slightly after being pulled from the hot oil, so you're looking for a light caramel color all over.

Using a spider (see page 374), remove the shallots from the oil and spread them across the prepared baking sheet to absorb excess oil. They will not be completely crispy when you first taste them, but they will crisp up with cooling. Fry the second batch the same way. When the paper towels become saturated with oil, replace with new ones. Sprinkle the fried shallots with the salt while still hot.

Allow the shallots to cool completely. Store in a paper towel–lined airtight container at room temperature for up to 1 week.

Herb Salad

SERVES 4 TO 6 AS A GARNISH

I use this as a garnish all the time. A simple herb salad that's lightly dressed with good vinegar and olive oil can totally transform a dish, giving it a pop of color and a bit of acid. Be sure to use a high-quality, light-colored vinegar.

> 1 cup loosely packed mixed herbs (such as flat-leaf parsley, celery leaves, chive batons, and tarragon)
> ⅛ teaspoon salt
> ⅛ teaspoon freshly ground black pepper
> ½ teaspoon high-quality vinegar
> ½ teaspoon extra-virgin olive oil

Immediately before serving, place the herbs in a bowl with the salt, pepper, vinegar, and oil and mix together using your fingertips.

Fried Garlic Chips

MAKES ¾ CUP

I put fried garlic on many dishes, such as Asparagus with Black Garlic Hollandaise (page 144), to add a little crunchy garlicky texture. It's one of my favorite snacks, and when we make large batches of it at the restaurant, we have to put it out of reach before we eat it all. Many thanks to Kristina Preka, who cooked with me at my bar Expatriate, for helping to develop this amazing recipe.

Peeled garlic is available in many Asian grocery stores. And despite the fact that I am generally against buying peeled garlic, the quality of the chips is not affected by it. In fact, the dryness of store-bought peeled garlic actually helps these chips fry up. If you're peeling it yourself, you'll need about 4 heads. Keep your oil at an even 275°F—the easiest way to ensure your oil maintains the correct temperature is to use a clip-on thermometer (see page 374).

> 30 large cloves garlic
> 3 tablespoons plus ⅛ teaspoon salt
> 8 cups canola oil

Working over a small metal mixing bowl, slice the garlic on a mandoline (see page 373). Each slice should be about as thick as two pieces of paper. It's imperative that all of the slices be the same thickness or they won't cook evenly.

Mix 1½ tablespoons of the salt into the garlic slices to season them and extract any extra moisture. Let the garlic sit for 2 minutes. Place the salted garlic in a fine-mesh strainer and rinse well under cold running water for 1 minute. Spin dry using a salad spinner.

Transfer the garlic back to the mixing bowl and season it with 1½ tablespoons of the remaining salt. Let the garlic sit for 2 minutes more, then place the garlic in a fine-mesh strainer and rinse one more time under cold running water for 1 minute. Rinse the mixing bowl, and then fill it with cold water. Add the rinsed garlic to the bowl of water and swish the water with your hands for 20 seconds, then pour the mixture back into the fine-mesh strainer. Spin dry the garlic in the salad spinner.

Line a baking sheet or large plate with a paper towel or a kitchen towel. Spread the garlic across the towel and lay another towel on top. Press down on the garlic with your hands, using medium pressure, to extract any moisture. Do not press so hard that you crush the garlic. Divide the garlic into four equal batches.

In a 6- to 8-quart Dutch oven or heavy pot, heat the oil to 275°F over medium heat. Line a baking sheet with paper towels and place it near the stove. When the oil is hot, gently drop in the first batch of garlic. Stir gently with a spider (see page 374) to help separate any garlic slices that have clumped together. Fry the garlic for 2 minutes, until no longer white; the slices should be very pale gold with no dark spots, as they will continue cooking after you remove them from the oil.

Using the spider, remove the garlic slices from the oil and spread them across the prepared baking sheet to absorb excess oil. Fry the three remaining garlic batches the same way, then sprinkle all of the chips while warm with the remaining ⅛ teaspoon salt.

Allow the chips to cool completely. Store in a paper towel–lined airtight container at room temperature for up to 1 week.

Pour the cream into a pint-size container with a lid and add the buttermilk. Cover the container and shake a few times to combine. Let the container sit on a countertop at room temperature (70°F to 75°F is ideal) for a day or two. The flavor is usually best after 2 days. The longer the crème fraîche sits, the more pronounced the sour flavor will be. Store in an airtight container in the refrigerator for up to 3 weeks.

Whipped Crème Fraîche

MAKES 2½ CUPS

If you haven't made your own crème fraîche, you can substitute a mixture of heavy cream and sour cream. Store-bought cultured sour cream will not whip on its own, but your homemade crème fraîche will whip up perfectly.

    1½ cups homemade crème fraîche (left),
    or 1¼ cups cold heavy cream plus ¼ cup sour cream
    2 to 3 tablespoons sugar
    ½ teaspoon vanilla extract

Grab a large, deep bowl—one that's much bigger than you think you need—and a large whisk. If you have the space, chill the bowl and whisk briefly in the refrigerator before you begin. In the bowl, stir together the crème fraîche, 2 tablespoons of the sugar, and the vanilla until the sugar dissolves. Taste for sweetness and add an additional 1 tablespoon of sugar if desired. (It is best to add the sugar now rather than later, when it won't have as much time to dissolve and the cream will be studded with tiny sugar crystals.)

Tilt the bowl to one side to create a pool of cream and start whipping it. Keep your wrist locked and draw a big circle with the end of the whisk, using your shoulder and elbow for most of the movement. This draws as much air into the cream with each motion as possible. Whip for 5 to 6 minutes. Stop when soft peaks form that droop a bit when you lift the whisk out of the bowl.

Whipped crème fraîche will not achieve the same stiff peaks as regular cream, and it will lose some of its shape after 30 minutes. Give it a few whisks to revive it before serving.

Crème Fraîche

MAKES 2 CUPS

Crème fraîche is simply a cultured cream. Store-bought versions are available, or you can make a very close approximation by letting cream and buttermilk sit together on a countertop for a few days. Use cultured full-fat buttermilk (sometimes called Bulgarian style) that doesn't have a lot of stabilizers in it, and avoid ultrapasteurized cream.

    1¾ cups heavy cream
    2 tablespoons cultured full-fat buttermilk

Vanilla Bean Whipped Cream

MAKES 2 CUPS

I love whipped cream—lightly sweetened and studded with fragrant vanilla seeds that give a little crunch as you eat the cream. It's a wonderful accompaniment to anything sweet. Learning to whip cream by hand is important because you'll never understand how the cream subtly evolves through the whipping process if you use a mixer. Working by hand gives you a denser, creamier result, too, and all but guarantees that you won't overwhip the cream into butter, which is a real risk with a stand mixer. Throw in a teaspoon or two of your favorite spirit (bourbon, rum, amaretto, Calvados) instead of the vanilla for a twist on the expected. And remember to keep your cream cold until just before you whip it: the colder the cream, the faster it whips.

1 vanilla bean

2 to 3 tablespoons sugar

1 cup cold heavy cream

½ teaspoon vanilla extract

Using a paring knife, cut the vanilla bean in half lengthwise. Use the knife to flatten the pod gently against the countertop, and then scrape out the seeds with the blade. Place the seeds in a small bowl with 2 tablespoons of the sugar and rub the seeds into the sugar with your fingers until evenly dispersed. Save the vanilla pod for another use: slip it into a bottle of rum to infuse the liquor, or bury it in a canister of sugar to make vanilla sugar.

Grab a large, deep bowl—one that's much bigger than you think you need—and a large whisk. If you have the space, chill the bowl and whisk briefly in the refrigerator before you begin. Add the cream, the vanilla and sugar mixture, and the vanilla extract to the bowl. Stir the ingredients together until the sugar dissolves, taste for sweetness, and add an additional 1 tablespoon of sugar if desired. (It is best to add the sugar now rather than later, when it won't have as much time to dissolve, leaving the cream studded with tiny sugar crystals.)

Tilt the bowl to one side to create a pool of cream and start whipping it. Keep your wrist locked and draw a big circle with the end of the whisk, using your shoulder and elbow for most of the movement. This draws as much air into the cream with each motion as possible. Whip for 5 to 6 minutes. If you're making soft whipped cream to dollop, stop when soft peaks form that droop a bit when you lift the whisk out of the bowl. If you're making cream for quenelles (see page 377), stop when stiff peaks form (they stand up and don't move when you lift the whisk).

Whipped cream will hold for about 6 hours in the refrigerator. Revive it with a few turns of the whisk just before serving.

VARIATION To make plain, unflavored whipped cream, follow the recipe above but omit the vanilla bean and vanilla extract.

Pâte Brisée

MAKES 1 (10-INCH) PASTRY SHELL

This pastry has a rich, buttery flavor and a crisp, flaky texture that works well for savory and sweet pies, tarts, and quiches. It is similar to the pâte sucrée recipe on page 358, but with less sugar and more tenderness (versus the sandy shortbread character of the pâte sucrée). I like to make this crust for Quiche with Wild Mushrooms, Gruyère, and Chives (page 204; see Note, facing page).

You must not overwork this dough, but it is totally fine to shape it and bring it together into a nice even disk before letting it rest. And because the dough has so much butter in it, you must chill it in the freezer as the final step before baking.

> 2 cups all-purpose flour (see page 376)
>
> 2 teaspoons sugar
>
> ¾ teaspoon salt
>
> 12 tablespoons cold butter, cut into ½-inch cubes
>
> 3 to 4 tablespoons ice water
>
> 1 egg white (see page 377), lightly beaten

Place the flour, sugar, and salt in a food processor and pulse 3 or 4 times for 3 to 4 seconds at a time to combine. Add all of the butter and pulse 6 to 8 times for 3 to 4 seconds at a time, until the mixture is fairly uniform, with the largest pieces of butter about the size of a corn kernel. Pour 3 tablespoons of the ice water evenly over the top of the mixture and pulse 6 or 7 times for 3 to 4 seconds at a time, until the mixture at the bottom of the bowl is just starting to come together in a different way from the rest (take a look from the side of the processor bowl). The mixture should not yet form a ball, but it should be gathering together a little bit. Pinch a handful of the dough beads together. If they hold together when you squeeze them, the dough will probably come together just fine. Add the remaining 1 tablespoon of ice water only if the dough seems extremely dry, and pulse again.

Turn the entire mixture out into a large metal mixing bowl. Working quickly, slightly break apart the dough and mix it with your fingertips to combine the wet and dry parts into a homogenous mass. This entire process shouldn't take more than 10 seconds.

Take out a handful of the dough and lay it in a loose pile on a clean, dry work surface. With the heel of your hand and using medium pressure, smoothly push the dough across the surface and away from your body, like a paint stroke. This method is called *fraisage* in French and is pictured on the facing page. This technique mixes the fat, water, and dry ingredients together quickly without causing toughening. Push that dough to the side and repeat with the remaining dough, one handful at a time.

Gather up all of the dough into a ball, press it together, and then shape it gently into a 4- to 5-inch disk. Turn the disk onto its edge and roll it across the surface like a wheel to firm up any uneven edges; this helps prevent cracking later. Wrap the dough in plastic wrap and refrigerate it for at least 2 hours and for up to 24 hours.

When you're ready to use the dough, remove it from the refrigerator, unwrap it, and lightly dust the countertop with flour. Wait for about 15 minutes for the dough to warm just enough so that it will not crack when you start to roll it. If you hit the dough hard across the surface with a rolling pin, there should be some good give to the dough. If it's not pliable enough, give it another 5 to 10 minutes to soften.

When the dough has some give, roll it out into a circle by moving your rolling pin from the very center to the edges in all four directions, then rotate it a quarter turn and roll again from the center in all four directions. Repeat this motion—rolling and then rotating the dough a quarter turn—until you have an even circle about 16 inches in diameter and 3⁄16 inch thick (the thickness of three quarters).

To line a tart or quiche mold (see Note, right) with the dough, gently fold the dough circle in half, and then fold it in half, again, forming a triangle. Carefully pick up the dough and place the tip of the triangle at the center of the mold. Carefully unfold the dough, and then very gingerly lift up the edges of the dough, and ease and press it into the sides and corner of the pan (where the bottom meets the walls). If there is an air gap between the pastry and the bottom of the pan, during baking the dough will sink into that space, making the sides too short. Now you can trim the top edge with a knife, unless you are making the quiche on page 204, in which case you should allow the crust to drape over the edge of the pan without trimming it further (see Note, right).

Prick the bottom of the pastry shell all over with a fork; see the photo on the facing page. (This is called docking, and it helps prevent the dough from puffing up when it is in the oven, ensuring more even baking.) Freeze the tart shell for 20 minutes. Preheat the oven to 400°F.

Remove the pastry shell from the freezer, line it with parchment paper, and fill it with pie weights, or with raw rice or dried beans reserved for this purpose. These weights will prevent the sides of the dough from sinking during baking. Make sure the parchment is large enough to cover the shell entirely or you run the risk of baking a piece of rice or bean into the shell.

Place the shell on a baking sheet and bake for 15 minutes. Remove the shell from the oven and remove the parchment and weights. Turn down the oven temperature to 350°F. When the oven has reached the lower temperature, return the shell to the oven and bake for another 15 minutes. Remove from the oven and brush the shell with the egg white to seal the holes on the bottom created by docking. Bake for 5 minutes more, or until the shell is light golden brown. Transfer the tart pan to a wire rack and let cool completely before filling.

NOTE If you are making the pâte brisée for the quiche on page 204, you must use a fluted quiche pan with a removable bottom or a springform pan that is 10 inches in diameter and 2 inches deep to ensure all of the filling will fit. Additionally, do not trim the excess pastry from the top of the shell until after the shell has been filled and baked. Finally, after washing and drying, before storing, make sure the pan is very dry; any moisture will cause it to rust.

Pâte Sucrée

MAKES 1 (10- OR 11-INCH) TART SHELL

This is a sweet dough with a rich, buttery flavor and a delicate, sandy texture that is perfect for sweet tarts. I use it for the Apricot–Brown Butter Tart on page 312. Roll out any scraps left over from making the tart shell, cut into any desired shapes, sprinkle with a little sugar, bake at 350°F for about 10 minutes, and enjoy these little bits as cookies.

This dough is slightly more forgiving to work with than the pâte brisée (page 356) because there is no water in the dough. However, it's still important not to overwork this dough. And as always, thoroughly chill it before baking. Use a 10- or 11-inch fluted tart pan with a removable bottom.

> 2 cups all-purpose flour (see page 376)
>
> ¼ cup sugar
>
> ½ teaspoon salt
>
> 14 tablespoons cold butter, cut into ½-inch cubes
>
> 1 egg yolk (see page 377)
>
> 2 tablespoons heavy cream
>
> 1 egg white, lightly beaten

Place the flour, sugar, and salt in a food processor and pulse 3 times for 3 to 4 seconds at a time to combine. Add all of the butter and pulse 6 to 8 times for 2 to 3 seconds at a time, until the mixture is fairly uniform, with the largest pieces of butter about the size of a grain of short-grain rice. Whisk the egg yolk and cream together in a small bowl until uniform. Remove the top of the food processor, drizzle the yolk-cream mixture over the flour and butter mixture, and replace the top. Pulse 3 to 5 times for 2 seconds. The dough should start to form at the bottom of the processor, yet may still look floury on top.

Turn the entire mixture out into a large metal mixing bowl. Working quickly, slightly break apart the dough and mix it with your fingertips to combine the wet and dry parts into a homogenous mass. This entire process shouldn't take more than 10 seconds.

Take out a handful of the dough and lay it in a loose pile on a clean, dry work surface. With the heel of your hand and using medium pressure, smoothly push the dough across the surface and away from your body, like a paint stroke. This method is called *fraisage* in French (see the photo, page 356). This technique mixes the fat and dry ingredients together quickly without fully blending them. Push that dough to the side and repeat with the remaining dough, one handful at a time.

Gather up all of the dough into a ball, press it together, and then shape it gently into a 5- to 6-inch disk. Turn the disk onto its edge and roll it across the surface like a wheel to firm up any uneven edges, which helps prevent cracking later. Wrap the dough in plastic wrap and refrigerate it for at least 2 hours and for up to 24 hours.

When you're ready to use the dough, remove it from the refrigerator, unwrap it, and lightly dust the countertop with flour. Wait for about 15 minutes for the dough to warm just enough so that it will not crack when you start to roll it. If you hit the dough hard across the surface with a rolling pin, there should be some good give to the dough. If it's not pliable enough, give it another 5 to 10 minutes to soften.

When the dough is pliable, roll it out into a circle by moving your rolling pin from the very center to the edges in all four directions, then rotate it a quarter turn and roll again from the center in all four directions. Repeat this motion—rolling and then rotating the dough a quarter turn—until you have an even circle about 16 inches in diameter and ³⁄₁₆ inch thick (the thickness of three quarters).

To line a tart pan with the dough, gently fold the dough circle in half and slip a dough scraper or your hand under the broadest area of the folded dough. Carefully pick up the dough and place it across half of the tart pan. Unfold it carefully, then very gingerly lift up the edges of the dough and ease and press it into the sides and corner of the pan (where the bottom meets the walls). If there is an air gap between the pastry and the bottom of the pan, during baking the dough will sink into that space, making the sides too short. The dough is very tender at this point and may tear a bit. If this happens, don't worry. Line the tart pan with the dough as directed and then repair any tears by patching with trimmings of dough. Now, using a knife or a rolling pin rolled across the top, trim the top edge even with the rim of the tart pan.

Prick the bottom of the tart shell with a fork at 1-inch intervals. Freeze the tart shell for 20 minutes.

Preheat the oven to 400°F. Remove the pastry shell from the freezer, line it with parchment paper, and fill it with pie weights, or with raw rice or dried beans reserved for this purpose. This will prevent the sides from sinking during baking. Make sure the parchment is large enough to cover the shell entirely or you run the risk of baking a piece of rice or bean into the shell.

Place the shell on a baking sheet and bake for 15 minutes. Remove the shell from the oven and remove the parchment and weights. Turn down the oven temperature to 350°F. When the oven has reached the lower temperature, return the shell to the oven and bake for another 12 minutes. Remove the shell from the oven and brush with the egg white to seal the holes on the bottom created by the docking (see the photo, page 356). Bake for 5 minutes more, or until the shell is light brown. Transfer the tart pan to a wire rack and let cool completely before filling.

NOTE After washing and drying, before storing, make sure the pan is very dry; any moisture will cause it to rust.

Biscuits

MAKES 12 BISCUITS

Halfway through writing this cookbook, I decided we needed a biscuit recipe. I was testing Milk-Braised Pork Shoulder (page 254) and had a little leftover meat and a lot of leftover sauce, which has a wonderful gravy-like consistency and flavor. The perfect thing to accompany these leftovers is fluffy southern-style biscuits, the kind my grandmother would approve of.

But mastering a perfect biscuit is an art, and this recipe took a lot of trial and error. I probably tested fifteen batches to get these just right, and at the time I was working on them, I had just moved, so I made really good friends with my new neighbors by off-loading all of my excess biscuits on them. This winning formula makes the beautifully fluffy, layered biscuits of my dreams.

Use lard only if you can get a high-quality product from a good source, like a trusted farmer; otherwise stick with vegetable shortening, but be sure to use an organic product. If you're unable to find full-fat buttermilk, whole milk mixed with 1 tablespoon plus 1 teaspoon white vinegar will work as a substitute.

18 tablespoons butter

6 tablespoons high-quality lard or organic vegetable shortening

2 cups cake flour (see page 376)

2 cups all-purpose flour (see page 376)

2 teaspoons salt

2½ teaspoons baking powder

1 teaspoon baking soda

2 teaspoons sugar

1½ cups cultured full-fat buttermilk, plus 2 tablespoons for brushing

Cut the butter and lard into small cubes (about ½ inch) and chill in the freezer for 20 minutes.

Place the flours, salt, baking powder, baking soda, and sugar in a food processor and pulse until well mixed, 20 to 30 seconds. Add the chilled butter and lard and pulse in brief spurts until the fats are in pea-size pieces, 7 to 10 pulses. Do not overmix.

Transfer the mixture into a large mixing bowl. It should look sandy and pebbly at this point. Make a small well in the center and add the 1½ cups of buttermilk all at once to the well. Use a wooden spoon to mix until the dough comes together, but don't mix any longer than necessary. The dough should look shaggy and a little rough, and you may have to press it in a few spots to get it to hold together. Turn the dough onto a lightly floured work surface. Gather the drier bits and gently press them into the wetter spots to make a more uniform ball.

Line a baking sheet with a Silpat baking mat (see page 374) or parchment paper. If the dough has any sticky parts, very lightly flour them. Then gently lift the dough to check the bottom side and flour if necessary. You don't want the dough to stick to the rolling pin or to the work surface during the next step.

Roll out the dough into a rectangle roughly measuring 9 by 12 inches. Fold the rectangle in thirds, like a letter (see figures 7 and 8, page 333). The dough will look like a book—with a spine (the folded edge) on one side and the open edge on the other. Now rotate the "book" so the spine is facing your body, parallel to the work surface's edge. Roll the dough out again to a 9 by 12-inch rectangle. Fold the rectangle in thirds again. Rotate the "book" one more time so the spine is facing your body and roll out the dough to a 9 by 7-inch rectangle. Cut four strips lengthwise and three strips crosswise so you have 12 roughly equal squares. Place the squares on the prepared baking sheet.

Place the baking sheet in the freezer to fully freeze the squares, about 1 hour. The biscuits can also be wrapped tightly on the baking sheet and frozen for up to 1 week before baking.

When you're ready to bake the biscuits, preheat the oven to 400°F. Take the biscuits out of the freezer and immediately brush them with the remaining 2 tablespoons buttermilk. Bake for 15 minutes, then lower the oven temperature to 350°F and continue baking until the biscuits are deep golden brown and puffy, 10 to 15 minutes. Serve hot. Reheat room-temperature biscuits in a 275°F oven for 5 to 7 minutes.

Quick Brioche

MAKES 1 (1-POUND) LOAF

This brioche recipe was passed down to my pastry chef, Ellen, from Robert Reynolds, a legendary figure in the Portland food scene. For many years, he ran an intensive cooking school that culminated in a trip to France, and when I first started catering, he taught me a great deal. He passed away in 2012, and it's important to me that this recipe lives on in his honor. The brioche needs to be made ahead of time if you're using it in Steak Tartare on Brioche with Quail Eggs (page 75). You'll have more brioche than you need for that recipe, but having extra brioche has never been a problem for me, as it makes excellent toast, French or otherwise.

¼ cup whole milk

¾ teaspoon active dry yeast

2¼ cups all-purpose flour (see page 376)

3 eggs

2 tablespoons sugar

1¼ teaspoons salt

13 tablespoons butter, melted and warm (not hot)

Lightly butter an 8½ by 4½-inch glass or metal loaf pan.

In a small saucepan over medium heat, heat the milk until warm (about 110°F), whisking often to ensure it doesn't burn. Set the milk aside to cool slightly (to about 100°F).

Place the warm milk, the yeast, ½ cup of the flour, and 1 of the eggs in a food processor and pulse a few times until the mixture comes together in a wet paste. Remove the top from the processor, add the remaining 1¾ cups flour, replace the top, and place the processor bowl (without mixing; the flour just rests on top) in a moderately warm (80°F) place for 1¼ hours.

Add the remaining 2 eggs, the sugar, and the salt to the food processor. Process until combined and the mixture is somewhat uniform, about 15 seconds. Note that the mixture will be soft and sticky, not like traditional dough. Set aside 1 tablespoon of the melted butter. With the machine running, pour in the remaining 12 tablespoons melted butter in a steady stream, pausing if it seems like it is not being incorporated. Wait for the last of the butter to be incorporated before adding more, to ensure the butter emulsifies properly.

Scrape the batter into the prepared loaf pan. Cut a piece of parchment paper to fit the pan and brush one side with the reserved 1 tablespoon of melted butter. Rest the parchment, buttered side down, on top of the loaf pan (it won't be touching the dough, but that's okay; the parchment keeps the dough from drying out). Let the dough rise in a warm place for 1 hour. The dough is ready when it doubles in volume and retains a faint impression when gently poked with a finger.

During the last 15 minutes of the rise, preheat the oven to 375°F.

Remove the parchment from the loaf, put the loaf in the oven, and immediately turn down the temperature to 350°F. Bake for 30 to 40 minutes, until the surface is golden brown. It's better to overbake here if you're not sure when the loaf is done.

Let the brioche cool to room temperature in the pan on a wire rack, then unmold the bread onto the rack. The brioche will keep, wrapped in plastic wrap, for up to 1 week.

Bread Crumbs

MAKES ABOUT 2½ CUPS

Chances are you have a hunk of leftover bread somewhere in your house right now. If you take a few quick minutes to make bread crumbs and store them in your freezer, you'll never have to pay for store-bought bread crumbs again.

½ large loaf artisanal bread (about 10 ounces)

For fine bread crumbs: Preheat the oven to 250°F. Cut off and discard the crust from the bread. Carefully slice the bread about ¼ inch thick, then tear the slices into ½-inch pieces. Spread the pieces on a baking sheet and bake for 40 to 45 minutes, until completely dry and brittle. You don't want any color, but the bread should shatter when broken and be completely dried out. Allow the bread to cool, then process to fine crumbs in a food processor.

For medium bread crumbs: Follow the instructions for fine bread crumbs for cutting and toasting the bread. Allow the bread to cool, then pulse briefly in a food processor until the pieces are roughly the size of a grain of rice. Run the crumbs through a fine-mesh strainer to shake out any bread dust, leaving you with medium-size crumbs.

For coarse bread crumbs: Follow the instructions for fine bread crumbs for cutting and toasting the bread. Allow the bread to cool, but do not process or pulse in a food processor. Instead, break the bread into roughly pebble-size pieces and place them between two sheets of parchment paper. Gently roll a rolling pin across the surface several times until the bread crumbs have the rustic texture you're looking for—larger than a grain of rice but smaller than a pea.

For panfried coarse bread crumbs to use as garnish (see Blistered Cauliflower with Anchovy, Garlic, and Chile Flakes on page 168): Heat ¼ cup extra-virgin olive oil in a sauté pan over low heat. Add 1 cup coarse bread crumbs, ¼ teaspoon salt, and ⅛ teaspoon pepper, and cook, stirring frequently, until golden brown, 5 to 7 minutes.

Homemade Ritz Crackers

MAKES ABOUT 40 (2-INCH) CRACKERS

This recipe makes a sizeable amount of dough, but it's a good thing to have around because you'll likely eat more of these flaky crackers than you think. They are delicious on their own and even better with cheese or Chicken Liver Mousse (page 67). Be sure to keep the butter cubes cold when you're mixing the dough, and keep the individual dough balls refrigerated until you roll them out. The rounds rise quite a bit while they're baking, and because you want thin, crisp, crackers, roll the dough out to the thickness of a nickel.

1¾ cups all-purpose flour (see page 376)

2½ teaspoons baking powder

1 tablespoon sugar

½ teaspoon salt

6 tablespoons butter, cut into 1-inch pieces, plus 2 tablespoons butter, melted

½ cup water

1 teaspoon flaky finishing salt

Place the flour, baking powder, sugar, and salt in a food processor and pulse 3 or 4 times to combine. Add the butter pieces and pulse about 4 times, until the butter breaks down into pieces about the size of corn kernels.

With the food processor running, add the water in a thin, steady stream. Stop when you have about 2 tablespoons of water remaining and check the dough to see if it will hold together in a loose ball without additional water. If you still see dry, floury bits and the rest of the dough doesn't look too wet, add a tiny splash of water to the dry sections and pulse 3 or 4 more times to combine.

Remove the dough from the processor, form it into 2 evenly sized disks, and wrap tightly in plastic wrap. Refrigerate for at least 1 hour and up to 2 hours. This allows the gluten in the dough to relax and the flour to hydrate.

Line 2 baking sheets with parchment paper. Lightly flour a countertop and roll out 1 disk of dough into a sheet the thickness of a nickel. Place the dough on a baking sheet. Using a 2-inch round cutter, cut out as many circles of dough as possible from the dough but leave the rounds in place on the baking sheet. Refrigerate the baking sheet. Repeat with the second piece of dough and let both baking sheets chill for 30 minutes.

Remove the baking sheets from the refrigerator and pull off and discard the scrap dough from around the circles. Brush the circles lightly with the melted butter and sprinkle with the finishing salt. Refrigerate the baking sheets one more time for about 15 minutes. Preheat the oven to 350°F.

Remove the baking sheets from the refrigerator and bake for 7 to 9 minutes, rotating the baking sheets 180 degrees after about 4 minutes, until the crackers are golden brown, layered, and very buttery. Remove from the oven and let cool completely on racks.

The crackers will keep in an airtight container at room temperature for 2 days. If you've stored them, reheat in a 350°F oven for about 2 minutes before serving to refresh.

Oat Thyme Crackers

MAKES ABOUT 35 (2-INCH) CRACKERS

There's something very satisfying about a thick whole-grain cracker, and these super nutty tasting and slightly sweet oat crackers fit the bill. Enjoy them with a sharp, salty cheese like an Irish Cheddar, Manchego, or fresh pecorino.

3 cups old-fashioned rolled oats

½ cup packed brown sugar

1 cup all-purpose flour (see page 376)

1 cup barley flour (see page 376)

1½ teaspoons salt

16 tablespoons cold butter, cut into ½-inch cubes

2 teaspoon chopped thyme

¼ cup hot water

1 teaspoon baking soda

Place the oats, brown sugar, flours, and salt in a food processor and process for about 1 minute, until the oats are finely ground but not entirely pulverized, so the crackers will have some

Continued

Clockwise from top right: Oat Thyme Crackers, Nigella and Sesame Crackers, Homemade Ritz Crackers, and Olive Oil and Black Pepper Crackers

texture. Add the butter cubes and the thyme and process for about 8 seconds. The butter should be in small uniform pieces roughly the size of grains of rice.

In a small bowl, mix together the hot water and baking soda. With the food processor running, drizzle the hot water mixture into the dough. Keep the processor running for another 3 seconds. The dough will still look quite dry but will come together in the next few steps.

Turn the dough out into a bowl and squeeze it together into a ball. Knead the dough a few times by squeezing the ball and turning it and pushing it against the bottom of the bowl. Divide the dough in half. Shape half of the dough into a ball and place the ball between two pieces of parchment paper. Press the ball out with the palm of your hand until the dough is about 1 inch thick, and then roll it out with a rolling pin until it is ⅛ inch thick. Transfer the dough to a baking sheet and remove the top layer of parchment. Refrigerate the first sheet of dough while you roll out the second half of the dough the same way.

Line two baking sheets with parchment paper. Using a 2-inch round cookie cutter or ring mold, cut the dough sheets into circles and use a large metal spatula or bench scraper to transfer them to the prepared baking sheets. Reroll the dough scraps to get a few more. Refrigerate the baking sheets for about 15 minutes so the dough will be cold when it goes in the oven. Preheat the oven to 350°F.

Bake the crackers for 8 to 10 minutes, until they smell toasty and the edges are lightly browned. Let cool completely on the baking sheets on racks. The crackers will keep in an airtight container at room temperature for up to 1 week. If they lose some crispiness, toast them in a 325°F oven for 2 to 3 minutes.

Nigella and Sesame Crackers

MAKES ABOUT 35 (2-INCH) CRACKERS

This is an easy cracker to make because you do not have to roll out the dough. Nigella seeds are common in Indian cooking and resemble black sesame seeds, with a mild, toasty onion flavor. If you can't find them, substitute poppy seeds. This cracker (see the photo, page 364) is a nice accompaniment to a cheese plate.

1 cup whole wheat flour (see page 376)

2 tablespoons sesame seeds

1 tablespoon plus 2 teaspoons nigella seeds

2 tablespoons brown sugar

¾ teaspoon salt

4 tablespoons cold butter, cut into ½-inch cubes

¼ cup plus 2 teaspoons heavy cream

1 teaspoon flaky finishing salt

Place the flour, 1 tablespoon of the sesame seeds, 1 tablespoon of the nigella seeds, the brown sugar, and the salt in a food processor and pulse a few times to combine. Add the butter and pulse for about 8 seconds, until the butter is in uniform pieces about the size of grains of rice.

With the processor running, drizzle in the cream and process until just combined, 15 to 20 seconds. Turn the dough out onto the countertop and knead a few times to bring it together. Form the dough into a log about 2 inches in diameter. Wrap the log in plastic wrap and chill for 1 hour. (Or freeze the log up to a month.)

In a small bowl, mix together the remaining 1 tablespoon sesame seeds, the remaining 2 teaspoons nigella seeds, and the flaky salt. Set aside.

Preheat the oven to 350°F. Line two baking sheets with parchment paper. Remove the dough log from the refrigerator (or from the freezer—no need to thaw first), unwrap it, and cut it into rounds no thicker than ⅛ inch. Place the crackers on the prepared baking sheets and sprinkle with the seed-salt mixture. Bake for 12 minutes, rotating the baking sheets 180 degrees after about 6 minutes, until the crackers are lightly browned at the edges. Let cool completely on the baking sheets on racks. The crackers will keep in an airtight container at room temperature for up to 3 days.

Olive Oil and Black Pepper Crackers

MAKES ABOUT 24 LARGE CRACKERS

You'll need a pasta machine or a pasta attachment for a stand mixer to make these thin, crisp crackers (see the photo, page 364). They get a nice kick from the pepper, are satisfying on their own as a snack, but they also pair well with a cheese plate and a glass of wine. Be sure the salt and pepper are not too coarse, as they can interfere with your efforts to make the dough as thin as it needs to be.

- ⅓ cup warm water (about 100°F)
- 1 teaspoon active dry yeast
- 1 teaspoon sugar
- 1 cup all-purpose flour (see page 376)
- 3 tablespoons semolina flour, plus more for rolling out the dough
- 1 teaspoon salt
- 1 teaspoon freshly ground black pepper
- ¼ cup plus 1 tablespoon extra-virgin olive oil
- 1 tablespoon butter, softened
- 1½ teaspoons flaky finishing salt

Mix together the water, yeast, and sugar in a small bowl. Set aside for 10 minutes to hydrate the yeast.

Combine the flours, salt, and pepper in a mixing bowl. Add the yeast mixture to the dry ingredients, then add the 1 tablespoon of oil and the butter and mix well until you have a uniform ball of dough, about 2 minutes. Turn the dough out onto a work surface and knead the dough by pushing it with the heel of your palm against the countertop, then pulling it up with your fingers and folding it over on itself until it is smooth and elastic, about 5 minutes. Place the dough back in the mixing bowl, cover with plastic wrap, and set the bowl in a warm spot for 1 hour.

Preheat the oven to 350°F. Line two baking sheets with parchment paper.

Turn the dough out onto a work surface and divide the dough into four evenly sized pieces. Sprinkle lightly with semolina flour to prevent sticking as needed. Using a manual pasta machine or a pasta attachment for a stand mixer, roll out each piece of dough: pass the dough through the machine's settings, starting with the largest and working through the thinner settings, until the dough has been passed through setting #5, or has the thickness of a dime. Transfer the dough sheets to the prepared baking sheets, cutting to fit as necessary.

Using a fork, dock the dough sheets by pricking them all over; this helps to keep the cracker sheets flat as they bake. Use a

pastry brush to brush the sheets evenly with the remaining ¼ cup oil. Sprinkle evenly with the finishing salt.

Bake for 8 to 12 minutes, until the crackers are golden brown. Check every minute after 5 minutes to make sure the crackers are not getting too dark. Let cool completely on the baking sheets on wire racks.

Break the cooled cracker sheets into large shards. Store in an airtight container at room temperature for up to 1 week.

Champagne-Poached Apricots

MAKES ABOUT 2 CUPS

Poaching dried fruit makes winter seem not so bad. These apricots, which are sweet but have a lovely acidity, are a welcome addition to a cheese plate and are delicious spooned over a bowl of yogurt or on top of a pancake. I always plump dried fruit in hot water before poaching because some fruits are much drier than others. Be careful to check the apricots frequently while they are cooking to ensure they don't overcook, especially if they seemed tender to start with.

> 8 ounces dried apricots (about ½ cup packed)
>
> 4 cups water
>
> ¾ cup Champagne or dry sparkling wine
>
> 1 cup sugar
>
> ½ teaspoon salt
>
> ½ teaspoon pink peppercorns
>
> 1 star anise pod
>
> 1 whole clove
>
> 12 green cardamom pods
>
> ½ cinnamon stick
>
> ½ vanilla bean
>
> 1 lemon zest strip (see page 375)
>
> 1 orange zest strip (see page 375)

Put the apricots in a small heatproof bowl. In a small saucepan, bring 3 cups of the water to a boil over high heat. Pour the boiling water over the apricots and let sit for 20 minutes to begin to soften.

Meanwhile, combine the Champagne, the remaining 1 cup water, the sugar, and the salt in a saucepan. Cut a small square of cheesecloth. Place the peppercorns, star anise, clove, cardamom, and cinnamon stick on the cheesecloth, bring the edges together, and tie securely with kitchen twine to create a small sachet. Using a paring knife, cut the half vanilla bean in half again along its length. Use the knife to flatten the pod gently against the countertop and then scrape the seeds onto the blade. Add the vanilla seeds and pod, the sachet, and strips of zest to the saucepan. Bring the mixture to a boil over high heat, reduce the heat to a simmer, and cook for 5 minutes to combine the flavors and reduce slightly.

When the apricots have finished their presoak, fish them out with a slotted spoon and add them to the saucepan with the syrup. Crumple a small sheet of parchment paper, then smooth it out a little and press it onto the surface of the apricots to keep them submerged. Simmer—just barely so the liquid doesn't reduce too much and the apricots don't fall apart—for about 20 minutes, stirring very gently every 5 minutes, until the apricots are nice and plump but haven't broken down. Remove the vanilla pod from the syrup and pour the apricots and the syrup into an airtight container. Let cool completely and refrigerate for up to 2 weeks. (If you're worried the apricots are overcooked or they look like they're falling apart, remove the fruit right away from the liquid and spread the pieces out on a baking sheet. Let both the fruit and the liquid cool completely, then recombine them in the container.)

Armagnac-Poached Prunes

MAKES 2 CUPS

I love having these prunes around for all sorts of things. They're an integral part of Cracked Green Olive and Armagnac Prune Relish (page 19), but they're also a nice addition to a cheese plate and are delicious inside Almond and Armagnac Prune Puff Pastries (page 325). They're versatile, beautiful, and keep well in the refrigerator.

The best prunes are already slightly soft, despite being dried fruit, and come in tightly sealed packages with some sulfur added to help keep their integrity. Whenever I poach fruit, I try to match the depth of flavor of the liquor to the fruit, and I like how prunes and Armagnac have a similarly rich, dark profile. You could substitute another brandy, but Armagnac gets the best results.

8 ounces prunes, pitted

4 cups water

¾ cup Armagnac

1 cup sugar

¾ teaspoon salt

Peel from 1 lemon (see page 375)

Put the prunes in a small heatproof bowl. In a small saucepan over high heat, bring 3 cups of the water to a boil over high heat. Pour the boiling water over the prunes and let sit for 20 minutes to begin to soften.

In a large saucepan over high heat, combine the Armagnac, the remaining 1 cup water, the sugar, salt, and lemon peel and bring to a boil. Reduce the heat to a simmer and cook until the fieriness is gone from the alcohol, about 5 minutes.

When the prunes have finished their presoak, fish them out with a slotted spoon and add them to the Armagnac mixture. Turn up the heat slightly until the mixture is gently simmering and cook until the prunes are just plumped (they should no longer feel like dried fruit when you touch them) but not falling apart, as little as 2 minutes and no more than 10 minutes.

Turn off the heat and allow the prunes to cool in the liquid, stirring gently to ensure even cooling. (If the prunes already feel very soft, remove them from the hot liquid right away and spread them out on a baking sheet to cool—you don't want to end up with prune mush! When both the prunes and the liquid are cool, return the prunes to the liquid.) Transfer the prunes and the liquid to an airtight container and refrigerate for up to 1 month. Leftover poaching liquid can be reused to poach more fruit, as a flavoring for sodas or cocktails, or added to Balsamic Braised Short Ribs (page 273).

Ingredients

People who cook with intention get used to talking about ingredients in a certain way. For example, most people these days understand that buying produce or meat directly from a farmer is better for both flavor and environmental impact. But the same principle applies to pantry ingredients, such as salt, vinegar, and oil. Using the best products possible makes a huge difference in the end result. Here are my essentials:

AGED BALSAMIC VINEGAR: I use balsamic vinegars with a DOC, or *tradizionale* certification, meaning they are products from specific regions of Italy that have been aged for a minimum of twelve years. A silver label means the vinegar has aged for eighteen years, and a gold label denotes aging of twenty-five years or more. The older the vinegar, the thicker and more viscous it will be. Although these are more expensive than supermarket brands, the trade-off is that you can use much less and still have a major impact on flavor—just a few drops will totally transform your plate. I like La Vecchia Dispensa and Villa Manodori brands.

AGED SHERRY VINEGAR: Sherry vinegars, much like balsamic, get more viscous and flavorful over time, and they take on a lovely nutty taste reminiscent of a fortified wine, like Madeira or port. I use BLiS 9-Year Old Sherry Maple Double Solera Vinegar, which is aged for nine years in single-barrel bourbon casks that were previously used to age maple syrup.

ANCHOVIES AND ANCHOVY PASTE: Use Sicilian olive oil–packed anchovies; Scalia is a good brand. To make anchovy paste, chop the anchovy fillets into small pieces, then move your knife across the fillets on the cutting board in a figure-eight motion—the same technique you use to make the garlic paste on page 344.

BLACK GARLIC: Black garlic has one of the most intense umami flavors I've ever tasted. It's like the vegetarian equivalent of *jamón ibérico*. It's made by slowly heating whole garlic heads over the course of several weeks, which turns the cloves inky black and gives them a pleasantly funky, slightly sweet taste. You don't cook black garlic; you pulverize or purée it to use as a condiment or to deepen the flavor of a vinaigrette or sauce. You can find it in many specialty groceries and online.

BUTTER: I recommend unsalted butter, ideally purchased from a local source. Buying local butter means you're probably buying a product that has been recently stocked, and fresher equals better. In most of these recipes, I call for butter in tablespoons. If you are using butter that's not in stick form, weigh the butter instead: 1 tablespoon butter weighs ½ ounce.

BUTTERMILK: I use cultured full-fat buttermilk, sometimes referred to as Bulgarian buttermilk. The full-fat versions have a better flavor and consistency than their nonfat counterparts. If you can't find full-fat buttermilk, substitute 2 parts nonfat buttermilk mixed with 1 part sour cream or crème fraîche.

COOKING WINE: Don't cook with wine you wouldn't drink. Also, if you find yourself with a leftover half bottle of wine, reduce it to a syrup for Caramelized Lentils du Puy (page 185), or use it as a base to make Beurre Blanc or Beurre Rouge (page 43). A wine reduction can also balance a demi-glace (see page 36). After reducing the wine, store it in an airtight container in the refrigerator for up to 1 week.

CRÈME FRAÎCHE AND SOUR CREAM: I use an organic cultured sour cream with no stabilizers and lots of fat. If you have access to a great dairy, I recommend doing the same. But if you don't have a good source, crème fraîche is a widely available alternative. You can also make your own crème fraîche (page 354), which is slightly thinner than some of the store-bought versions but tastes amazing and allows you to control how sour it is. Plus, when you make your own, it whips up like a dream.

FISH SAUCE: I prefer Red Boat brand because it has a deep, pure umami flavor and full caramel notes without any fillers or artificial ingredients. I use fish sauce much in the same way Worcestershire sauce is used, to add depth of flavor to soups, sauces, and braises.

HONEY: I never buy commercial honey, and I recommend that you don't, either. The global bee population is declining, which has serious environmental repercussions, so one of the best ways to support the future health of our planet is to buy local honey, which also has deeper and more interesting flavors than the commercial stuff.

NUTS: It's important to buy your nuts from a farmers' market or other reputable source that has a high product turnover, such as nuts.com. The difference in taste between stale walnuts (many of which are rancid) and fresh cannot be overstated. You'll know the second you bite into a sweet, fresh one.

OLIVE OIL: I cook almost everything in extra-virgin olive oil, which doesn't have to be expensive. (I use an organic Arbequina olive oil from California that costs about fifteen dollars for a 750-milliliter bottle.) Use olive oil that has a flavor you enjoy, whether you're using it for cooking or dressing a salad. Do some taste tests and find a bottle that suits you.

Occasionally I use a lemon-pressed olive oil, such as Agrumato brand, which is olive oil pressed with the rinds of lemons. It's a lovely finishing oil or a garnish for the celery velouté on page 93 or the seared rib eye on page 263.

PRESERVED TOMATOES: I always buy tomatoes in glass jars or aseptic packages. I've found that tomatoes packed in cans have a metallic aftertaste. Even jarred tomatoes are technically "canned" because they go through a water bath canning process during packaging. As a result, I call for canned tomatoes in these recipes even though they are not preserved in metal. My preferred brands are Mutti, which comes in glass jars, and Pomi, which is aseptic-packed, though many aseptic-packed tomatoes are a fine substitute if you can't find jarred.

SALT: All of the recipes in this book were tested with fine-grained, medium-moisture sea salt from Guatemala. I strongly recommend using a natural sea salt for your everyday cooking, and I like using one that's fairly dry and composed of irregularly shaped, yet evenly sized crystals, as opposed to flakes. If your sea salt is very fine, dry, and tightly packed, use slightly less than called for in these recipes.

I don't recommend kosher salt or table salt, despite the fact that kosher salt has been widely popularized by chefs in recent years. Unlike sea salt, which occurs naturally, kosher salt is an artificially manufactured product. Table salt is also an artificial product and should be avoided.

I use small amounts of pink curing salt no. 1, which has sodium nitrite, to prevent oxidation and preserve the color of meat. Recipes will work if you don't include the curing salt, but the finished dish won't look the same. It's available online at Butcher & Packer and at kitchen supply stores.

Flaky finishing salt is bigger and flakier than the sea salt I use in cooking. I sprinkle it atop salads and pastries for texture. Versions from Halen Môn or Murray River, available online at themeadow.com and in specialty shops, are my favorites.

STOCK: If you're unable to make the stock on page 346, substitute the highest-quality beef or chicken stock from a specialty grocer or sustainable butcher who makes it in-house. Avoid canned or aseptic-packed stocks. They usually have an insipid onion flavor and are very watery, with little flavor resemblance to their homemade brethren.

SUGAR: Sugars have widely varying flavors. For baking, I almost always use regular 100 percent cane sugar. For more savory applications, I use maple or muscovado sugar to add complexity and depth.

WONDRA FLOUR: This is a quick-mixing, enriched flour that contains both wheat and barley. It has a very dry texture and doesn't get sticky like regular flour when wet. I use it for frying foods such as Sole Piccata on page 221 or Lamb Scallopini on page 285.

Equipment

I don't call for a lot of special equipment, but I strongly recommend investing in a few things that will make you a better cook.

BLACK STEEL PAN: This is one of the most used pieces of equipment in my kitchen, whether I am searing meat or vegetables or frying eggs. It allows you good control over temperature because its walls are thin and smooth, which means the pan both heats up quickly and cools down fast. It's also lightweight, so you can flip ingredients easily on the stove top, and it transfers effortlessly to the oven. Black steel frying pans are inexpensive and widely available online and at restaurant supply stores. I recommend buying a 10-inch pan. Never put anything acidic (vinegar, wine, tomatoes) in a steel pan, black or otherwise, as it will immediately impart an unpleasant metallic taste to your dish.

Alternatively, use a well-seasoned cast-iron skillet, but note that it will take about three times as long to preheat cast-iron as it does black steel.

CHINOIS: A chinois is a conical fine-mesh strainer. I call for it often in soup recipes because its shape and size make it easy to pour in liquids and press them down with a ladle to get a better yield. If you don't have a chinois, a fine-mesh strainer lined with cheesecloth will also work.

CONVECTION OVEN: Every recipe in this book that calls for oven cooking can be adapted to a convection oven (because of its even heat distribution, a convection oven is actually my preference). If using convection, simply drop the temperature called for by 25 degrees.

COPPER MIXING BOWL: An unlined copper bowl is great for whipping egg whites because the copper reacts chemically with the whites in the same way cream of tartar does to help create volume and stability. If you're whipping egg whites in a copper bowl for a soufflé or other use, omit the cream of tartar.

CUTTING BOARD: I use only wooden cutting boards. Plastic cutting boards are brutal on your knives. I also like to save one of my boards for cutting garlic and onion exclusively. That way, I'm sure that when I cut fresh fruit or do pastry work, I will not be passing along a garlicky or oniony bite. Also, smell your board before cutting anything on it and wash it as necessary. The best way to maintain wooden cutting boards is to wash them with mild soap and water, and to apply a cheap mineral oil to the surface about once a week. Let the oil soak in and then wipe away the excess with a paper towel. Regular mineral oil can be purchased at a pharmacy for little money. It's not worth spending big bucks on fancy board oil.

DIFFUSER: If you have a high-powered stove, it can be hard to get the flame low enough to cook some of the more delicate recipes in this book. A diffuser can help solve this. It's an enameled cast-iron disk that fits directly over the burner to help diffuse the heat. It's particularly useful if you'd like to be away from the stove for a little while, as it ensures even, low heat.

FISH SPATULA: This sharply angled, highly flexible slotted spatula allows you to gently and carefully remove a piece of fish (or other delicate food, such as a crêpe or a fried egg) from a pan.

HANDHELD TORCH: Suggesting a torch might seem fussy, but it's impossible to achieve a sheet of crystallized sugar, such as in Figs with Foie Gras Mousse (page 60), without one. Buy an inexpensive model at a hardware store; they're often stocked in the welding aisle.

HOTEL PAN: Also known as a steam table pan or counter pan, this is a standard piece of equipment in professional kitchens, and it's useful for making the stock on page 346. It's a lightweight stainless-steel roasting pan measuring about 12 by 20 inches and with tall walls (usually 2, 4, or 6 inches deep). A half hotel pan is the same thing but half the size and is good for smaller projects, such as smoking onions (see page 377).

KITCHEN SCALE: Weighing ingredients is an excellent way to ensure accuracy, control, and precision when cooking. I like the digital models from Escali, which are inexpensive and lightweight.

MANDOLINE: This handy slicer with adjustable blades is indispensable for cutting ingredients more thinly and evenly than a chef's knife can. It's essential for slicing foods that will be deep-fried, like garlic chips (page 353), so each piece cooks evenly. Pay close attention when using a mandoline, as the blades are extremely sharp. Stop slicing your ingredient before your fingertips get too close to the blades—even experienced chefs run the risk of a painful nick. That said, it's well worth the risk when you see how thin and even your slices are. I usually use the lightweight and inexpensive Japanese Benriner brand; when the blades dull, you can just replace the slicer.

MASKING TAPE AND MARKER: These are the two items that most separate home cooks from restaurant cooks. Restaurant cooks label everything, and it's not just because we have to for health-code reasons. It's to keep track of what to use first, and it also helps with menu planning, so we can easily see what we have around and what we need to use. I recommend you do the same at home.

MICROPLANE GRATER: The Microplane company makes a line of handheld rasp-type graters for grating and zesting cheese, chocolate, citrus, and more. I have a variety of Microplane graters with different-size teeth. The one with the smallest holes is perfect for citrus, and I often use the larger-rasp grater for hard cheeses. Once you have two or three Microplane graters, you'll wonder what you ever did without them.

MISE EN PLACE BOWL: These can be anything, really. I have a set of half-size vintage jelly jars that I use most often, along with random sets of different-size ramekins. I use almost every one of them on a daily basis, and I am often fishing around in my dishwasher for more. You can't have enough. I use them to keep spices separate when making involved recipes, and they are indispensable when gently scooting an egg into simmering water for poaching.

PASTRY BAG: I recommend having at least one 16- or 18-inch pastry bag with two or three round and starred tips of various sizes to pipe fillings into decorative shapes or designs. To fill a pastry bag, bend up the tapered neck of the bag so the tip is pointing up and your filling doesn't come pouring out. Then stand the bag up in a quart container or measuring cup and fold the wide end of the bag down around the edges of the

container like you would a garbage bag over a garbage can. Use a rubber spatula to scrape the filling into the pastry bag. If you don't have a pastry bag, a resealable bag with the corner cut off will work in a pinch.

SAUCE SPOON: Chef Gray Kunz, formerly of Lespinasse, designed this spoon, which has a large bowl that holds exactly 2½ tablespoons, a tapered edge, and a shorter handle than most spoons. Although a saucing spoon is not strictly necessary, its unique size and shape makes it perfect for forming quenelles, saucing dishes, basting meats, and more. Buy one online at jbprince.com.

SILPAT BAKING MAT: These silicone-coated nonstick baking mats come in a variety of sizes and are inexpensive and reusable. In most cases, a Silpat mat can be used interchangeably with parchment paper, though a mat is necessary when making the Gruyère crisps for the kale salad on page 134.

SPICE GRINDER: I don't recommend buying an actual spice grinder. I find the best tool for grinding spices and herbs is a small, inexpensive electric coffee grinder (I have tried a lot of brands and found the best to be a standard-issue Krups model) that's reserved specifically for that purpose.

SPIDER: This is a skimmer with a wide, shallow wire-mesh basket and a long handle. I use it in lieu of a slotted spoon to pull ingredients quickly out of hot liquid when frying or blanching. Spiders are inexpensive and widely available in Asian markets and online.

THERMOMETER: I use two types of thermometers, a digital probe thermometer for testing the temperature of cooked meats, liquids for proofing yeast, and the like, and a clip-on digital thermometer for deep-frying. Maintaining the correct temperature is essential when deep-frying, and a clip-on thermometer allows you to keep your hands free and concentrate on cooking. For deep-frying, I like the digital version from CDN that beeps when the oil reaches the correct temperature.

Techniques

This is the real reason I wrote this book: to help illustrate the most valuable techniques I've learned over time. These are, simply put, the techniques that will make you a better cook.

AERIAL SALTING METHOD (ASM): Sprinkle salt from high above to distribute it evenly across the surface of whatever you're salting. It's my method for salting everything, especially meats. Start with a four-finger pinch of salt (my four-finger pinch weighs about 2 grams, or about ¼ teaspoon). Hold your fingers at least 4 inches above the surface of whatever you're seasoning and, twisting your fingers back and forth, evenly spread the salt across the surface. Even though I call this ASM, the same technique also applies to black pepper.

BLANCHING AND SHOCKING: This technique cooks ingredients in simmering water and helps preserve and even heighten color while infusing seasoning. The basic formula for blanching a small amount of green vegetables is to bring 2 quarts water and 2½ tablespoons salt to a boil in a 4-quart pot. Set up a mixing bowl with 4 cups water, 4 cups ice, and 1 tablespoon salt for shocking. When the blanching water reaches a full rolling boil, dunk the ingredient into it. As soon as it wilts, or is tender, depending on the directions in the recipe and what you are blanching, use a spider (see facing page) to transfer the ingredient immediately to the ice water to arrest the cooking and cool to the touch. Transfer the vegetables to a plate lined with kitchen towels to dry.

To blanch and shock round fruit such as peaches or tomatoes, follow the method above for blanching and shocking, but omit the salt. (Use an 8-quart stockpot and 6 quarts of water to blanch large quantities of large fruit.) When the blanching water reaches a full rolling boil, working in batches of 3 or 4 fruits, dunk the fruit into the water and let it blanch for 45 to 60 seconds, until the skin of the fruit begins to curl back slightly. Use a spider to transfer the ingredient immediately to the ice water to arrest the cooking and cool to the touch. Transfer the fruit to a plate lined with kitchen towels to dry.

CHECKING MEAT FOR DONENESS: A digital probe thermometer (see facing page) is invaluable for this task, but you'll be a better cook if you use a few methods to check for doneness.

For example, you can press firmly against the thickest part of the meat with two fingertips to feel if it springs back slightly, or you can very gently insert a sharp knife into the natural breaks in a piece of fish to look for opaqueness versus translucence. The more you touch meat or fish to check for doneness, the more skilled you'll become—and soon you may not even need a thermometer.

CITRUS TECHNIQUES

LEMON WEDGES: To make the perfect seed-free lemon squeezer to serve alongside fish or vegetables, start by quartering a lemon lengthwise. Cut off the strip of membrane in the center. Pick out the seeds with the tip of a paring knife before using.

PEEL: Using a vegetable peeler, remove a thin strip of just the colored peel—not the white pith—from the citrus.

RIND: Using a sharp paring knife, remove the colored peel—including the white pith—from the citrus. This is used when supreming citrus.

SUPREME: Supreming citrus is the classic French way of saying "cut the fruit into neat segments." Slice off both the blossom and branch end of the fruit, cutting as closely as possible to where you think the pith will end. Turn the fruit on one of its flat ends and, using a sharp paring knife, cut downward, following the contour of the fruit, to remove the peel and all of the pith. (It usually takes me 6 to 8 passes with the knife, depending on the size of the fruit.) Carefully following along the membrane of each segment of the exposed fruit, cut out individual wedges by making two small V-shaped incisions. An individual section of citrus is called a "citrus supreme." Make sure to remove any white pith or membrane that may still be stuck to your beautiful work.

ZEST: Run a washed and dried citrus fruit over a fine-holed Microplane grater (see facing page) set over a cutting board. When measuring citrus zest, pack it tightly into the spoon.

FOLDING EGG WHITES INTO A SOUFFLÉ BASE: In a metal or copper mixing bowl, whisk the egg whites, adding the cream of tartar after about 30 seconds if not using a copper bowl, until stiff, almost shiny peaks form. Scoop approximately one-third of the whipped egg whites into the egg yolk mixture. Using a rubber spatula, thoroughly mix everything together, using a light hand to retain as much air as possible, until fully incorporated. This lightens the thick base significantly so that the two mixtures are more evenly matched when you add the remaining whites. One of the most vital steps in making a soufflé is incorporating the final two-thirds of the egg whites. This needs to be done using an extremely soft touch. Scoop all of the remaining egg whites on top of the base. With a rubber spatula, cut down the middle of the bowl, then bring the spatula back up toward the top scraping along the curve of the bowl and carefully scooping some of the base up over the whites. Repeat this cut-and-scoop motion as many times as you need, giving the bowl a quarter turn after each scoop, but do not fully incorporate the whites. The fully folded mixture should still have some white streaks.

FRYING SAGE LEAVES: Melt 6 tablespoons butter in a small sauté pan (no larger than 6 inches in diameter) over medium heat. Test the heat by dropping in a sage leaf; the butter should begin to bubble immediately. If the butter is hot enough, add up to 6 sage leaves and stir with a slotted spoon until the edges of the leaves begin to curl slightly and a leaf pulled from the oil looks translucent. (If the butter is turning dark brown, lower the heat.) Always fry in batches of no more than 6 leaves; it's acceptable to use the same butter for multiple batches. When the leaves are done, transfer them with a slotted spoon to paper towels to drain. Sprinkle lightly with salt while still warm. Leaves should stay crisp for about 1 day if cooled completely and kept in an airtight container.

GRINDING PARMIGIANO-REGGIANO: Do not buy grated Parmigiano-Reggiano cheese. It lacks moisture and flavor and is likely not real Parmigiano-Reggiano from Italy, which is the only kind of Parmesan cheese you should buy, if possible. Instead, chop a small block of Parmigiano-Reggiano cheese into rough ½-inch cubes and place the cubes in a food processor. Pulse until the cheese moves freely, then process until the cheese becomes very small, pebbly pieces with a fine, even texture akin to coarse cornmeal.

KNIFE SKILLS

FINELY CHOPPING HERBS: After washing the herbs (if necessary), dry them thoroughly (I have a small herb spinner for this purpose in addition to a large salad spinner). Your herbs must be very dry when you cut them or they will stick together and bruise as you chop. Pile the washed and picked herbs in a bowl near your cutting board. If chopping a large amount of herbs, work with a small handful at a time. Using a chef's knife with at least a 6-inch blade, slice the herbs into very thin strips, then cut across the strips to create a fine, uniform chop.

CARING FOR KNIVES: Every knife is different, so instead of providing a tutorial on how to sharpen knives, I urge you to get to know your knife. Buy one from a reputable knife store and talk to the person who works there about the best way to sharpen it. Cooking with a sharp knife is essential to cooking well. It gives you control and precision and makes cooking more enjoyable. In the same way that you should always start with the best ingredients possible, you should also start with the sharpest knife possible. I prefer Japanese steel over German because it is a bit easier to sharpen and maintain an edge and is generally lighter weight. If you don't want to buy a whetstone for your home (which is what I recommend), find a local professional with good reviews to sharpen your special tools.

MEASURING FLOUR: So the flour isn't packed too tightly, scoop flour with a large spoon into a measuring cup and scrape off the top with the flat edge of a knife.

MEASURING WITH QUARTERS: I keep four quarters in a kitchen drawer to help me estimate thickness. One quarter is 1/16 inch, two stacked quarters are 1/8 inch, three quarters are 3/16 inch, and four quarters are 1/4 inch. Using quarters as a thickness guide is very helpful when slicing or rolling dough out.

SEARING MEAT: Searing is an integral step in achieving an all-important crust on the outside of meat. The correct way to sear is to get your pan (I use a black steel pan; see page 373) very, very hot, then add the oil just a few seconds before adding the meat, as you don't want the oil to begin to denature and smoke. Press down on the meat (with tongs or a heavy bowl or plate, depending on the shape and size of the cut) to ensure that it gets an even sear across its entire surface.

SEPARATING EGGS: The easiest and cleanest way to separate eggs is to crack all of the eggs into a bowl and then pull out the yolks. Set up a bowl for the whole eggs and a small bowl for the yolks. The fresher and colder the eggs, the easier they will be to separate. Crack the eggs on a flat surface like a countertop rather than the edge of a bowl, so pieces of shell aren't pushed into the interior of the egg. Use clean hands to fish out the egg yolks, resting them in your cupped fingers. Let the whites filter through your fingers and use your opposite hand to pull the whites from the yolks. Place the yolks in the small bowl. If an egg yolk breaks as you are removing it from the bowl of whites and you will be whipping the whites (yolk—or any fat—is death to nicely whipped egg whites), immediately use half an eggshell to fish out the yolk that is suspended in the white.

SHAPING QUENELLES: Making oval-shaped quenelles is a beautiful way to garnish pastries or soup with whipped cream or mousse, though the technique itself can be used to shape all kinds of foods (ice cream, pâtés, butter, and so on). To make a quenelle, pour about 1 cup of just-boiled water into a small heatproof dish. Put a long, small metal spoon in the hot water for 1 minute. Tap the spoon lightly on a dry towel before dipping it into the ingredient you want to shape into a quenelle. Drag the hot spoon toward you across the surface of the food to make an egg (oval) shape. Brush whatever you're scooping against the side of the container to form two distinct points on either end. Gently turn out the quenelle on top of your dish.

SMOKING ONIONS

To smoke onions, you'll need two pieces of equipment that you're willing to sacrifice to the smoking gods: a half hotel pan (see page 373) and a perforated half hotel pan insert (both are available at restaurant supply stores) or a wire rack that fits inside the half hotel pan. (If you're using a charcoal grill, you'll need only a perforated half hotel pan insert.) Reserve these for smoking, as the pans will get burned and be unusable for other cooking (but you can continue to use them to smoke other foods in the future). The onions can be smoked up to 1 week ahead of time.

TO SMOKE INDOORS: Soak 2 cups wood chips in 3 cups water for 10 minutes. Open your windows, disarm your smoke alarm, and turn on your hood vent if you have one. Place the soaked wood chips in the hotel pan and place the perforated insert inside the pan on top of the wood chips. Peel and slice 2 large yellow onions in 1/8-inch half moons and place them on the insert. Wrap the entire pan with aluminum foil, and wrap the edges of the pan with another piece of foil to ensure a very tight seal.

Heat the pan on the stove top over high heat. The metal pan may pop and warp; this is normal. Keep the pan over high heat until a little bit of smoke begins to rise, about 5 minutes. If you see a lot of smoke escaping, place a little more foil at that point to keep the seal tight. Turn the heat down to low and cook for 45 minutes.

Remove the pan from the heat but don't unwrap it. Allow it to cool for 2 minutes, then take the whole thing outside (or near a window) before removing the foil, so you don't release a big billow of smoke directly into your house.

TO SMOKE ON A GAS GRILL: Follow the instructions for smoking indoors, but use your grill instead of your stove top. Don't worry about opening the windows or moving the pan outside before lifting off the foil since you'll already be outside.

TO SMOKE ON A CHARCOAL GRILL: Stack about 16 charcoal pieces in your grill. Light the charcoal and let it burn down until the coals are covered with white-hot ash, 20 to 30 minutes. Slightly spread out the coals, then place the soaked wood chips directly on top of the coals. Place the sliced onions in the perforated hotel pan insert and set the insert directly on the grill grate. Cover the grill and smoke the onions for about 45 minutes.

SWEATING VEGETABLES: Sweating is the act of gently cooking vegetables in fat while stirring frequently so all of the liquid emitted evaporates and the vegetables don't take on any color. Sweating usually results in tender and sometimes translucent pieces.

TOASTING SPICES: Toast spices in a black steel pan (see page 373) over medium-high heat for 30 to 45 seconds, depending on the spice. Most spices can be toasted whole, but cinnamon sticks should be broken into ½-inch shards by hitting them with the bottom of a heavy pan or with a meat mallet. Toasting is a bit of a misnomer here, as you're really releasing a spice's aromatic oils, so be attentive to the heat (spices burn easily) and don't let the spices take on too much color. If you will be grinding the freshly toasted spices, let them cool, then grind them in a spice grinder (see page 374). When a recipe calls for a measure of ground spice, you should measure it *after* grinding. You will need to grind slightly more of the whole spice than called for in the ingredient list to get the amount needed.

WASHING AND STORING SALAD GREENS AND HERBS: Most salad greens are perkier and hold dressing better if they're cool, crisp, and dry before serving. When I get home from the market, I fill the basin of a salad spinner with water and 4 or 5 ice cubes or very cold tap water, then I pick through the greens or herbs and drop them into the cold water. (The exception is basil, which should be kept unwashed and dry in a resealable plastic bag on your countertop. This may seem counterintuitive, but it works like a charm.) Let them sit for about a half hour to refresh, and then drain them and spin them very, very dry. For spinach, which tends to be very dirty, follow the instructions above but agitate the water every few minutes so the dirt drops to the bottom. Pour out the water, then rinse the basin, and repeat up to two more times until the spinach is clean. Line a resealable plastic bag with a kitchen towel or paper towels and place the dry greens inside, then squeeze out all of the excess air and seal the bag closed. Most greens will keep for several days when stored this way.

WEIGHING ICE FOR WET BRINES: Because all ice is shaped differently, use a scale to measure it rather than a measuring cup, which can easily throw off the percentage of salt in a brine solution. Cooling with ice allows you to use the brine right away, but if you don't have a kitchen scale (see page 373), substitute cold water instead, measuring 2 cups water for every 1 pound ice. Wait until the brine has cooled to room temperature before using it.

WHIPPING EGG WHITES BY HAND: In a metal or copper mixing bowl, begin to whisk the egg whites. When the egg whites are foamy, after about 30 seconds of steady whisking, add a pinch of cream of tartar, which helps keep the whites from deflating. (If using a copper bowl, the cream of tartar can be omitted; see page 373.) Continue whisking until soft peaks form. Carefully continue whisking just a few more seconds until stiff, almost shiny peaks have formed. When they're ready, you'll be able to pull your whisk out of the egg whites to make a peak with a shape that does not fall (like a mountain). You will know you've gone past the optimal stage if the whites begin to release a clear liquid or break apart from each other rather than being a cohesive mass. If this happens, you've overwhipped your egg whites and must start over. Next time, you will have a better idea of when to stop.

Acknowledgments

First, I must thank Jamie Feldmar, whose fortunate lust for adventure brought us together at a party and eventually lead to traveling and eating our way through Southeast Asia. Your dedication to perfection (and possible masochism) allowed you to say yes to this project. Thank you; your words perfectly captured my spirit.

After hundreds of phone calls, four trips from Portland to New York and back, two flights from Australia (for my incredible photographer, Chris Court), and two truckloads of props faithfully brought from San Francisco by Glenn Jenkins (the very best stylist in the business), we now have this beautiful book. Chris and Glenn, if every day were as driven, fun, and gratifying as the photo shoots we did together, I would quit my day job and work with you forever. Here's to the next book.

To Ellen Laing, because without you, I would be short a best friend, and this book wouldn't have a desserts chapter(!). Thank you; you stood for sixteen hours a day while seven months pregnant to help with every photo that we styled and directed together. Some of the hardest working days and most fun I have ever had were with you. You are this book and this book is you.

My agent, Kim Witherspoon, has believed in this project since the beginning. You are a powerhouse of a woman and an incredible role model, wife, mother, and friend. How you do it all, I hope to someday understand. I look forward to a long partnership.

To Emma Campion at Ten Speed Press, who put up with my constant meddling in design detail. Your unwavering pursuit of excellence ended up making something more beautiful than I could have imagined. To Julie Bennett and Kate Bolen, who worked with our many, many words until they fit together and flowed perfectly.

To Tristan Blash, who dutifully tested every one of my not-so-simple recipes with a smile—and asked all the right questions.

For building me the sexy working kitchen where we shot the book's photography: Matthew Peterson. For loaning me crazy, awesome knives: the Portland Knife House. For giving me all the garnishes I could ever want: Manuel Recio and Leslie Lukas-Recio at Viridian. For bringing me a whole salmon on the exact day I needed it: Sonny Davis.

To David Howitt for his unwavering support and belief, Erin Tewes for her amazing read-through, and Jody Stahancyk for her years of support and for teaching me the value of depending on myself.

To my current, past, and future staff: You hold the keys. Your hard work and passion have created and pushed this project and others to come forward. Believe it is never about the woman or man standing out front—no one in this (or any business) is worth a damn without the people who create the show. I love you.

To Mika Paredes for every bit of work that lead to being able to make this book. Beast will always be you and me, and I can never repay you for the years of service and friendship.

To those who helped launch my career: My ex-husband and father to my daughter, Michael Hebb, who followed big dreams, won, lost, and won again, and for teaching me about perseverance and believing in myself. And to the earliest guys I hired who were all more talented than me and who taught me what I didn't learn in books—you were my real teachers: Dan, JB, Morgan, Tommy, Gabe, and Jason, you know who you are to me, and I am beyond grateful.

To Jean Kowacki from Caio Main in Ashland, Oregon, for teaching me how this work can suck you in and take over your life, and showing me that I should try for balance.

To my daughter, August, whose patience throughout my career is the only reason I've reached the levels I have. I literally owe it all to you, and watching you grow and evolve is my biggest source of inspiration.

Continued

To my husband, Kyle Linden Webster. Finding absolute and true love has been the single most important thing in my life. It radiates out into the universe and makes all things possible.

To my mother, Karen, whose drive to teach herself to cook as I was growing up and to patiently involve me in all aspects of making a meal fostered my ability to wake up every day loving my work, and consequently, my life. Thank you so much.

To my dad, Toby, for never, ever stopping until the moment you feel it is as good as it can possibly be. I learned the pursuit of perfection by watching you. And to Ronna, for taking the time to teach (me and others).

To my late grandmother Vivian, from whom I realized the value of subtlety, because that was the one thing she wasn't. You taught me that curries should taste as good as they smell, and that sometimes you don't have to say everything you think. Here's to learning from observing the successes and failures of our elders. Thank you, Grandma, you're always with me.

Most importantly, I dedicate this book to the farmers. Without you, we cooks have no inspiration. Thank you for all of your hard work and dedication.

Merci to all.

About the Author

Naomi Pomeroy won the James Beard Award for Best Chef Pacific Northwest in 2014, was named a Best New Chef in *Food & Wine* in 2009, and has been featured in *Bon Appétit*, *Elle*, and *O* magazine, along with appearances on *Top Chef Masters* and *Knife Fight*. After launching Family Supper, clarklewis, and Gotham Tavern, she opened Beast in 2007 and with her husband, Kyle Linden Webster, the bar Expatriate in 2013. She lives in Portland, Oregon.

Index

Copyright © 2016 by Naomi Pomeroy
Photographs copyright © 2016 by Chris Court

Library of Congress Cataloging-in-Publication Data is on file with the publisher.

Hardcover ISBN: 978-1-60774-899-1
eBook ISBN: 978-1-60774-900-4

Printed in China

Design by Emma Campion
Food styling by Naomi Pomeroy
Food styling assistance by Ellen Laing
Prop styling by Glenn Jenkins

10 9 8 7 6 5 4 3 2 1

First Edition